ARMOR

— AND —

BLOOD

ARMOR

— AND —

BLOOD

THE BATTLE OF KURSK
THE TURNING POINT OF WORLD WAR II

Dennis E. Showalter

RANDOM HOUSE

NEW YORK

Published in the United States by Random House, an imprint of The Random House
Publishing Group, a division of Random House, Inc., New York.

RANDOM HOUSE and the HOUSE colophon are registered trademarks of
Random House, Inc.

LIBRARY OF CONGRESS CATALOGING-IN-PUBLICATION DATA
Showalter, Dennis E.
Armor and blood: the battle of Kursk: the turning point of World War II /
Dennis E. Showalter.
pages cm
Includes bibliographical references and index.
ISBN 978-1-4000-6677-3
eBook ISBN 978-0-8129-9465-0
1. Kursk, Battle of, Russia, 1943.   2. World War, 1939–1945—Tank warfare.   I. Title.
D764.3.K8S56 2013   940.54'2735—dc23   2012047086

Printed in the United States of America on acid-free paper

www.atrandom.com

First Edition

2   4   6   8   9   7   5   3   1

Book design by Christopher M. Zucker
Maps by Robert Bull

03149 8767

CONTENTS

List of Maps

INTRODUCTION

THE BATTLE OF KURSK is a continuing paradox. On the one hand, it is regularly described as a military epic: history's greatest armored battle, the first stage on the Red Army's road to Berlin, an ultimate test of Nazi and Soviet military/political systems. On the other, it is strangely blurred. Compared with Stalingrad or Barbarossa, it remains obscure, its narrative fostering myth as much as history. In the context of Western, particularly English-language, writing on World War II, Kursk is part of an imbalance that focuses on Anglo-American operations. The sheer scale of the fighting, the absence of significant cultural and political reference points, and an understandable interest in the deeds of one's own countries combine in a literature acknowledging the Russo-German War after Stalingrad as a vital factor in the war's development and outcome but restricting it to the periphery in terms of page counts.

A recent development in the historiography of the Russo-German War integrates it into the related perspectives of total war and genocide. Sometimes it becomes pivotal, as in Niall Ferguson's *The War of the World* and in Timothy Snyder's *Bloodlands*. In other works, such as Stephen Fritz's *Ostkrieg* or Catherine Merridale's *Ivan's War,* Kursk, when it appears, becomes a footnote in a wider story of Armageddon and apocalypse.

In the context of the Russo-German War as a subject of military analysis, Kursk remains blended with what Germany's Military History Research Institute, the Militärgeschichtliches Forschungsamt, calls the "forgotten year" (from summer 1943 to summer 1944), a time of inglorious retreats on the German side and inglorious victories for the Soviets—both achieved at excessive cost and neither offering much inspiration or value to students of the art/science/craft of war. In that sense, Kursk becomes a counterpoint to Passchendaele and Chemin des Dames in World War I, or the American Civil War's Wilderness: a tribute to uninspired hard fighting and colossal human suffering.

Well before John Keegan's *The Face of Battle* focused military writers' attention away from the map movements of abstract red and blue blocks to the mechanics of battle as they apply to men at the sharp end, Kursk generated accounts of memory and explanation. Two master narratives emerged. The German version depicted a heroic struggle, wearing down massively superior Soviet defenders, climaxing with the SS Panzer Corps's destruction of the Fifth Guards Tank Army at Prokhorovka—only to have their victory thwarted by Hitler's micromanaging and indecision. The Soviet counterpart depicted a German attack first ground down by a scientifically created, dauntlessly defended fortification system, then defeated by the intrepid attack of the Fifth Guards Tank Army at Prokhorovka.

Addressing the contradictions between the two memes has been complicated until recently by a virtual German monopoly of Eastern Front narratives. The USSR's determination to control the story of the Great Fatherland Patriotic War was complemented by a discouraging of memory and memoir at every rank from private to marshal of the Soviet Union. The improved post-Soviet access to archives, memories, and battlefields has combined with postreunification developments in German military historiography to revitalize, indeed revolutionize, the academic and general-audience writing on Kursk and its matrices.

The general intention of this book is to synthesize the material and the perspectives that have in some cases been upheld and in others modified, reshaped, or revised. It is operationally structured, but not operationally focused. The events of the battle are used to contextualize wider issues of operations and strategy, institutional structure and state policy, and to convey some of the Eastern Front's human dimension.

This work has a specific purpose as well: to structure and clarify the newly available mass of detail, official, tactical, and personal, on the fighting. Kursk was a battle before it became anything else. That makes it worthwhile knowing who did what, where, when, with what, to whom, and above all *why*. This requires collating, comparing, and critiquing official and personal accounts, contextualizing them in a geography significantly unfamiliar to all but a few potential readers, then presenting the results in a way that is comprehensible without being condescending.

For the sake of clarity, the text uses Russian orthography for geographic features. It addresses the two-hour difference between German and Russian official time by citing the time noted by the subjects of the narrative: German when the actors are German, Russian for Russian. The text also minimizes references to the obscure villages and low heights that were the usual foci of orders and reports and challenge the most detailed and costly tactical maps. In each case of this kind of judgment call, the author acknowledges any misjudgments and requests charity.

For the sake of another kind of clarity, the linguistically and orthographically complex ranks of the Waffen SS have been translated into their U.S. Army counterparts.

The same acknowledgment and the same request apply to the book's subtext. That is, to avoid "war porn," whether in contexts of heroism, pathos, horror, or voyeurism. Should it succeed in nothing else, may that objective stand.

Order of Battle, Operation Citadel

German

Army Group Center—
Field Marshal Günther von Kluge

9th Army—General Walter Model

    XX Corps

45th, 72nd, 137th, 251st Infantry Divisions

    XLVI Panzer Corps

7th, 31st, 102nd, 258th Infantry Divisions

    XLVI Panzer Corps

2nd, 9th, 20th Panzer Divisions, 6th Infantry Division

    XLI Panzer Corps

18th Panzer Division, 86th, 292nd Infantry Divisions

    XXIII Corps

78th Assault Division, 36th, 216th, 383rd Infantry Divisions

Army Group South—Field Marshal Erich von Manstein

4th Panzer Army General Hermann Hoth

    XLVIII Panzer Corps

3rd, 11th Panzer Divisions, Panzer Grenadier Division
Grossdeutschland, 167th Infantry Division

II SS Panzer Corps

SS Panzer Grenadier Divisions Leibstandarte, Das Reich, Totenkopf

LII Corps

57th, 255th, 332nd Infantry Divisions

ARMY DETACHMENT KEMPF— GENERAL WERNER KEMPF

III Panzer Corps

6th, 7th, 19th Panzer Divisions

XI Corps

106th, 320th Infantry Divisions

XLII Corps

39th, 161st, 282nd Infantry Divisions

RUSSIAN

CENTRAL FRONT—GENERAL KONSTANTIN ROKOSSOVSKY

13th, 48th, 60th, 65th, 70th Armies, 2nd Tank Army, 9th, 19th
Tank Corps

VORONEZH FRONT—GENERAL NIKOLAI VATUTIN

6th, 7th Guards Armies, 38th, 40th, 69th Armies, 1st Tank
Army, 35th Guards Rifle Corps, 2nd, 5th Guards Tank Corps

5th Guards Army, 5th Guards Tank Army assigned from Steppe
Front during Citadel as reinforcements

ARMOR

— AND —

BLOOD

Chapter I

GENESIS

"IT'S TIME TO WRITE THE LAST WILL!" one SS trooper grimly noted in his diary on July 5, 1943, while awaiting the order to advance. Across the line, Soviet soldiers swapped their own grim jokes—like the one about the tanker who reported that almost everyone in his unit had been killed that day. "I'm sorry," he replied, "I'll make sure I burn tomorrow."

Everybody on the long-designated battlefield knew what was coming. In mounting Operation Citadel, Adolf Hitler and his generals were seizing a high-risk window of opportunity: a last, best chance to regain the initiative in Russia before Soviet material power grew overwhelming and before the Western Allies could establish themselves in Europe. The Russians faced a graduation exercise: a test of their ability to handle a major and intricate combined-arms battle against a first-class, heavily armored, and experienced enemy.

For weeks, the Germans and the Russians had been massing men, tanks, guns, and aircraft from every sector of the Eastern Front into and around a hundred-mile salient centered on the

Ukrainian city of Kursk, about four hundred miles south of Moscow. All that remained indefinite were the starting time and the precise locations, which Soviet intelligence had been unable to determine. Adolf Hitler had postponed the date repeatedly. At least three times the Soviet high command, known as the Stavka, had issued false warnings. Then, on the evening of July 4, 1943, the Germans sent their men the infallible signal: a special ration of schnapps. An Alsatian serving in the Waffen SS promptly deserted—and convinced a high-status interrogation team, including Voronezh Front's commander, General Nikolai Vatutin, and a forty-nine-year-old political adviser named Nikita Khrushchev, that the German offensive would be under way before dawn on July 5. Giving the Germans the advantage of tactical surprise might be fatal. Khrushchev promptly reported to Moscow. Joseph Stalin returned the call and—according to Khrushchev—asked for his opinion. Khrushchev replied that "we will make the enemy pay in blood when he tries to break through." At 10:30 P.M., more than six hundred heavy guns and rocket launchers began the overture to the Battle of Kursk by blasting German artillery positions and assembly areas in Voronezh Front's sector.

I

The groundwork for this epic armored battle had been laid almost two years earlier, when the Wehrmacht had failed to overrun the Soviet Union in the lightning campaign projected by Operation Barbarossa. The long list of specific German mistakes can be conveniently grouped under two headings: overextension and underestimation. Both reflected the general sense of emergency that had informed Hitler's Reich from the first days of its existence. Time was always Adolf Hitler's chief enemy. He believed that only he could create the Thousand Year Reich of his visions, and to that end he was willing to run the most extreme risks.

Hitler's generals shared that risk-taking mind-set and accepted the apocalyptic visions accompanying it. That congruence shaped Barbarossa's racist, genocidal nature. Worse than a crime, it was a mistake antagonizing broad spectrums of a population that could have been mobilized to work for and with the conquerors and in some cases even act against the Soviet system. But to behave differently would have required Nazis to be something other than Nazis—and, perhaps, German generals to be something other than German generals, at least when confronting Slavic Bolsheviks.

More directly significant was an operational plan that lacked a decisive point. Instead, Barbarossa's armored spearheads were positioned on what amounted to a starting line sent in extrinsic directions toward Leningrad, Moscow, and Kiev and increasingly worn down by being shifted from sector to sector to deal with emergencies as the Red Army fought back fiercely and effectively. Behind the front, the Soviet government mobilized resources and developed skills to frustrate the invasion, capture the initiative, and discredit the myth of an inherently superior German way of war.

The initial result was a stalemate as Soviet counteroffensives staggered the Wehrmacht but failed to shatter it. During the winter of 1941–42, both sides regrouped and reconceptualized. On April 5, 1942, Hitler issued Directive 41, outlining the operational plan for the summer of 1942. Its focus would be in the south: a major drive toward the Caucasus to destroy Soviet forces in the region and seize the oil fields vital to both Soviet and German war making. A secondary objective was Stalingrad—not for its own sake, but to cut the Volga River, isolate the Russians south of the industrial city, and cover the main assault's flank.

The offensive's aims were no less ambitious than Barbarossa's had been. It would be launched on a five-hundred-mile front. Its objectives would create a salient, a bulge, of over thirteen hundred miles—something like the distance from New York City to the middle of Kansas. Road and rail networks would grow thinner as the Germans advanced. Scheduling the main attack for the end of

LIST OF MILITARY SYMBOLS

	GERMAN	RUSSIAN	
Army Group	XXXXX	XXXXX	Front
Army	XXXX	XXXX	Army
Corps	XXX	XXX	Corps
Division	XX	XX	Division
Infantry	⊠	⊠	Infantry
Panzer Grenadier	⊗	⊗	Mechanized
Panzer	⬭	⬭	Tank

Leningrad

XXXX
18

XXXXX
NORTH

XXXXX
LENINGRAD

XXXXX
VOLKHOV

XXXX
16

XXXXX
NORTHWESTERN

XXXX
3 Pz.

XXXXX
CENTER

N

XXXXX
WESTERN

● Moscow

RUSSIA

● Smolensk

XXXX
4 Pz.

BELORUSSIA

EASTERN FRONT
Beginning of March 1943

XXXXX German Army Group
XXXX German Army
XXXX German Panzer Army
XXXXX Russian Front

0   50   100   150km.
0   50   100   150mi.

XXXX
2

Bryansk
Orel

XXXXX
BRYANSK

XXXX
9

Kursk

XXXXX
VORONEZH

XXXX
3 Pz.

XXXX
4 Pz.

● Kharkov

XXXXX
SOUTHWESTERN

UKRAINE

XXXXX
SOUTH

XXXX
1

XXXX
6

XXXXX

Sea of Azov

XXXXX
SOUTHERN

XXXXX
A

XXXX
17

CRIMEA

Black Sea

June left at best four or five months before rain and snow put an end to major mobile operations. Even if the offensive succeeded, there was no guarantee that the Soviet Union would collapse or cease fighting de facto. It had other domestic sources of oil. It had as well the support of the United States and Great Britain, committed to keeping Russia in the war at all costs.

The operation nevertheless made sense to Hitler and his high command. It offered the opportunity to consolidate the Reich's military and economic position against the establishment of a second front in Europe—something Hitler considered possible as early as 1943. It extended the land war into Asia Minor and beyond, where the immediate pickings and possibilities seemed somewhat easier. And it offered a second chance for the German army to do what it so far had done best: win a mobile campaign in a limited time.

Initially, Stalin and his principal military advisers expected the Germans to attack—but in the direction of Moscow, replicating their failed final drive of autumn 1941. The supreme leader, the Vozhd, proposed to respond by seizing the initiative as soon as possible with half a dozen local offensives across the entire front. His staff planners were less sanguine and less eager. Chief of Staff Boris Shaposhnikov and Aleksandr Vasilevsky, who assumed the post in May 1942 when Shaposhnikov resigned due to ill health, expected the Germans to attack again. Let them again break their teeth on Red Army defenses, then the Soviets would mount a full-scale counterstroke. Field commanders such as Semyon Timoshenko and Georgi Zhukov, who had bloodied and blunted the first German onslaught, were dubious about dissipating the strength of a still-rebuilding army, short of men and material at every level. But Zhukov was not, or not yet, the man to cross Stalin directly. And Timoshenko believed his Southwest Command Sector offered an opportunity for a major offensive to recapture the city of Kharkov, in German hands since October 1941. Stalin approved the plan.

By May 12, the men and material were in place. For the first few days, it achieved a series of local successes. Then German air and armored forces counterattacked. It took them three days to reduce the Red Army's attack to prisoners and corpses: six hundred thousand casualties, two full armies, and two of the new tank corps destroyed, over twelve hundred tanks lost. German casualties totaled around twenty thousand—no bagatelle, but an exchange ratio suggesting strongly that Ivan was still no match for Hitler's panzers at any level.

In fact, the Soviet offensive suffered as much from bad staff work, inadequate intelligence and reconnaissance, and chaotic logistics as it did from German tactical sophistication. For a Führer and a high command still concerned with straightening the line in the northern and central sectors, and with clearing the stubbornly defended Crimean Peninsula, Kharkov nevertheless seemed a sign from Bellona herself that even delaying the main offensive to clean up details and replace losses would have no consequences. Indeed, a later start might have advantages: the faster the pace, the less likely an effective Soviet response.

Operation Blue tore the southern front wide open beginning on June 28. Its plan was audacious to the point of recklessness. An armored spearhead, the Fourth Panzer Army, was to thrust toward the Don River and the rail hub and industrial center of Voronezh, then turn south to trap and finish off the Reds driven east by the First Panzer Army and its accompanying infantry. Meanwhile, the Sixth Army would advance to the Volga and Stalingrad, while the First Panzer Army struck down the Volga to Baku and the Caucasus.

Stalin and his high command, Stavka, responded by launching a series of offensives against German Army Groups North and Center and committing more of their steadily increasing reserve forces to successive offensives around Voronezh. These were not mere counterattacks, but parts of a systematic effort to regain the strategic initiative secured in December 1941 and now apparently slipping away. That effort was frustrated by consistently poor execution, operationally and administratively, at subordinate levels.

Compensating by micromanaging only compounded the problem. The Germans consistently got within Red Army decision/implementation loops and just as consistently surged forward.

The problem was that they were surging to nowhere in particular. Instead, the offensive was pursuing two objectives simultaneously rather than sequentially, as in Blue's original conception. This was no simple manifestation of Hitler's unfocused, dilettantish interference in command decisions. Soviet pressure on the attack's left flank was convincing the German high command as well as the Führer that for the Caucasus and its oil fields to fall, Stalingrad must be not merely blockaded and screened, but captured.

The result across the offensive's front was an increasing division and diversion of German forces, in particular the panzer and motorized divisions, which were barely sufficient for Operation Blue had it gone as expected. In the Caucasus sector, Soviet resistance combined with dust, broken terrain, fuel shortages, and unreplaced losses in men and tanks to halt the Germans well away from the oil fields of Grozny and Baku by the end of September. A final desperate German lunge only delayed the inevitable retreat. At the same time, Stalingrad developed into a magnet and a killing ground for German forces sacrificed to the high command's conviction that maintaining the initiative was better served by continuing into the city than enveloping it and blocking the Volga with air and artillery.

On August 26, Stalin bit a bullet of his own and appointed Zhukov his deputy supreme commander. Zhukov typified a new generation of Red Army generals: as fearless as they were pitiless, ready to do anything to crush the Germans, and not inhibited by threats from either front or rear. He shared his superior's conviction that Stalingrad must be held—but in a strategic context. The summer of ripostes was over. Since September, Stavka, urged on by Zhukov, had been developing plans for a decisive winter campaign involving two major operations. Operation Mars would be launched in mid-October against a seemingly vulnerable sector on the front of German Army Group Center: a salient around the city of Rzhev. It would be followed in two or three weeks by Operation Jupiter, an attack in the Bryansk sector, to the south, intended to link up with Mars and shatter Army Group Center. Operation Uranus would begin in mid-November and commit large mobile forces north and south of Stalingrad, encircling and destroying enemy forces in the resulting pocket. Uranus was to be followed by Operation Saturn, which would finish off whatever remained of the Germans in Stalingrad and leave those in the Caucasus isolated, ripe for the picking.

Described for years in Soviet literature as no more than a diversion, Mars was in fact a complement to Uranus, a double penetration intended to put the Red Army on the high road to Berlin. It was, to say the least, an ambitious strategy for an army still reeling from the seismic shocks of Barbarossa and Blue. Its prospects depended entirely on the ability of Stalingrad's defenders to hold. Hold the Red Army did, in an epic defense that reduced the city to a wilderness of rubble, smoke, and ash. Two graffiti on the remnants of a wall told the story. One read "Here Rodimtsev's Guardsmen stood to the death." Below it was a coda: "They stood, and defeated death."

On November 19, the tide turned. Stavka had held its hand for a month, waiting for the rains to end and the ground to freeze. Two tank-headed sledgehammers struck the Romanian armies holding the flanks of the Stalingrad salient. A million men, a thousand modern tanks, fourteen hundred aircraft, fourteen thousand guns—all of it went undetected by a German intelligence blinded by Soviet deception measures and by its own belief that the Soviets were as locked into Stalingrad as the Germans were. On November 23, the Soviet spearheads met fifty miles west of Stalingrad.

The resulting catastrophe might well have metastasized except for an overlooked German victory to the north. Operation Mars, the other half of Operation Uranus, was delayed a month by heavy rains and began only on November 24. German intelligence for once accurately predicted something like the massive Soviet forces involved.

Had the Soviets been able to get out of their own way, the German front in the East might have broken from the attack's sheer mass: thirty-seven rifle divisions, forty-five tank and mechanized brigades, and dozens of independent artillery regiments. Instead, traffic and supply problems slowed the Red Army columns just long enough for the Germans to mount a series of counterattacks that cut off Soviet tank spearheads and stabilized the front.

With his reputation, perhaps his position, and possibly his neck at stake, Zhukov brought together the offensive's senior commanders on November 28 for counseling and admonition. The attack resumed with predictably renewed vigor the next day, featuring everything from tank attacks to cavalry charges. The weather grew more bitter in the first days of December. This year, however, the Germans were well supplied with winter clothing and had learned how to use trees and drifts to keep from freezing. The *Landser,* the foot soldiers and tankers, held—just barely, but it was enough. The Red Army stood down in mid-December. Soviet casualties exceeded two hundred thousand men, half of them dead. Over eighteen hundred of the two thousand tanks committed had been lost. Grimly, the Germans reported fewer than five thousand prisoners: quarter was neither asked nor given in most times and places in the Rzhev salient.

The historian David Glantz correctly describes the original strategic plan for Mars as too ambitious and Zhukov as too stubbornly optimistic to modify it. Operationally and tactically, however, Rzhev was a watershed. This was the last time in a major sector that the Red Army made the adolescent mistakes characteristic of its post-Barbarossa reconstruction: poor tank-infantry-artillery cooperation, inflexibility at all command levels, a tendency to reinforce failure at the expense of exploiting success. Rzhev, seen from a Soviet perspective, resembles the French offensives of 1915 in the Champagne and the British experience on the Somme a year later: a high learning curve imposed by an instructor charging even higher tuition.

On the other hand, Operation Uranus, the attack at Stalingrad, threatened to eviscerate the entire German position in Russia. The suddenly threatened forces in the Caucasus were too involved in their own withdrawal to assist the now surrounded Germans in Stalingrad. No significant reserves were available elsewhere in Russia or anywhere else under Nazi rule. The garrison's faint hopes ended definitively on December 16, when the Soviets responded to their initial success in that sector by launching a modified version of Operation Saturn. "Little Saturn" belied its name: it involved thirty-six rifle divisions, over a thousand tanks, and five thousand guns and mortars. As Soviet tanks and cavalry ran wild in the virtually undefended German rear areas, Field Marshal Erich von Manstein made a decision. One of Germany's outstanding experts on armored war, Manstein had been given command in the Stalingrad sector because earlier in the Russo-German War he had earned a reputation as a troubleshooter from Leningrad to Sebastopol. By December 19, it was clear to him that Stalingrad could not be relieved. The best hope of salvaging the situation involved sacrificing territory—most of the territory, in fact, gained during the entire summer campaign.

For Manstein, that was the necessary first step in restoring the maneuver warfare that was the German army's great strength—and by now perhaps the Third Reich's best hope. That restoration had two immediate prerequisites. One was administrative: a united command in the southern sector. The second prerequisite was doctrinal: trading space for time on levels and to degrees unheard of in the Prussian/German military experience. Manstein recognized the latter's applicability on an unprecedented scale, and he had the intellectual force and the moral courage to convince Hitler that operational exigencies overrode the strategic and economic arguments presented against them. As a result, Hitler authorized a single Army Group South under Manstein's command.

Encouraged by Little Saturn's initial success, the Soviet high command decided to extend the offensive toward Rostov. This was part of a Stalin-devised grand strategic plan to drive the Germans back across the entire Eastern Front while the winter held and establish an intermediate stop line extending from Narva to the Black Sea.

With Soviet pressure increasing across the front, Manstein oversaw a fighting retreat on a shoestring into the Donets Basin, north of Rostov, shortening the arc of his front while simultaneously preparing a counterattack as the Russians outran their supply and overextended their communications. Forward units were living off the resources they carried for up to two weeks at a time—acceptable for food, less so for fuel and ammunition. Soviet commanders' contact with higher headquarters was increasingly tenuous—and initiative even at corps level was not a Red Army hallmark. But the prizes that seemed within reach encouraged Stavka to go a stage further.

At the beginning of February, Russian Operations Gallop and Star retook the city of Kursk. Red Army spearheads drove forward, toward the industrial center and transportation hub of Kharkov, where they launched a counterattack. Hitler insisted on giving the city's defense top priority. And now some of Manstein's subordinates were unwilling to continue conceding ground on Manstein's scale. Manstein as a rule receives correspondingly high marks for a second major act of cool calculation: conceding the loss of Kharkov in order to lure the Soviets forward, into a better position for the counterstroke he was preparing.

Manstein did not sacrifice the city in order to recapture it. He saw the loss instead as the unpleasant but acceptable consequence of the few days needed to convince a visiting Hitler of the advantages of concentrating real reserves for a real counterattack. The Führer was dubious enough to consider dismissing Manstein. When Kharkov fell on February 16, the city's loss seemed to prefigure disaster in the wake of Stalingrad. But the next day Manstein struck, two panzer armies in tandem catching the Soviets off balance. By February 28, the Germans were back on the Donets and a Soviet retreat was turning into a rout. Kharkov was retaken by the SS Panzer Corps, newly arrived in Russia on March 15 after four days' hard fighting. The German air force, the Luftwaffe, played a vital role, mounting as many as a thousand sorties a day while shifting its emphasis between the two panzer armies. The weather also worked in the Germans' favor just as they reached the Donets, with the spring thaw, the *rasputitsa*, setting in and immobilizing Soviet reserves.

The Germans took pride in their comeback, and Kharkov did cost the Red Army half a dozen tank corps and ten rifle divisions destroyed or mangled. Soviet casualties were around eighty thousand. But by Eastern Front standards, both were bagatelles easily made up. For Stavka, and for the field commanders, Kharkov's consequences lay in what did not happen. The defeat did not shake Russian confidence that the initiative had passed to the Red Army. "Next time!" became an unspoken watchword.

Manstein's performance between December and March was considerable. Drawing from commanders, staffs, and soldiers the best they had left to give, he achieved a reversal of fortunes that had seemed inconceivable and remains a lodestone to historians and aficionados of maneuver war. "Miracle" is still widely used to describe the event; "genius" is a familiar appellation for its architect. Manstein compared his approach to a tennis player's "backhand blow": a difficult shot, but one that when made effectively can mean game, set, and match. Close examination of the sequence of events suggests a better athletic metaphor might be that of a scrambling quarterback in U.S. football—an improvised response to pressure by a defense, avoiding a tackle while looking for an opportunity to reverse the situation.

Manstein's success in restoring and stabilizing the southern sector of the German front has inspired arguments that Hitler and the high command should have continued the offensive instead of throttling back and preparing for a later climactic battle. The obvious counter is that despite Manstein's careful stewardship, his army group was fought out by the end of March, needing rest and reinforcement before going anywhere. Indeed, both Germans and

Russians were like boxers in the late rounds of a bruising fight: exhausted, punch-drunk, working more from reflex than calculation. The Eastern Front's fighting line on April 1 strongly resembled its spring 1942 predecessor and accurately reflected the state of play. The game, however, was far from over. "Strongly resembled" does not mean "identical." The Red Army had driven a hundred-mile bulge around the city of Kursk into the German lines during the winter fighting. The salient's reentrant, German-held, was just to the north, around Orel. On a large-scale map, the two resembled a large, upside-down *S*. It was the kind of anomaly no staff planner was likely to ignore.

II

The armies that drew apart snarling in the spring of 1943 had changed significantly from those that confronted each other at the start of Barbarossa. The Red Army was still in the process of re-covering from two disconnects. The most fundamental was insti-tutional. From its early revolutionary days under the guidance of Leon Trotsky, the army had been seen as a major instrument for creating the New Soviet Man. Free from the snares and delusions of the past, this archetype was to be materialist and collectivist in his essence, eager to sacrifice himself for the Soviet system and for Communist ideology. Military service would facilitate and con-cretize this transformation while simultaneously creating an in-strument of war and revolution that would showcase Soviet power and deter Soviet enemies.

Reality was far more pedestrian. Initial concepts of building this army around a core of class-conscious proletarians foundered with the simultaneous military and industrial expansions inaugu-rated by the five-year plans that began in 1925. The conscript in-takes were increasingly composed of poorly educated peasants with negative cultural memories of military service under any system. Ethnic and regional frictions further induced entropy down to platoon level. "Nationalist in form; socialist in content" became in practice another empty slogan.

These tensions were exacerbated by a pervasive scarcity. From barracks to dispensaries to latrines, facilities were comprehensively swamped; everyday life was marginal even by czarist standards. Shortages of uniforms, weapons, and equipment could not be made good by an economy that, especially before the mid-1930s, had more of a civilian emphasis than is generally recognized or conceded. The result was a collective malaise, informed by an attitude of *nichevo,* which created a culture of minimal compliance: the antithesis of ideological hopes and expectations. *Nichevo* is usually translated as "never mind" and is presented as a trope of passivity. It incorporates as well a strong element of "F— it; don't mean a thing"—what the British Army called "bloody-mindedness" and punished as "dumb insolence."

The situation could not be changed by an officer corps whose professionalization was consistently retarded not only by the crosscurrents of Communist Party demands, but by a significant sense that a commission was a route of upward mobility in the Soviet order and that in a continuing environment of scarcity, officers deserved special treatment and special privileges. At regimental levels, the officers never set a comprehensive example—never became a bridge between the conscripted lower ranks and the Soviet system. Nor did the noncommissioned officers (NCOs) develop as a facilitating body between men and systems in the Western fashion.

Stalin's Great Purge of the late 1930s did not spare the Red Army. Recent statistics indicating that less than 10 percent of the officers were actually removed overlook the ripple effects, in particular the diminishing of the mutual rapport and confidence so important for the kind of war that the Germans brought with them and that the Soviets proposed to wage. In response to substandard performances in Poland and Finland, the Red Army restored a spectrum of behaviors and institutions abolished after the Revolution of

1917, designed collectively to introduce more conventional discipline and reestablish the authority of officers and senior NCOs. These changes did not sit well with the "reluctant soldiers" of the rank and file. Nor did they fit well on officers who were themselves profoundly uncertain of their positions.

One result was a significant decline in training standards already mediocre. Western images shaped largely by German myths describe the Russian soldier of World War II as a "natural" fighter, whose instincts and way of life inured him to hardship in ways foreign to "civilized" men. The Red Army was in fact based on a society and a system whose hardness and brutality prefigured and replicated military life. Stalin's Soviet Union was a society organized for violence, with a steady erosion of distinctions and barriers between military and civilian spheres. If armed struggle never became the end in itself that it was for fascism, Soviet culture was nevertheless comprehensively militarized in preparation for a future revolutionary apocalypse. Soviet political language was structured around military phrasing. Absolute political control and comprehensive iron discipline, often gruesomely enforced, helped bridge the still-inevitable gaps between peace and war. But in the summer of 1941, too many officers and men, active soldiers and recalled reservists, were ignorant of such basics as minor tactics and fire discipline. They would fight—but too often did not know how.

That disconnect was replicated at the levels of doctrine and planning. For the emerging Soviet Union, war was not a contingency but a given. The external class enemy, the capitalist states surrounding the USSR, sought its destruction from their own objective dynamics. Preparing for war, total war, was a pragmatic imperative, implemented in a context that defined war as a science. Marxism-Leninism, the USSR's legitimating ideology, was a science. The Soviet state and Soviet society were organized on abstract, scientific principles. Studied systematically and properly applied, these principles made it possible to anticipate the consequences of decisions, behaviors—even attitudes. War making too was a science. The application of its objective principles by trained and skilled engineers was the best predictor of victory.

In that matrix, a rising generation of technocrats saw the Soviet Union's military future in terms of a mass mechanized army. In the mid-1920s, instructors at the Red Army Military Academy described the total destruction of enemy forces by a series of "deep operations": shock armies for breakthrough, mobile echelons for exploitation and pursuit. Mikhail Tukhachevsky, appointed deputy people's commissar for military and naval affairs in 1931, was the focal point of a school of thought arguing that mechanization vitalized and extended revolutionary war. A technologized mass army could export communism as well as defend it. "Reluctant soldiers" would be transformed into enthusiasts by experiencing directly what the Soviet Union could do to its enemies. They would become part of a new proletariat, able to make optimum use of the military technologies created under communism.

Stalin internalized and epitomized the conviction that the non-Communist world embodied an irreconcilable hatred for the Soviet system. Even the Great Depression did not change his mind: capitalism in its death throes might be even more willing to undo history by turning its armed forces against the USSR. However intensely managers, soldiers, and officials might dispute specific policies or details of production, the basic assumption of isolation in a mortally hostile world went unchallenged throughout the period. Moderation in defense planning was criminal. Cycles of purge, disruption, and reorganization characterized the defense industry well before they became a general norm in the late 1930s.

The Red Army's unwavering support for Stalin in the intraparty struggles of the 1920s reflected its appreciation for Stalin's support of military spending at the expense of balanced budgets and civilian production, to a permanent "half war, half peace" level. "Deep battle" became a comprehensive doctrine that included air-supported, fully mechanized mobile groups taking the fight into the enemy's rear at a rate of twenty-five or thirty miles a day. By 1938, the Soviet order of battle included four tank corps and a large number of tank brigades. But in November 1939, these formations were disbanded, replaced by motorized divisions and tank brigades designed essentially for close infantry support.

One reason for this measure—the public one—was that the Spanish Civil War had shown the relative vulnerability of tanks, while large armored formations had proved difficult to control both against the Japanese in Mongolia and during the occupation of eastern Poland. Reinforcing operational experience was Stalin's concern for the armored force as a potential domestic threat. Not only were the top-level advocates of mobile war, men like Tukhachevsky, eliminated—all but one commander at brigade level and 80 percent of the battalion commanders were replaced as well.

The successes of Hitler's panzers combined with the winding down of the purges to encourage reappraisal. Beginning in 1940, the People's Commissariat of Defense began authorizing what became a total of twenty-nine mechanized corps, each with two tank divisions and a motorized division: thirty-six thousand men and over a thousand tanks each, plus twenty more brigades of three hundred light T-26 tanks intended for infantry support. The numbers are mind-boggling even by subsequent Soviet reckoning. But low maintenance standards kept field strength down, and the sheer size of the mechanized corps defied all but the best efforts at command and control.

As the Germans drove toward Moscow in 1941, the Red Army began rebuilding virtually from the ground up. Infantry, the rifle divisions, remained the backbone, but their authorized strength was reduced to around eleven thousand and their supporting arms and services were cut to minimums. Even vehicles were reduced by two-thirds, and most of those were horse-drawn. These frugal formations were supplemented by a large number of brigades less than half their size. The new structures reflected not only the heavy losses in men and equipment during Barbarossa,

but also the fact that effective command of more complex formations was simply beyond the skill of the colonels and junior generals who took the places of those killed, captured, or replaced.

Higher command structures were correspondingly simplified.
Divisions—four or five, sometimes more—were for a time assigned directly to rifle armies, which also controlled most of the
service and support elements. During 1942, as supplies of armor
and artillery increased, communications improved, and staff work
grew more competent, the rifle corps reemerged to enhance flexibility. A rifle army might field three or four of them, each with
three or four divisions, sometimes upgraded from the independent brigades, which disappeared in their turn.

Divisional allocations of guns and automatic weapons increased, but the bulk of supporting assets remained pooled at
army level, assigned as needed. Throughout 1942, Soviet rifle formations were seldom anywhere near their authorized numbers. In
theory and practice, they were regarded as expendable: to be kept
in the line until reduced to cadre strength, then either broken up
or completely rebuilt. Shock troops or cannon fodder? It depended
on perspective. Nineteen-year-old Boris Gorbachevsky entered
the army in January 1942. He first saw combat in August, in front
of Rzhev, in a mixed-bag rifle company of "Russians, Ukrainians,
Cossacks, and Uzbeks. . . . We now no longer belong to ourselves;
we have all been seized by the incomprehensibly savage element of
battle. Shell bursts, shell fragments, and bullets are sweeping away
the infantry lines. . . . The remnants of former companies and battalions have turned into a senseless mass of onward-charging, desperate men." Like so many Red Army attacks in 1942, this one
collapsed in a welter of blood and bodies. Wounded and hospital-
ized, Gorbachevsky encountered his regiment's Communist Youth
organizer, also a casualty: "How are we fighting? Everyone from
the army commander down to the company commander . . . drives
the soldiers forward into the chopping machine. And the result!
We don't have enough paper for all the funeral notices!"

Yet many a veteran *Landser* has recalled that for all the high-tech terrors of the Eastern Front, the T-34 tanks, the Shturmovik attack planes, the Katyusha rockets with their eldritch scream, nothing was worse than the deep-throated "Urraa! Urraa!" accompanying the charge of the Red Army's infantry.

The armored force, prime target on all of Barbarossa's fronts, was eviscerated in a matter of weeks. On July 15, 1941, the elephantine mechanized corps were disbanded. The signature unit became the tank brigade: initially around two thousand men and ninety-three tanks, two-thirds of them light T-60 tanks, whose 20 mm popguns and thin armor made them meat on the table for the panzers. Even that low strength proved materially unsustainable and beyond the capacity of most commanders. In December, the brigade was cut back to eight hundred men and forty-six tanks, about the strength of a Western battalion.

These small formations made predictably little headway in the winter counterattacks. In March 1942, the first four tank corps were authorized. Between April and September 1942, twenty-five more joined the order of battle. Their final configuration on paper was three tank brigades and a motorized rifle brigade: just short of ten thousand men and 165 tanks. A third of those tanks were T-60s. Their more complex stablemates, the medium T-34s that became the Red Army's signature armored vehicle, were still entering mass production.

The 1942 order of battle remained the standard tank corps framework for the rest of the war. Light tanks were replaced by T-34s in a structure that was armor-heavy by developing Western standards, lacking both artillery to deal with German infantry and antitank guns and infantry to hold the ground it might gain. The former shortcoming would eventually be modified by increasing the number of turretless assault guns, the latter by creating mechanized corps built around truck-borne infantry. But the tank corps's structure was a function of its mission: exploiting the breakthroughs made by infantry- and artillery-heavy "shock forces" as described before the war.

That mission was easier defined than accomplished. The new

tank corps underwent their first serious test in the Soviet Kharkov offensive in May 1942. Over thirteen hundred armored vehicles were concentrated for the attack. Early successes gained by mass could not be sustained against a flexible German defense built around coordinated air and armor strikes. The tank corps lagged too far behind the fighting lines to intervene quickly, then kept going as a German counterattack closed off the neck of the salient they formed.

A similar, albeit smaller-scale, armored debacle took place in the Crimea, where a single understrength panzer division took the measure of superior forces employed piecemeal. As Russian survivors fought delaying actions on the long retreat to the Don River, Russian staffs emphasized surprise, exploitation, and improved logistic support for future offensives. All of these appeared in the Stalingrad offensive. The rally and the counterattack orchestrated by Manstein showed that the Germans still mastered the armored battlefield. Mastered—but no longer dominated. Beginning with the new year, frontline commanders were reporting unpleasant tactical surprises. Red armor was no longer following its familiar pattern of engaging German strongpoints and exposing itself to paralyzing local ripostes by the panzers. Instead the tankers were bypassing the "hedgehogs," driving past them deep into the German rear. Lower-unit leadership was becoming more flexible, more situationally oriented.

Four hundred thousand tankers were trained during the war. More than three hundred thousand died in battle—a ratio matching the often-cited losses of the Nazi U-boat service, but in numbers ten times greater. The execution squads of the security police, the People's Commissariat for Internal Affairs, or NKVD, were seldom to be found riding with the tankers. And the fatalism characteristic of the Red Army for almost a decade was beginning to develop among the tank crews into a determination, still unfocused but increasingly powerful, to take as many Hitlerites as possible along with them.

The armored force attracted quality recruits—country boys

who had dreamed of driving tractors for the machinery collective, factory workers attracted by the technical and mechanical aspects: socialist modernization on treads. Russia's military heritage included elements other than brute force. It had a raiding culture as well, a concept of freewheeling mobility dating back to the Cossacks of the Zaporozhian Sich, the flying columns that devastated Napoleon's army during its retreat from Moscow, the mounted buccaneers of Semyon Budenny's Konarmia (Cavalry Army) during the Russian Civil War. Given the right catalyst, a Red Army tank corps was a potentially lethal compound.

The Red Army was also developing a supporting infrastructure—most significantly in its artillery. Guns had been important in the Russian army since the eighteenth century. Stalin would call artillery "the Red god of war." And here if anywhere, mass was dominant. Western armies emphasized fire mobility. The Soviets emphasized tubes. The Red Army lacked the electronics and the technicians to implement a Western-style approach. Decentralization was in any case not a part of Soviet principle or practice. Guns, on the other hand, were easier to manufacture than tanks, and heavy mortars were even simpler than conventional artillery pieces. By October 1943, there were enough of them that Stavka authorized twenty-six artillery divisions, each with over 200 guns and howitzers plus 108 heavy (120 mm) mortars. At the same time, four rocket-launcher divisions were created. By the end of 1943, there were seven, each able to fire a salvo of over 3,400 rockets.

The effect was an ability to saturate a battle zone in the fashion attempted by the Allies on the Western Front in 1916–17. It was as sophisticated as a baseball bat to the kidneys, and just as effective. Even when the guns were deployed in forward, exposed positions, German counterbattery fire and air strikes (when these were available) were simply absorbed by the sheer number of targets. Artillery commanders were responsible to artillery superiors, creating a chain of command and control that enabled artillery to be used independently, without particular and changeable commitments to the infantry and armor. The potential of the adjusted system was only marginally apparent during the Stalingrad campaign. At best it had its limits. Against stationary targets or massed formations, it could have effects prefiguring those later projected for a tactical nuclear bomb. The best counters were dispersion, mobility, flexibility. At Kursk the Germans would deny themselves all three, and Soviet gunners would make them pay.

For the men in the Red Army's ranks, the war's second summer seemed to offer "neither victory nor hope." Another third of a million men, another two thousand tanks, had been lost. The survivors were caught up in what seemed an endless retreat across the steppes, broken by last stands on temporary stop lines. Sergey Bondarchuk, himself a veteran of four years' wartime service, presented a sanitized dramatization in his 1975 epic film, *They Fought for Their Country*. It follows the remnants of a shattered rifle regiment as they make their way toward the Don and Stalingrad, facing the scorn of the civilians they abandon and wondering why their efforts so far have been so futile, until finally they turn and fight, unfurling their banner and following it to glory on the Volga.

The film's tone of determined optimism interspersed with bits of comedy and nostalgia parallels that of its Western counterparts of the 1940s and 1950s in that it reflects an official policy that endured virtually until the Soviet Union's final implosion. Russia's soldiers and Russia's people behaved heroically. Should they not in fact live up to the trope—that was why the police system existed, and from privates to generals, all went in fear of the NKVD. Its presence was ubiquitous, but its behavior remained random until July 28, when Stalin issued Order No. 227, which called for an end to retreat and demanded that every foot of Soviet soil be defended. Penalties ranged from service in a penal battalion to summary execution: more than 150,000 Red Army soldiers were formally sentenced to death. The number of summary executions will never be known.

High morale was a soldier's duty, not his right. But Stavka did not base morale on executions alone. Part of the mythology of Soviet recovery from Barbarossa involves Stalin's willingness to call on religion and nationalism. Orthodox prelates met with Stalin himself. Churches were opened, seminaries authorized. Accompanying this was a near cultic emphasis on the "motherland," its heroes and its symbols. Motherland became a form of "sacred space," combining emotional abstraction with geographic reality. Films and lectures celebrated legendary generals such as Bohdan Khmelnytsky, Aleksandr Suvorov, Mikhail Kutuzov—and Stalin, revolutionary defender of the city that now bore his name. Uniforms were smartened up with shoulder boards and standing collars. Military bling returned to fashion: a structure of medals, orders, and decorations that could literally cover the entire chest of senior officers such as Zhukov and his counterpart and rival, Ivan Konev. Enlisted men from cooks to snipers had their own badges recognizing "distinguished" service.

As early as September 1941, the title of "Guards" was reintroduced. Not Red Guards, as might have been expected—just Guards, referring both to the revolutionary formations and to the elite troops of the czarist empire. Units from independent battalions to entire armies that distinguished themselves in combat were rechristened and renumbered. Members of the units were titled Guardsmen—and the honorific accompanied them if they were transferred.

The new spectrum of recognitions was welcome enough. But for the surviving veterans of 1941, for the wartime conscripts, and for the recovered wounded returning in increasing numbers, the sting of defeat was beginning to mask the cultures of buck passing and scapegoating developed under two decades of postrevolutionary terror. The material and human devastation left in the Nazis' wake had become general knowledge. For some in the ranks, it generated anger at losing the results of generations of sacrifice and deprivation. The impulse to spiral into nihilism was counterbalanced by a growing conviction, even among the cynical and the disaffected, that nothing was wrong with the Soviet Union that the Germans could fix—or wanted to.

A comprehensive and enduring propaganda campaign worked

tirelessly to encourage and systematize hate—to make killing Germans a pleasure and a habit. Training, never exactly a humanitarian enterprise in the Red Army, inculcated toughness by such exercises as having tanks drive over recruits in slit trenches—sometimes trenches they had dug themselves. An "accident" or two was a sovereign cure for reluctance to dig in and dig deep.

A common Red Army type never developed even in the homogenizing context of total war and despite an official Soviet policy of stressing the collective nature of its sacrifice and victory. Age and ethnicity, background and culture, sustained individual identities. Confidence and comradeship, hope of recognition and fear of punishment, ideology and tradition—all played roles in renewing and refocusing combat motivation. Underpinning them all, even at the war's middle stage, was the frontline soldiers' increasing hope that their sacrifices would bring about postwar reform—"communism with a human face," purged of prewar hatreds and misunderstandings, productive capacities adjusted to civilian needs and wants, leaders and people committed to the same goals.

Boris Gorbachevsky, by then a captain, recalls a postwar discussion with half a dozen of his men around the kind of campfire that inspired swapping confidences even with an officer present: "If only the authorities would give us freedom, spare us from Kolkhoz troubles and think up something like the NEP. If only they'd set us free, we could rebuild all of Russia within five years." Illusion and delusion were not Third Reich monopolies.

III

The Red Army's background is best understood in the context of disconnects: between the party and the military, and among the major combat arms. The German army of 1943 is best understood in terms of synergies: among army, party, and society and within the army's fighting components.

The Nazi Party has been compared by scholars with almost

every possible human organization, even medieval feudalism. The one adjective that cannot be applied is "patriarchal." Change and progress were the movement's flywheels. Nazi nostalgia found its essential expression in domestic kitsch. It had no place in military matters. Hitler's initially enthusiastic wooing of the soldiers was based on his intention of using them first to consolidate his hold over both the Nazi Party and the German people, then as the standard-bearers of territorial and ideological expansion until they could safely be replaced by the SS. National Socialist views of war differed in important, arguably essential, respects from those of the Reichswehr. But on such subjects as anti-Marxism, anti-pacifism, and hostility to the Versailles Treaty, the military's values were not incongruent with those avowed by Nazi theorists and propagandists.

The armed forces and the Nazis also shared a common commitment to the future rather than a vision of the past. General Hans von Seeckt during the Great War had established a reputation as one of the army's most brilliant staff officers. He became head of the Reichswehr high command in the newly established Weimar Republic. From the beginning, he challenged the concept of mass that had permeated military thinking since the Napoleonic Wars, instead insisting on the principle of pursuing quick, decisive victories by offensive action.

Boldness was Seeckt's first rule; flexibility was his second. The Treaty of Versailles, however, specified the structure of the Reichswehr in detail: a force of one hundred thousand, but, forbidden tanks, aircraft, and medium or heavy artillery, it badly needed force multipliers. Versailles did authorize each Reichswehr division a motor-transport battalion, and Seeckt saw their vehicles as an increasingly valuable supplement to the conventional combat arms. Beginning in the early 1930s, war games focused on not merely the combination but the integration of mobility and striking power—quality enhanced by technology. In 1934, the first "experimental armored division" was authorized. The next year Hitler reintroduced conscription and officially initiated rearmament. In return, the armed forces gave the Nazis a free hand in Germany's "reconstructuring."

This decision reflected neither simplemindedness nor moral blindness. The Reichswehr understood, better than any army in the world, that total war and industrial war had generated new styles of combat and new methods of leadership. The officer no longer stood above his unit but functioned as an integral part of it. The patriarchal/hegemonic approach of the "old" Prussian/German army, parenting youthful conscripts and initiating them into adult society, was giving way to a collegial/affective pattern, emphasizing cooperation and consensus in mission performance. "Mass man" must give way to "extraordinary man"—the combination of fighter and technician who understood combat as both a skilled craft and an inner experience.

The soldiers were confident that once Germany's young men changed their brown shirts and Hitler Youth uniforms for army field gray, their socialization away from National Socialism would be relatively easy. The army knew well how to cultivate them from its own resources. The new Wehrmacht had new facilities. Leave policies were generous. Food was well cooked and ample. Uniforms looked smart and actually fit—no small matters to young men on pass seeking to make quick impressions.

The conscripts were motivated, alert, and physically fit. Thanks to the eighteen months of compulsory labor service required of all seventeen-year-olds since 1935, they required a minimum of socializing into barracks life and were more than casually acquainted with the elements of close-order drill. Officers and noncommissioned officers were expected to bond with their men, leading by example on a daily basis.

The army was still the army, and NCOs had lost none of their historic set of tools, official and unofficial, to "motivate" recalcitrants and make them examples for the rest. But military service had for over a century been a major rite of passage for males in Prussia/Germany. The army's demands had generally been understood as not beyond the capacities of an ordinarily fit, well-adjusted young man. That military service had been restricted during the Weimar years gave it a certain forbidden appeal. And a near standard response of older generations across the republic's social and political spectrum to anything smacking of late-adolescent malaise or rebellion was that what the little punks needed was some shaping up in uniform.

Recruit processing differed significantly from both pre-1914 practice and the patterns in contemporary conscript armies. While not ignoring experience, aptitude, education, and even social class, the German sorting and screening system paid close attention to what later generations would call "personality profiles." Determination, presence of mind, and situational awareness were the qualities most valued. Initial training in all branches can best be compared to a combination of the U.S. Army's basic training with its advanced infantry training, informed by the Marine Corps's mantra of "every man a rifleman." That reflected the belief that infantry warfare's moral and physical demands were the greatest. A soldier who could not meet them was less than an effective soldier no matter his level of technical proficiency. Misunderstandings and mistakes in combat were to be expected. Overcoming them depended more on character than intellect. And character in the context of combat meant, above all, will.

The question of nature versus nurture did not significantly engage the Wehrmacht. Long before Leni Riefenstahl celebrated Hitler's version of the concept, the armed forces acted on the principle that a soldier's will was essentially a product of cultivation. Drill was the means to develop the reflexive coordination of mind and body. Troops trained day or night, at immediate notice, in all weather, under conditions including no rations. Combat conditions were simulated through the extensive use of live ammunition. Casualties were necessary reminders of the dangers of carelessness and stupidity.

A persistent mythology continues to depict the German army of World War II as a "clean shield" force, fighting first successfully and then heroically against heavy odds, simultaneously doing its best to avoid "contamination" by National Socialism—a "band of brothers" united by an unbreakable comradeship. That concept of comradeship is arguably the strongest emotional taproot of what John Mearsheimer has memorably dubbed "Wehrmacht penis envy." Soldiers and scholars inside and outside Germany have consistently cited "comradeship" to explain the "fighting power" the Reich's opponents found so impressive.

Particularly in the context of the Russian front, the concept of comradeship has been described as an increasingly artificial construction, based on Nazi ideology, generated by material demodernization and consistent high casualty rates that destroyed "primary groups" that depended on long-standing relationships. Small relational groups based on affinity, proximity, and experience were above all survival mechanisms. A man physically or emotionally alone in Russia was a casualty waiting to happen. The ad hoc, constantly renewed and reconstructed communities resulting from heavy losses were held together by the old hands—sometimes of no more than a few days' standing—who set the tone and sustained by the newcomers not only seeking but needing to belong in order to survive physically and mentally.

"Good" was in fact frequently defined as any behavior that strengthened the fragile, fungible, ad hoc community against external or internal challenges. But however deep ran their brutalization, the ground forces, army and Waffen SS alike, never degenerated collectively into what Martin van Creveld called "the wild horde." Lawless and disorganized, committed to destruction for destruction's sake, self-referencing to the point of solipsism, the horde can neither give nor inspire the trust necessary for the kind of fighting power the Germans demonstrated to the end.

Comradeship helped them to remain soldiers, not warriors or killers. And after 1945, for German veterans comradeship became the war's central justifying experience. Few were willing to admit they had fought for Hitler and his Reich. The concept of defending home and loved ones was balanced, and increasingly overbalanced, by overwhelming evidence that the war had been Germany's war from start to finish. What remained were half-processed memories nurtured over an evening glass of beer or at the occasional regimental reunion—memories of mutual caring, emotional commitment, and sacrifice for others. Traditionally considered to be feminine virtues, these human aspects of comradeship made it possible to come to terms morally and emotionally with war's inhuman face—and to come to terms with the nature of the regime one's sacrifices had sustained.

If the Soviets saw war as a science, the Germans interpreted it as an art. Though requiring basic craft skills, war defied reduction to rules and principles. Its mastery demanded study and reflection but depended ultimately on two virtually untranslatable concepts: *Fingerspitzengefühl* and *Tuchfühlung*. The closest English equivalent is the more sterile phrase *situational awareness*. The German concept incorporated as well the sense of panache: the difference, in horsemen's language, between a hunter and a hack—or, in contemporary terms, the difference between a family sedan and a muscle car. It emphasized speed and daring, maneuvering to strike as hard a blow as possible from a direction as unexpected as possible.

The mobile way of war was epitomized in the panzer divisions. From its inception, the division was conceptualized as a balanced combined-arms force. Tanks and motorized infantry, motorcyclists and armored cars, artillery, engineers, and signals would train and fight together at a pace set by the armor. The panzer division would break into an enemy position, break through, and break out with its own resources, thereby solving the fundamental German problem of World War I. But the panzer division could also create opportunities on an enemy flank or in his rear areas. It could conduct pursuit and turn pursuit into exploitation. It could discover opportunities with its reconnaissance elements, capture objectives with its tanks, hold them with its infantry, then regroup and repeat the performance a hundred miles away.

No less significant was the rapid development of radio—and the accompanying sense that commanders of mobile forces could and must be at the head of their units. Helmuth von Moltke the Elder's familiar aphorism that "no plan survives contact with the enemy" acquired a new context. In the future, mechanized commanders and mechanized forces would be able to make, remake, and implement plans immediately reflecting changing situations. War by timetable in the fashion of 1914–18 would become war by stopwatch.

The critique of mass war developed in German military thought after 1918 had never excluded numbers per se. Its goal had been the eventual creation of a force able to achieve decisive tactical and operational results initially, thus avoiding the spiral of escalation forcing Germany into a war of attrition—exactly the kind of war the professional soldiers had warned for decades that Germany had no chance of winning. The army that took the field, however, was the product of improvisation. The steady pace originally projected by the general staff and the high command was submerged by a rearmament that rapidly became its own justification and increasingly outran available human and material resources. Even after the Blood Purge of 1934 eliminated the possibility of using the Sturmabteilung (SA), the paramilitary brownshirts, as the basis for an alternative military system, the army continued to fear dual loyalty in an increasingly Nazified society. Total war of the kind Hitler seemed willing not merely to risk but to affirm remained in strategic terms the wrong kind of war for Germany. And in social/political contexts, a mass war involving the German *Volk* was likely to benefit the Nazis far more than the soldiers.

Since the Napoleonic Wars, the Prussian/German army had stressed the desirability of a high average. The general staff developed as a leaven to the officer corps as a whole, rather than as a self-absorbed elite. In operational terms, one regiment, division, or corps had been considered as capable as any other. When reserve divisions were organized on a large scale as part of the run-up to World War I, they were structured as far as possible to the active army's norms and from the beginning used in the same way as active formations. In 1939, however, most of the divisions were formed by "waves" (*Wellen*), each with differing scales of equipment, levels of training, and operational effectiveness. Now, in planning for war, the army had developed a hierarchy of dependability, with the peacetime divisions of the "first wave" at its apex—and the mobile divisions at the apex of the first wave.

That situation offered the army a political and military window of opportunity. The tactical, doctrinal, and institutional concepts developed by the Reichswehr and refined after 1933 provided the prospect of decisive offensive operations executed not by a small professional army, but by specialized technocratic formations within a mass. High-tech force multipliers favored developing an elite—not in the racial/ideological sense, but a functional elite, based on learned skills. Its professionalism would enable the employment of ways of war, inapplicable by homogenized mass armies in the pattern of 1914–18, that would produce victories.

Soldiers and academics alike in recent years have been at pains to discredit and deconstruct the concept of blitzkrieg. Reduced to its essentials, the critique is that the German victories of 1939–41 were not consequences of doctrine or planning. They developed from a series of accidents and coincidences reflecting improvisations born of the necessity to avoid a war of attrition and responding to imperatives generated by the random nature of the National Socialist regime.

Blitzkrieg was not a comprehensive principle for mobilizing and employing Germany's resources. Nor was it a structure of concepts expressed in manuals, taught in schools, and practiced in maneuvers. To say that blitzkrieg was an ex post facto construction nevertheless makes as much sense as to assemble the components of a watch, shake the pieces in a sack, and expect to pull out a functioning timepiece. Blitzkrieg was the latest manifestation of mobile war, the historic focus of Prussian/German military planning that Seeckt and his contemporaries sought to restore after 1918. Blitzkrieg also gave a technologically based literalness to an abstract concept. Mobile war waged with human and animal muscle power had always been more of an intellectual construction than a physical reality. In blitzkrieg, the combination of radios and engines made it possible for an army literally to run rings around its enemy—if, and it was a big if, its moral and intellectual qualities were on a par with its material.

Between 1939 and 1941, that was the case from France and Belgium to Yugoslavia and Cyrenaica. The stresses of making war in Russia, however, transmuted blitzkrieg's strengths to its weaknesses. Production lagged behind expenditures. Casualties exceeded replacement capacities. The gap in capabilities and effectiveness between the mechanized elite and the foot-marching, horse-drawn infantry divisions grew into a chasm. One consequence was the progressive devolution of the mechanized forces from spearhead to backbone: the necessary element of every operation from holding the front in the winter of 1941 to leading the way street by street in Stalingrad a year later. Infantry divisions remained so chronically understrength that by 1943 they were in the process of being reduced to six battalions instead of the original nine. New weapons like the MG-42 light machine gun and a family of man-portable antitank rockets enhanced the infantry's firepower. But the reconfigured divisions lacked the staying power to sustain operations, offensive or defensive, against a Red Army increasingly able to depend on more than its own determination.

As the panzers became more of an elite, their responsibilities expanded beyond any original intentions. The mobile divisions were increasingly expected to use their own resources to hold ground, recover it, and secure it, at the expense of generating and sustaining offensive momentum. By the end of the winter fighting in 1942, the eighteen panzer divisions on the Russian front had a combined strength of only around six hundred serviceable tanks. The shortages of trucks and other supporting vehicles were even greater. Replacing casualties and equipment had become a haphazard process—almost random, depending on which division could be pulled off the line, how far back it could be moved, and what was available in the depots and workshops.

A second consequence was tunnel vision: a focus on "hitting the next target," an emphasis on action at the expense of reflection at all levels and in all aspects of war making. Prussian/German military planning historically tended to devolve downward, privileging operational art at the expense of strategic projection and privileging tactical virtuosity at the expense of both. A chronic shortage of staff officers at all levels, often uncritically praised as reflecting a "lean and mean" profile, in practice too often meant chronic overwork and no time to think about next week. Improvisation was a necessity in the German way of mobile war. But improvisation on the Eastern Front too often tended to the verge of randomness—and beyond.

Third, and arguably most serious in the long run, was a culture, a mentality, that had developed into something combining convenience and indifference, embedded in a matrix of "hardness." Hardness was neither cruelty nor fanaticism. It is best understood as evolving from prewar concepts, as will focused by intelligence for the purpose of accomplishing a mission. It was a mind-set particularly enabling the brutal expediency that is an enduring aspect of war and was underwritten and nurtured by Nazi ideology.

Hardness transmuted expediency into a norm and redefined it as a virtue. Impersonalization and depersonalization went hand in hand. Interfering civilians or inconvenient POWs might not be condignly and routinely disposed of—but they could be, with fewer and fewer questions asked externally or internally. The culture of hardness was centered in the army's junior officers. With the outbreak of war, combat experience became the dominant criterion for a commission. By the end of 1942, any German over sixteen could become an army officer if he served acceptably at the front, demonstrated the proper character, believed in the Nazi cause, and was racially pure—and the final three criteria were as much a matter of square filling as rigorous investigation.

This relative democratization in good part reflected the growing synergy between National Socialist ideology and the demands of the front. Hitler wanted young men "as tough as leather, as fleet as greyhounds, and as hard as Krupp steel," correspondingly un-burdened by reflection or imagination. The Red Army at its best did not offer sophisticated tactical opposition. What regiment and division commanders wanted in subordinates was tough men physically and morally, willing to lead from the front and publicly confident in even the most desperate situations. One might specu-late, indeed, that a steady supply of twenty-something lieutenants with wound badges and attitudes helped older, wiser, and more tired superiors to suppress any developing doubts about Hitler and his war.

Chapter II

Chapter II

———

PREPARATIONS

THE BATTLE OF KURSK developed in the wider contexts of a war that the Reich's leadership, from Hitler downward, understood hung in the balance. In the aftermath of El Alamein, Hitler had heavily reinforced defeat in North Africa. The result was a few tactical victories, won against inexperienced troops, that proved operationally barren and strategically empty.

I

Erwin Rommel, the Desert Fox, was worn down mentally and physically. He halted one attack when the American artillerymen facing it had a fifteen-minute supply of ammunition remaining. He managed to concentrate three panzer divisions for an attack against the British Eighth Army advancing from the east, the largest armored attack the Germans made in the entire campaign. But radio intercepts gave Field Marshal Bernard Law Montgomery an outline of his enemy's intentions, with the result that the Germans ran into a multilayered, prepared defense that tore the heart out of the panzers. "The Marshal has made a balls of it," Montgomery pithily observed, and within a day Rommel called off a battle that by all odds ranks as his most embarrassing.

Three weeks later, on March 26, 1943, the British Eighth Army enveloped the Mareth Line. On April 19, the British First Army and the U.S. II Corps attacked in the west. Despite Hitler's continued reinforcing of failure, there could be no serious doubt of the final outcome.

Hopes for the U-boat campaign, and faith in new weapons from nerve gas to super-long-range cannon to rocket bombs, were balanced against an Anglo-American round-the-clock aerial offensive absorbing increasing amounts of the Reich's high-tech capacities. They were further dimmed by the prospects of a cross-Channel invasion sometime in 1943 by an alliance demonstrating in North Africa an uncomfortably high learning curve, albeit on a small scale. The domestic situation was no less disquieting. In 1942, the Eastern Front alone had cost the army an average of more than a hundred thousand dead each month. Not counting the completely unfit and the indispensable war workers, as of March 1943 the Reich was down to its last half million warm bodies not yet in uniform. In 1942, the Eastern Front had also cost fifty-five hundred tanks, eight thousand guns, and almost a quarter-million motor vehicles. Two-thirds of the twenty thousand written-off aircraft had been lost in Russia. These material losses were being successfully replaced—but for how long?

Complicating the answer was Hitler's fundamental distrust of both the German people and his own apparatus of repression and control. He believed firmly that Germany had been "stabbed in the back" by the collapse of its home front in 1918. "Total mobilization" as practiced in Russia and Great Britain—conscripting women for war work, shutting down civilian-oriented production, combing the economy ruthlessly for men—was highly risky and to a great extent beyond the capacities of the haphazard, inefficient Nazi system.

Paradoxically, from Hitler's perspective the strategic situation seemed most promising on the Russian front. Postwar historians in general have followed the generals' memoirs in blaming the defeat at Kursk on the Führer. Hitler is indicted, tried, and convicted first for refusing to accept the professionals' recommendations and shift to an operational defensive, replacing the losses of the winter campaign and temporarily trading space for time, while allowing the Red Army to extend itself in a renewed offensive, then for using the refitted mobile divisions in counterattacks such as Manstein's post-Stalingrad "backhands." Once having forced through the concept of an offensive, Hitler is described as first delaying it while the Russians reinforced the sector, then abandoning it when, against the odds, the generals and the *Landser* were on the point of once more pulling the Reich's chestnuts from the fire.

Reality, as might be expected, is a good deal more complex. As early as October 1941, Japan had offered to act as an intermediary in negotiating a Russo-German peace, in the interest of focusing the Axis against Great Britain and the United States. Even before the Soviet offensive at Stalingrad, Hitler had rejected Italian suggestions for either seeking terms with Russia or shutting down the Eastern Front and transferring resources to an increasingly threatened western theater.

Hitler rejected both possibilities repeatedly and emphatically. For the Führer, the Reich's blood-bought living space was not a negotiable asset. Defeat and retreat, moreover, meant material losses were permanent, while in an offensive, damaged weapons and vehicles could often be repaired by a maintenance system whose efficiency had improved by necessity. Hitler's specific insistence that south Russia's resources were too significant for sustaining Germany's war effort to be casually fought over, much less abandoned, could not be simply dismissed. Neither could his argument that the slightest hint of negotiations between Germany and the USSR would only encourage the Anglo-Americans to intensify their air offensive and step up their invasion plans.

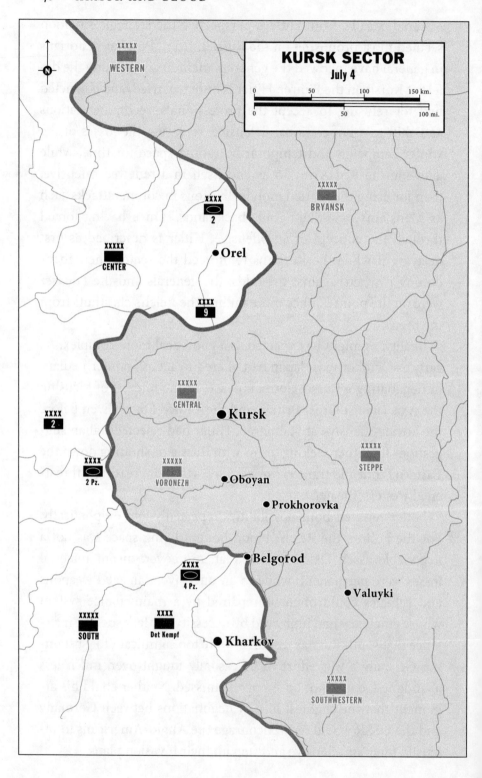

KURSK SECTOR
July 4

Instead, with the turn of the year Hitler increasingly focused his strategic thinking on the East. Italy and Hungary were withdrawing their forces from Russia. Romania was reducing its commitment. Finland had always fought a parallel war. A major victory was badly needed to impress these wavering allies. Russia offered the best immediate prospect of such a victory: a victory that might convince even Turkey to join the war. And prospects for negotiations with Stalin—which seemed more likely than discussing peace with Winston Churchill—was better undertaken from a position of strength than one of stalemate. Perhaps as early as the coming autumn, when weather again closed down the front, something might be undertaken in that quarter.

By any rational calculation, the Reich's short-term prospects of total victory were close to zero. Without Hitler's iron determination, Germany would probably have been ready to conclude peace in 1943. But by that time, the National Socialist Führer state had so far eroded the principal institutions of government, party, Wehrmacht, and society that neither institutional nor personal forums for debating the issue in any consequent way existed. Not only was no one but Hitler responsible for the whole—no one (above all, no one in the military) was willing to risk looking beyond operational factors, considering the larger strategic issues, and concluding that the war might be unwinnable, much less acting on such a conclusion. Like many another Third Reich design, the Kursk offensive would take on a half-life of its own.

In the spring of 1943, the Army High Command (the OKH, Oberkommando des Heeres), responsible for the war in Russia, was divided evenly on the specific issue of attack and defense on the Eastern Front. Heinz Guderian was one of the many generals supplanted during the *Ablösungswinter* ("relief winter") of 1941–1942. In February 1943, he was restored to power and favor as the newly created inspector general of armored troops. From his first weeks in office, he argued against any major offensive during 1943 in favor of rebuilding a mechanized force that had been stretched to its limits by the fighting at the turn of the year. Wait until 1944,

Guderian urged. Build a mobile reserve strong enough to hold any Western front the British and Americans could open. Then strike in the East with divisions built around a new generation of heavy tanks, with increased numbers of half-tracks, assault guns, and self-propelled artillery pieces.

Manstein, by this time the doyen and guru of the Russian front, at least in his own mind, believed Guderian took too little account of the Red Army's growing size and effectiveness. Manstein's answer was elastic defense: giving ground before a Soviet offensive, then striking the flanks. This, he believed, would maximize German officers' mastery of mobile warfare and German soldiers' fighting power. However, the concept was Manstein's personal brainchild: barely articulated, tested over no more than a few months, and for practical purposes unfamiliar even in the panzer force. Nor was elastic defense a panacea. Its success depended on an obliging enemy, making the right mistakes at the right time. The Red Army of 1943 was less and less obliging.

Manstein made his case to the army's chief of staff, Kurt Zeitzler, on March 7–8, 1943. Zeitzler had held the post since September 1942, replacing the dismissed Franz Halder. Although no lapdog, he had deliberately sought closer contact with Hitler in order to improve the eroding relationships among policy, planning, and command. Also, like many interwar-trained staff officers, he was more in the model of a troop staff officer than a traditional general staffer. It is an overlooked irony that the often criticized Versailles Treaty, by abolishing the general staff in its historic form, may have contributed significantly to the tunnel vision so characteristic of the German high command. Certainly Zeitzler was more concerned with resting the mobile troops than with long-term strategic planning. Manstein responded by explaining that he could not defend a 450-mile front with twenty-five divisions. It was either sustain the initiative and attack or be forced back again, sacrificing any material and moral gains made since Stalingrad's surrender.

Manstein had a chance to make his case in person when Hitler visited his headquarters on March 10. On one level it was propaganda theater, with sixteen senior generals present as a chorus line to celebrate the latest achievements of "the greatest warlord of all time." The Führer was in a correspondingly mellow mood and listened when Manstein reiterated the importance of resuming mobile operations. Another "backhand," frustrating and then rolling back a Soviet attack, was a possibility. A better option was a "forehand stroke" to eliminate what Manstein called the Kursk "balcony."

Elastic defense was for Manstein a temporary expedient, to wear down Soviet forces and prepare for a grander design. The backhand solution promised the greatest results. But what if the Soviets did not cooperate by attacking? Or if the Red Army chose a different sector, not graced with Manstein's presence? What if the British and Americans were somehow inspired to seize the operational initiative in the West and deplete the reserves Manstein considered necessary for an effective backhand stroke? Manstein's compromise concept was a combined general offensive by his Army Group South and Army Group Center against the Kursk salient. A large-scale double penetration would not only cut off Soviet forces in the salient, but draw Soviet reserves in the entire region onto a German anvil in the fashion of 1941. With the Russians significantly weakened, and with the front shortened by 150 miles, German reserves could more readily be deployed for further operations against the Soviet flanks and rear.

The long-range prospects of such operations were above the field marshal's pay grade—or perhaps his professional horizons. What he did insist on was that something must be done quickly, before Soviet material power grew overwhelming and while the Germans could take advantage of the dry season. And before the Western Allies could establish themselves on the continent.

Hitler's distrust of his generals had in no way lessened. He made no secret of his belief that they deceived him at every opportunity. But on March 13, he issued Operations Order No. 5. It called for a spring offensive to regain the initiative, but its objectives remained vague. Manstein repeatedly informed Zeitzler that Kursk was within the Germans' immediate grasp. Clearing the salient, however, would require the participation of Army Group Center. It was correspondingly disconcerting when Günther von Kluge's Army Group Center replied that it lacked the strength to participate in the kind of assault Manstein projected. That refusal made Manstein's commitment to the Kursk operation even firmer. It was a high-risk window of opportunity that must be seized even with limited resources.

Adolf Hitler once described his field marshals' horizons as "the size of a toilet seat." Manstein's version of that plumbing item, however, seems to have been too large for the Führer's comfort. On March 21, Hitler took Kursk off the table. Was he concerned for the still-continuing muddy season, the *rasputitsa,* which bogged down tanks and trucks? Was he anxious about the steadily mounting, as yet unreplaced losses of men and equipment? Did he worry about securing the gains of Manstein's previous offensives? Perhaps he feared nurturing an overmighty subject by sustaining his freedom to act. Guderian noted at the time Hitler's inability "to tolerate the presence of so capable and soldierly a person as Manstein in his environment."

The question became temporarily moot when Manstein's eye problems compelled his return to Germany for treatment on March 30. He kept in touch with his headquarters, but recovery absorbed his energy. The fifty-seven-year-old Manstein had pushed himself hard since 1940, and minor surgery—in this case sick leave for treatment of a developing cataract—kept him away. Manstein's absence cleared Zeitzler's field. He was also attracted by the prospects of eliminating the Kursk salient, albeit for less ambitious reasons than those of his subordinate. He considered weakening the Russians in the southern sector and shortening the front quite enough to be going on with—particularly given the increasing Russian concentration in and on the salient. On April 11, he submitted a recommendation to Hitler. It called for a pincer attack, utilizing a reinforced army from the north and Manstein's army group from the south. They would meet at Kursk.

The hundreds of thousands of Russian prisoners would be sent to Germany as slave labor in the overextended war industry. With the shortened Eastern Front line, Germany could reinforce the western theater against the inevitable invasion and free reserves for further operations in Russia. A dozen or so panzer divisions, the chief of staff suggested, should be enough to complete the job.

On April 15, Hitler responded. The opening paragraph of Operations Order No. 6 spoke of "decisive significance . . . a signal to all the world." The attacking forces were to be concentrated on "the narrowest possible front" and "break through the enemy at one blow." The earliest date for the attack was set at May 6. The code name was Operation Citadel.

In sharp contrast with the far-reaching objectives set in 1941 and 1942, Citadel's operational geography was so limited that it requires a small-scale regional map to follow. Order No. 6 insisted on the sovereign importance of maintaining surprise through "camouflage, deception, and disinformation." Success depended even more on preventing reserve-siphoning Soviet breakthroughs elsewhere. Army Groups South and Center must prepare as well for defensive battles on the remainder of their respective fronts. "All means" must be used to make all sectors secure. But recognizing that the shining times of 1940–41 were past did not make Kursk a limited offensive. Success offered a chance to damage the Red Army sufficiently to at least stabilize the Eastern Front and perhaps even develop a temporary political solution to a militarily unwinnable war.

In principle and in reality, the offensive was promising. Strategically, even a limited victory would remove a major threat to German flanks in the sector and limit prospects for a Red Army breakout toward the Dnieper. In Barbarossa and Blue, the Germans won their victories at the start of campaigns and ran down as they grew overextended. Citadel's relatively modest objectives seemed insurance against that risk. This time, forward units would not be ranging far beyond the front in a race to nowhere in particular. There were no economic temptations like those the Ukraine offered in 1941 or the Caucasus in 1942. Kursk would be a straightforward soldiers' battle. As for what would happen next, sufficient unto the day was the evil thereof. It was a line of thinking—perhaps a line of feeling—uncomfortably reminiscent of Erich Ludendorff's approach to the great offensive of March 1918: Punch a hole and see what happens.

In its immediate contexts, Kursk nevertheless seemed eminently plausible: the kind of prepared offensive that had frustrated the Soviets from divisional to theater levels for eighteen months. Geographically, the sector was small enough to enable concentrating overstretched Luftwaffe assets on scales unseen since 1941. Logistically, the objectives were well within reach. Operationally, the double envelopment of a salient was a textbook exercise. Tactically, from company to corps, the panzer commanders were skilled and confident. Materially, for the first time since Barbarossa they would have tanks to match Soviet quality.

That last point calls for explanation, particularly since "Kursk" and "armor" are symbiotically linked in most accounts of World War II. German armor doctrine stressed avoiding tank-on-tank encounters; German tank designs emphasized mobility and reliability as opposed to protection and firepower. From Poland to North Africa, the system worked. In Russia, it faltered—not least because of the growing presence of the Soviet T-34 tank, which could do anything its German counterparts could do, was better armored, and carried a powerful 76 mm gun. Prior to Barbarossa, German tank crews and tank officers had been a significant, albeit intangible, force multiplier. But the technological discrepancy between the Mark III and IV panzers and the T-34 diminished it. In human terms, the German armored divisions were about as good as they were likely to get given the limits of flesh, blood, intelligence, and character. In numerical terms, every calculation demonstrated inability to outproduce the Soviets. Technically, the

Panzer III, backbone of the armored force through 1942, could be upgunned no further.

That left three options. One involved taking advantage of the large turret ring and robust chassis of the Mark III's stablemate, the Mark IV, and upgrading what had been designed as a support vehicle to a main battle tank. Technically, the reconfiguration was highly successful. However, it was achieved at the expense of production numbers and repair statistics. The second possibility was copying the T-34, either conceptually or by reverse engineering. In the latter case, the Russian vehicle's cast turret and its aluminum engine would have challenged German capacities and resources. The two-man turret diminished the crew's effectiveness—still a German strongpoint. In any case, the lead times involved were an almost certain guarantee that when German imitations reached the front, the Red Army would be another generation ahead.

That left a new design, which became the Panther. Its design and preproduction absorbed most of 1942, and delivery projected by May 1943 was only 250. Its 75 mm L/70 was the most ballistically effective tank gun of World War II. But apart from the predictable teething troubles, two fundamental issues emerged. One was protection. Would the Panther's well-sloped frontal armor suffice against the weapons likely to be introduced as a counter? Its side armor, moreover, was not much better than that of its predecessors. The Panther's other problem was the engine. The tank weighed forty-five tons. Its Maybach 230 delivered a power-to-weight ratio of 15.5 horsepower per ton: low enough to strain the entire drive system and make uparmoring problematic. "Not perfect, but good enough" was the verdict rendered in the developing crisis of the Eastern Front.

The Panther's counterpoint, the Panzer VI, better known as the Tiger I, lent its aura to the whole German armored force. Even experienced British and U.S. troops were likely to see Tigers behind every hedgerow and leading every counterattack. There have been at least a hundred books in English, French, and German devoted to the Tiger's origins and performance. The first Tiger was a birthday present for the Führer in April 1942. Its initial production runs were set modestly, at fifteen a month by September. The Russians were expected to be defeated by the time the new tanks could take the field.

"The Tiger was all muscle, a slab-sided beast as sophisticated as a knee in the groin." Incorporating components from several firms and several design projects, it was always high maintenance. That does not mean unreliable. "Tiger was like a woman," in the words of one old hand. "If you treated her right, she'd treat you right." Tiger was also not a cheap date. Range on a full tank was only 125 miles. Speed was on the low side of adequate by previous panzer standards: about twenty miles per hour on roads, half that and less cross-country. But far from being a semimobile "furniture van" (*Möbelwagen*), Tiger was intended for offensive operations: exploitation as well as breakthrough. Its cross-country mobility was as good as that of most of its contemporaries. And with an 88 mm gun behind more than 100 mm of frontal armor, the Tiger could outshoot anything on any battlefield. Tested in small numbers from Leningrad to Tunisia beginning in August 1942, the Panzer VI seemed ideal for the conditions developing around Kursk, although it could be deployed only in small numbers—128 at the start of Citadel.

In one sense, that was Hitler's problem—the tank and the situation fit together too well for comfort. As early as April 18, the Führer inquired whether a preferable alternative might be to do the really unexpected and attack the salient's relatively vulnerable nose. In 1914, with war only hours away, German emperor Wilhelm II reacted to a vague hint of French neutrality by saying that now the whole army could be sent to the Eastern Front. His chief of staff never recovered from the shock. Kurt Zeitzler had a stronger nervous system. The time lost in shifting forces, he replied, would impose unacceptable delay, sacrifice prospects for surprise, and encourage a Soviet attack as the Germans redeployed.

Hitler calmed down for a week. Then he received a disconcerting report from the commanding general of the army responsible for Citadel's northern half. Walther Model is best remembered as a tactician, a defensive specialist shoring up broken fronts in the Reich's final years. But he had made his bones with the panzers, commanding a division and then a corps before being assigned to Army Group Center's right-flank Ninth Army in January 1942. He was also a trained staff officer, and the details of his army's proposed mission were not reassuring. The plan allowed too little time for preparation. It took too little account of the defense system the Soviets were constructing in Model's zone of attack. It allotted too few men and tanks to underwrite Model's original estimate of two days to achieve a breakthrough. As corroborating evidence mounted, six days seemed a more reasonable figure.

Hitler respected this tough, profane battle captain enough to schedule a one-on-one meeting for April 27. He rejected Model's suggestion that a preferable alternative was to shorten Army Group Center's line and await a Soviet attack. But he was impressed by the visual aids Model proffered: aerial photos showing a spiderweb of Soviet fortifications and trench lines matching anything in World War I. He responded by postponing the start of the offensive to May 5, then to May 9; and he spoke privately with Zeitzler about dropping it back to mid-June.

In May, the Führer took his concerns to a conference in Munich. The key meeting was on May 4; the principal participants were Zeitzler, Manstein, Kluge, and Guderian, plus Luftwaffe chief of staff Hans Jeschonnek. Hitler began by explaining in almost an hour's worth of detail his reasons for postponing the attack—essentially the same ones offered by the absent Model. When called on to reply, Manstein reiterated the necessity for an early success in the East, noting that by June the Red Army's overall abilities to mount its own offensives would be significantly enhanced. Rather than lose time reinforcing the armor, Manstein asked for more infantry—at least two divisions—to facilitate breaking through the Red Army's defenses. Hitler responded that none were available; tanks would have to compensate.

Kluge was next, and he spoke out strongly against postponement. He described Model as exaggerating Russian strength and warned that Citadel's delay increased the risk of a major Soviet attack elsewhere on his army group's front. Hitler shut him down by replying that he, not Model, was the pessimist here. Guderian promptly asked permission to speak. He called the Kursk operation pointless. It would cost armor losses the Reich could neither afford nor replace. And if the Panthers were expected to make a difference, they were still suffering from teething troubles and should not be counted on. Guderian concluded by recommending that should Citadel be allowed to proceed, the armor should be massed on one front to achieve total superiority—in other words, to create a decisive point, the *Schwerpunkt* that had been a feature of German planning for a century. Jeschonnek agreed, along with mentioning that the Luftwaffe had no chance of matching the Red Air Force's concentration in strength if the delays continued.

By this time, Hitler had a well-developed approach to dealing with the senior officers he disliked and mistrusted. He structured conferences around his own remarkable memory for detail, bolstered by information provided directly by his staff. If he failed to carry a point by drowning it in statistics, he insisted that decisions were best made spontaneously: instinct processed data more reliably than did calculation. Almost disconcertingly, neither of these behaviors was in particular evidence on May 4. Instead, Hitler seemed to weigh events and balance prospects.

The Axis position in Tunisia was collapsing with unexpected speed. Formal resistance ended on May 13. For ten days before that, increasing numbers of Germans and Italians were on their way to POW camps. The final tally was nearly a quarter million— worse than Stalingrad, without even the possibility of spinning the catastrophe into a heroic last stand.

Hitler obsessively saw himself as working against time. In contrast with Marxist-based radicalism, which ultimately understood itself to be on the side of history, Hitler's clock was always at five minutes to midnight. That in turn reflected Hitler's increasing sense of his own mortality, combined with the self-fulfilling para-

dox that Hitler's self-defined role had no place for a genuine successor. But his reflexive compulsion to action was in this case
arguably balanced by Model's photographs. Hitler's identity was
also shaped by his experiences as a Great War combat veteran, a
Frontschwein, "front hog," who understood battle in ways alien to
the grand gentlemen of the general staff. And what he had seen—
studied, indeed, with a magnifying glass—was all too reminiscent
of a Western Front that had ultimately defied German efforts at a
breakthrough.

Inaction was not an option. Neither was a second failure. In the
first half of May, Hitler's thoughts—and more important, his
feelings—turned to the new tanks as he increasingly came to view
technical superiority as the key to defeating enemies committed to
mass war. Moreover, since 1940 the panzers had been Germany's
arm of decision, challenging and overcoming space, time, and
numbers in every conceivable situation; this time they would do it
again.

The May 4 meeting did not result in a decision. But on May 5,
Citadel's date was reset to June 12. When Guderian warned again
that the Panthers could not be made combat-ready in five or six
weeks, Hitler abandoned his own initial sense of urgency, disregarded his field commanders' emphasis on haste, and postponed
the operation until early July.

While the Führer delayed, the soldiers moved. In Model's sector, XX Corps, with four infantry divisions, would hold down the
Ninth Army's right flank. Next came XLVI Panzer Corps. It had
only a few tanks under command, but its four infantry divisions
were as good as any in Russia and expected to fight their way
deeply enough into the Russian defenses to draw their reserves
away from Model's *Schwerpunkt.* That was provided by XLVII
Panzer Corps: three panzer divisions and another good infantry
division, commanded by Lieutenant General Joachim Lemelsen,
who had commanded mobile troops since 1938 and had no illusions about what he was expected to do. Next to Lemelsen was
another panzer corps: Josef Harpe's XLI. With the 18th Panzer Di-

vision, two infantry divisions, and several battalions of heavy armored vehicles, Harpe's corps was Lemelsen's left shoulder, to cover his advance and develop his success. The XXIII Corps, which concluded Model's sector to the east, was tasked with mounting a secondary attack toward the town of Maloarkhangelsk. It had two infantry divisions and a one-of-a-kind "assault division," an experimental formation whose strong component of antitank guns would make it possible for the corps to hold any positions captured. In reserve were three mobile divisions, two panzer and one panzer grenadier (motorized infantry with some armored half-tracks). These were under Kluge's control, not Model's, and would be committed only when the breakthrough was secured.

Model thus commanded in total around 335,000 men, six hundred tanks, and three hundred assault guns. These were tank chassis with guns mounted in the hull. Their heavier caliber made up for limited traverse compared with their turreted counterparts. There were no Panthers, and a single Tiger battalion would join Lemelsen's corps only at the start of the attack. As compensation, Model received two battalions of Ferdinands: 88 mm assault guns built on the chassis of a Tiger design rejected for production. Often dismissed by critics because of their bulk and because they lacked machine guns for close defense, the Ferdinands drew no criticism from their crews or the infantry, who welcomed their big guns as tank killers and bunker busters.

The Second Army held the salient's nose. With seven understrength infantry divisions and fewer than a hundred thousand men, it was assigned no role in Citadel beyond maintaining the link between the Ninth Army and Army Group South—which was configured to do the heavy lifting. Model's deployment reflected what was expected: a straightforward collision of men and tanks, with the Germans essentially muscling their way through the Russian defenses. Hermann Hoth's Fourth Panzer Army had to perform a trifecta: break in, break through, and break out into the rear of the salient.

To do it, Hoth had almost a quarter million men, including some of the best troops in the German army. Hoth formed his *Schwerpunkt* by allotting the left half of his sector to LII Corps and its three infantry divisions. In the center, XLVIII Panzer Corps had an infantry division as maid of all work, two panzer divisions, and the elite Grossdeutschland Division (GD). Designated a panzer grenadier, or mechanized infantry, division, Grossdeutschland was configured as a full-fledged panzer division and was at the head of the Wehrmacht's list for replacements and equipment. The corps also included an independent tank brigade with no fewer than two hundred brand-new Panthers, giving it a total of around six hundred armored fighting vehicles. Next to XLVIII was an arguably even more formidable instrument of war. The SS Panzer Corps had three divisions, 1st Leibstandarte, 2nd Das Reich, and 4th Totenkopf: the pick of the litter in Heinrich Himmler's already metastasizing Waffen SS. They had fought separately until assembled for Manstein's counteroffensive in early 1942, and earned reputations as warriors who never expected quarter and gave it only when convenient. Designated panzer grenadier divisions, they were panzer formations in all but name: the corps had around five hundred tanks and assault guns, including forty-two Tigers, and each division had six panzer grenadier battalions—two more than their army counterparts.

Neither Otto von Knobelsdorff of XLVIII Panzer Corps nor Paul Hausser of SS Panzer Corps—the corps's official title was changed to II SS Panzer Corps in June, but the original title remained in common use during Citadel—particularly stood out among the senior panzer officers as tacticians. The British phrase "good plain cooks" is not damnation with faint praise here. But both had reputations as soldiers' generals with the decorations to prove it, and Citadel did not look like the kind of battle that would offer much opportunity for finesse. Should that quality be required, Hoth had an ample supply of it. In the spring of 1943, he was the most experienced, and in many judgments the best, army-level commander of mobile forces in the German army. He had led a corps and a panzer group in 1940–1941, survived Hitler's purge in the winter of 1941–42, taken over the Fourth Panzer Army in June 1942, and taken it to Stalingrad and beyond in a series of virtuoso performances that impressed even Manstein. And through all that, his men called him "Pop" (*Vati*). Much depended on him. Hermann Hoth expected to deliver.

Army Detachment Kempf stood on Hoth's right. This was an ad hoc formation above a corps but below an army. It had nine divisions by early July, three of them panzers in III Panzer Corps commanded by another "comer," Hermann Breith. Werner Kempf was the right man to oversee Breith's debut in high command. He had led a brigade, a division, and a corps well enough to be promoted to the ad hoc force bearing his name in early 1943. Manstein trusted him: as good a recommendation as any tank man might wish. Kempf's detachment was originally intended as a blocking force, but its role grew as it became apparent that the defenses on its front might be a little less formidable than those facing Model and Hoth. Breith's corps added an infantry division, then a Tiger battalion, to its original strength of more than three hundred armored fighting vehicles (AFVs)—a formidable strike force in its own right, able to create opportunities as well as exploit them.

Army Group South had reserves as well: an army panzer division and the 5th SS Panzer Grenadier Division Wiking. But with only around a hundred tanks between them, they were more derringer than belt gun: better able to restore positions or exploit situations than to turn the tide of battle by themselves. They came, moreover, with a string attached. The Army High Command had to approve their commitment—a virtual guarantee of delay and distraction under conditions demanding Manstein's total concentration.

By this time, what "wave" a German infantry division belonged to was more or less irrelevant. The ones assigned to spearhead the offensive usually had solid cadres of veterans and as many replacements and as much new equipment as the overstretched rear echelons could provide. As late as mid-May, fewer than four hundred recruits and convalescents had on average reached Model's divisions. They would go into action as much as 20 percent under strength—a level even higher in the rifle companies. Training was another problem. Attacking the kinds of positions mushrooming in the Kursk salient was a specialized craft, and field commanders were willing enough to trade the offensive's repeated delays for a chance to improve training and increase firepower, giving their men a better chance in the close-quarters fighting to be expected.

The mobile troops were no less weary. By the end of the winter fighting, the eighteen panzer divisions in the East were down to around six hundred tanks. "Motorized" battalions were moving on foot and by wagon. Friedrich von Mellenthin, XLVIII Panzer Corps's chief of staff, widely accepted in postwar years as a final authority on mobile operations, declared that "hardened and experienced" panzer divisions were ready for another battle as soon as the ground dried. But Mellenthin was a staff officer: a bit removed from the sharp end. Hoth informed Manstein on March 21 that men who had been fighting day and night for months now expected a chance to rest. Even hard-charging regiment and division commanders had to drive instead of lead because of widespread apathy in the ranks.

Staff officers and line officers alike were openly critical of Citadel's repeated postponements. But delaying the attack provided the breathing space, the *Verschnaufpause,* the Germans so badly needed. It gave the newcomers a chance to shake down and the old hands a chance to relax. Gerd Schmückle, who would end a long and checkered military career as deputy commander of NATO in Europe, in 1943 was a junior officer in a panzer division. His memoirs nostalgically recall elaborate alfresco dinner parties, friendly Russian peasants, visits to the Kharkov opera—and one particular ballerina. There was even time to put on a show for a delegation of Turkish officers: clean shaves, clean uniforms, and all medals on display, with a cameraman on hand to record a Tiger put through its paces for the benefit of the Reich's newsreels.

The backdrop for all this was a buildup like few had ever experienced. Reactions, even among the cynics and grumblers, oddly resembled those widespread in the British Expeditionary Force in the weeks before the Battle of the Somme in 1916. This time, there was just too much of everything for anything to go seriously wrong!

II

Ironically, the Russians were coming to a similar conclusion. The Soviet victories at Stalingrad and in the Caucasus had not been won in isolation. On January 18, the Red Army had opened a corridor to the besieged city of Leningrad. Small-scale actions in the central sector had also favored the Soviets. Evaluating the results, Stalin interpreted the success of Manstein's post-Stalingrad counterattack as anomalous. He believed Soviet forces could shift directly to the offensive and win decisively. In response, the Soviet high command initially planned a major offensive: a deep battle, initiated by sequential attacks on a front extending from north of Smolensk down to the Black Sea, followed by theater-scale mechanized exploitation.

But the price of recent Soviet success had been high. The Germans, against expectations, had staged another remarkable recovery. Stalin might cultivate an image as Vozhd, supreme leader, source of all wisdom and authority. He may have been able to strike mortal fear into the most senior of generals and party officials. But he had learned the risks of taking immediate counsel of his own confidence. As Chief of Staff Vasilevsky noted, Stalingrad in particular added an operational dimension to his chief's thinking. In an Order of the Day issued in February, Stalin acknowledged the German army's recent defeat, but noted that there was no reason to assume it could not recover: "It would be stupid to imagine the Germans will abandon even a kilometer of our country without a fight."

Like many of the Red Army's common soldiers, Stalin understood, viscerally if not always intellectually, that the long retreat during the summer of 1942 could not be repeated, whatever the prospective advantages of further overextending the invaders. For practical purposes, there was nowhere left to go. Stalin understood as well, however unwillingly, that the kinds of strategic offensives the Red Army had conducted since the winter of 1941 had a way of turning into poorly coordinated, systematically mismanaged, hideously costly sector attacks, no matter how heavy Stalin's hand might lie on the responsible generals.

Should a reminder have been necessary, the still-incomplete relief of Leningrad was a depressing account of operations depending primarily on mass impelled by callousness and brutality, grinding forward a few miles, then stalling as much from internal frictions as from any German efforts. Commanders and formations alike showed repeated, glaring ineptitude in reconnaissance, communications, and combined-arms operations.

One of the Soviet Union's major advantages to date had been the ability to renew its forces to a degree impossible to the overextended Wehrmacht. But even Russia's resources, human and material, were not infinite. Significant evidence indicates Stalin seriously considered the prospects of a separate peace with Hitler, or with a successor government willing to respond. Tentative contacts between the respective diplomats, most of them indirect, began in Sweden during the spring of 1943 and continued for most of the year. Germany had worked out an agreement with the Soviet Union in 1939, and the USSR had demonstrated beyond question that it could defend itself essentially from its own resources. A separate peace, even temporary, would provide time for recovery. The second front long promised by the Western Allies still consisted of promises and substitutes. The suitably leaked possibility of an end to the fighting might impel Great Britain and the United States to step up the pace of their operations. And if the capitalist powers continued their war with one another, that as well would be to the USSR's long-term advantage.

Nothing came of the prospect, but while the diplomatic theater played itself out, military developments began focusing Stalin's attention elsewhere. On March 16, Stalin sent Zhukov down from Leningrad, where he had been assigned to organize an operation to relieve the city for good, to restore the situation at Kharkov. It was too late for that, but the transfer put Zhukov on the site as ground patrols and aerial reconnaissance, information provided by partisans and deserters, reported a rapid and increasing buildup in the Kursk sector. By early April, Zhukov was confident of enemy intentions as well as capabilities.

Rudolf Roessler, a German Communist who had relocated to Switzerland, had been running a spy ring that allegedly possessed high-level contacts in the Wehrmacht. The exact nature of the relationship of the "Lucy ring" to those contacts, and to Swiss military intelligence, remains obscure. But Lucy had established its credibility during 1942, repeatedly transmitting accurate and actionable information on the German offensive Operation Blue. Put temporarily out of business during the Kharkov operation, when Manstein limited his electronic connection to Hitler, by March Roessler was able to transmit an increasing amount of raw data on both German plans for an offensive at Kursk and the new material they were planning to deploy.

British intelligence passed on through the Military Mission in Moscow similar information, describing a projected May attack against the Kursk salient. The intelligence had been obtained as part of the Ultra operation, the intelligence coup based on cracking the codes of the "unbreakable" German Enigma cipher machine. Ultra was Britain's ace in the hole: the last strategic advantage retained by an overextended and exhausted empire. Its paradox was that its value depended on secrecy. Should the Germans even suspect Enigma was compromised and fundamentally reconfigure its electronic communication system, Ultra would have the value of a buggy whip.

Anglo-American intelligence cooperation may have been a necessary relationship, but it was also a cautious collaboration. The British were as determined as any ecdysiast to secure reci-

procity in return for revelation. That attitude governed as well
their dealings with the USSR. On June 12, 1941, the Soviet ambas-
sador to London was presented with detailed information on not
merely the projected German attack, but its precise starting date.
British intelligence forwarded similar information through a double agent, the deputy head of the Soviet espionage network in
Switzerland. The underlying hope was to frustrate Hitler's designs
and in the process improve currently distant relations with the
USSR. But Stalin ignored the information, as he did most of
the "Very Special Intelligence" subsequently made available to
Moscow—with its origins carefully camouflaged. Stalin was in
principle suspicious of any clandestine material that came from
the West. The comprehensively obsessive secrecy generated by the
Soviet secret police system kept information closely compartmen-
talized and tightly wrapped, restricting the development of alternative channels that might have compensated for Stalin's refusal to
share. So the British turned off the taps—until Churchill, recognizing the sovereign importance of keeping Russia in the war, ordered the Kursk material forwarded, albeit with its sources
camouflaged.

Stalin's doubts were overcome because the data was not only
confirmed but enhanced by a Soviet agent inside the Ultra project
itself. John Cairncross was the "fifth man" in the Cambridge spy
ring, whose highly placed traitors fed Soviet intelligence from the
world war into the Cold War. Assigned to Ultra in mid-1942, he
delivered to his handlers weekly decrypts of the same material
Ultra was processing. This was the kind of information from multiple sources that Stalin found difficult to resist.

Zhukov was in another category of credibility. He was not only
a field commander, but a Stavka troubleshooter, sent from crisis to
crisis with near plenipotentiary powers: "the high justice, the middle, and the low," disciplining, dismissing, or executing as deemed
necessary. By this time Stalin's ace troubleshooter, Zhukov impressed the Vozhd himself with his ruthlessness. So when on April
8 he sent a message predicting that the end of the *rasputitsa* would

be followed by a major German offensive against the Kursk salient as the first stage of a renewed drive on Moscow, Stalin was not prone to dismiss it as defeatism. Zhukov's recommended action was a different story. Preempting the German attack, he argued, was to invite a repetition of the recent defeat of Kharkov. Instead, reinforce the salient with every available man and gun, button up, dig in, and deploy major armored forces outside the immediate zone of operations. Wear out the Germans, wear down their tanks, and then shift to a counterattack as part of a full-scale, end-the-war counteroffensive. Vasilevsky, who was at Stalin's side when the dispatch came out of the teleprinter, fully endorsed his colleague's recommendations and the reasoning behind them. Stalin was not so sure. He saw the Kursk salient as a springboard and proposed to use the two fronts occupying it in a preemptive strike toward Kharkov and into the rear of the German Army Group Center. He called for a top-level conference.

On the evening of April 12, Zhukov and Vasilevsky entered Stalin's study—his "power room," whose layout and furnishings were configured to intimidate anyone not already intimidated and to silence anyone not inflexibly convinced of his position. This time, according to Zhukov, Stalin listened "more attentively than ever before" when Zhukov made his case. The Germans faced a grim paradox. Because mobile war was their best force multiplier, the increasingly irreplaceable losses suffered in the winter of 1942 compelled them to attack. Because their reserves were so limited, the attack could be made in only a limited sector of the front. And a cursory study of the situation map showed that German armored and motorized formations were steadily concentrating around the Kursk salient.

A Soviet offensive, whether the general operation originally bruited about or a more focused preemptive strike, made correspondingly no strategic or operational sense. The Germans still had a decisive edge in encounter battles, and the kind of concentration taking place around Kursk only enhanced that advantage. Rzhev might have been scrubbed from official memory. Zhukov had not forgotten. Neither had Stalin. It nevertheless took two months for the Soviet leader to commit definitively to standing on the defensive at Kursk and wearing out the German mobile forces as the first stage in a massive strategic offensive. This was not mere stubbornness. Zhukov, Vasilevsky, and the senior commanders on the ground were confident the Red Army could hold the Germans and grind them down in the Kursk salient. Stalin was less optimistic. As repeated German delays strained his equanimity and goodwill—neither present in oversupply—he developed two simultaneous approaches.

One involved creating a massive regional reserve under Stavka command. This Steppe Front by July would be built up to five rifle armies, the Fifth Guards Tank Army, three independent tank and mechanized corps, and an air army—almost six hundred thousand men and more than sixteen hundred armored fighting vehicles, deployed in a mutually supporting semicircle around the salient as a backstop against a German breakthrough. Steppe Front was also intended as the muscle behind an eventual counterattack—not in the Kursk sector, but north of it: around Orel. The Germans were weaker there and likely to be focusing on events at Kursk. The offensive, complemented by lesser diversionary attacks elsewhere in the southern theater, would compel the Germans to transfer mobile formations away from Kursk and eventually create a tactical overstretch enabling operational breakthrough and strategic exploitation.

As an ultimate insurance policy, Stalin insisted on transforming Kursk into the most formidable large-scale defensive system in the history of warfare. Like almost all of Stalin's initiatives in the war's second half, the policy had an obvious agenda and a hidden one. It was designed to transform Kursk into a killing ground. It was also designed to fix the Germans' attention. The elaborate construction work and the extensive movements of men and equipment in a relatively small area were impossible to conceal completely. So to borrow once more the metaphor of a burlesque theater, the object was to keep the mark looking in the wrong

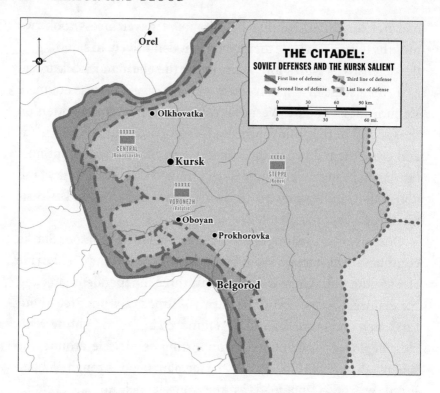

places. Let the Germans think that their opponent had committed itself to a defensive battle. Let them focus intelligence, reconnaissance, and planning on the Kursk salient. Their surprise, like that of a disappointed customer, would come when the Red Army rang down the curtain from the wings as the dance continued onstage.

The salient's transformation into a fortress began in mid-April. Initial talk of evacuating civilians was quashed by military authorities who said that this would have an adverse effect on troop morale—and on the labor supply. By June, more than three hundred thousand civilians, most of them women, were working on roads, bridges, and airfields in the salient's rear. Forward construction was the soldiers' responsibility—250 engineer companies, supported by every man the infantry could spare on a given day. The defensive system was configured as a labyrinthine combination of battalion defensive sectors, antitank ditches and strongpoints, machine-gun positions, barbed wire, minefields, roadblocks, and obstacles whose positioning at times seemed almost random.

Each frontline rifle army had a forward zone, a second line, and an army defensive line, plus a trip wire of outposts and small forlorn-hope strongpoints designed to frustrate German ground reconnaissance before the attack and compel early German deployment once the offensive started. The salient's forward zones alone included 350 battalion positions, 2 or 3 to a rifle regiment, networks of mutually supporting trenches, blockhouses, and bunkers. There were as many as six successive defensive zones, each with two or three layers. The first two zones were fully occupied, the middle ones were held by units in reserve, and the final two were left empty, as fallback positions or to be occupied by reinforcements. These extended as far as fifty miles into the salient's rear. And behind them were two more positions constructed by the Steppe Front, which extended the zone of defensive operations to something approximating two hundred miles—an unmatched record in the history of war, and one likely to remain unchallenged.

Other statistics are no less daunting. In their final form, the defenses absorbed almost a million men. They were supported by almost twenty thousand guns and mortars, three hundred rocket launchers, and thirty-three hundred tanks. The engineers supervised the stringing of over five hundred miles of barbed wire and the laying of around 640,000 mines. There were so many minefields, and with their well-camouflaged layouts so often overlapped, it became necessary in the Soviet rear areas to post sentries and warning signs to protect unwary men and vehicles. Minefields averaged more than twenty-four hundred antitank mines and twenty-seven hundred antipersonnel mines per mile—about one mine per foot. Many of these were "box mines" in wooden casings, substitutes for scarce steel. As a rule, their explosive force was too diffused to destroy tanks, but they remained effective against treads and suspension. They also had the advantage of being undetectable by standard minesweeping equipment. Clearing such a field too often meant probing the ground with bayonets. As a deterrent to prospective heroes, the minefields also included improvised flamethrowing devices based on a mine linked to several gasoline bombs.

The minefields were laid out so as to "encourage" the panzers to move into antitank killing zones. Those were the domain of the PTOPs, the *protivtankovye opornye punkte,* antitank strongpoints. Sited in checkerboard fashion, usually a half mile apart and in zones up to five miles deep, they included infantry and engineers tasked with using hand-carried explosives to finish off disabled tanks. But their core was the 76 mm gun. This high-velocity, flat-trajectory piece was both the army's standard light field gun and a formidable antitank weapon, able to penetrate the frontal armor of any armored vehicle the Germans had deployed to date. Some strongpoints included as well self-propelled versions of the 76, artillery pieces up to 152 mm gun-howitzers, and prepared positions for T-34 tanks. The heavy weapons were supported by large numbers of antitank rifles and light 45 mm guns. Both were long obsolescent. Both were most useful at close range. Both were proof of Stavka's commitment to a finish fight on the steppe.

There was no room in these crowded positions for vehicles to remove the guns. To improve concealment and make the point that withdrawal was not an option, gun wheels were sometimes removed. To maximize the advantages of fixed positions, crews were trained and ordered to hold their fire until point-blank range. The engineers devoted all their considerable skill at camouflage to conceal the entrenchments. Their success is indicated by German aerial photos taken before and during the battle that show miles of territory with only limited signs of life. Once exposed, the strongpoints could call for support from any guns and rocket launchers within range—which was most of them. But in the end, the antitank strongpoints were expendable. The watchword for their garrisons was "stand or die." "Hold and die" was to prove no less appropriate.

The static fixed defenses were coordinated with mobile antitank and armor reserves. The former ranged from a few guns and some antitank riflemen at regimental level to a full antitank battalion, built around a dozen 76 mm guns, for an army corps. The forward infantry units could also count on direct tank support: a company for a battalion, a regiment or brigade for a division. The dispersion of armor ran against Soviet doctrine and experience. But the tankers too were expendable, there to do as much damage as they could, to keep German break-ins from becoming breakthroughs.

Kursk was projected as a managed battle, a scientific exercise. To that end, the communications network was developed with unprecedented care and precision. Radios, phones, and messengers were coordinated to complement one another. Command posts even at regiment and battalion levels became electronic centers. Landlines were buried deeply and duplicated, sometimes tripled, in critical sectors. This time, no excuses based on failure to receive orders would be accepted.

This emerging defensive maze was designed to work in three stages. The German infantry, Zhukov had argued, seemed less capable of offensive operations than in 1942. As it was worn down, the German armored forces would have to rely on their divisional infantry to lead the way and secure the rear zones. That would have the effect of separating tanks and infantry, breaking the combined-arms cohesion on which German tactics depended. And when the increasingly isolated tanks played their familiar card and maneuvered in search of weak spots, they would find that none existed—at least none that the worn-down panzers could exploit.

Deception, the *maskirovka* at which the Red Army had come to excel, was comprehensively employed to obscure details. Dummy airfields, simulated communications centers, and false gun positions saturated the salient. Daylight movement was kept to a minimum. Planes flew into forward bases at twilight, hugging the ground. Rear-echelon supply and maintenance units were sited in the narrow valleys and gorges that dotted what seemed to be the steppe's open grasslands. In 1914 and again in 1941, Russian communications security had often been an oxymoron. At Kursk, radio security was rigidly maintained, and ground lines and messengers did most of the work. Even the frontline visits of senior party members and generals were discouraged—in some cases forbidden.

Morale was the responsibility of the front political departments. They intensified the usual high level of party activists. Political officers, Communist Youth, and party members were expected to set examples in everything from weapons care to combat training. Though the ultimate sanctions were not abolished, they faded into the background as the Kursk salient prepared for a finish fight.

Partisan operations were also part of the general plan. By 1943, the Soviet presence behind enemy lines had developed into a formidable mass movement, supplied, armed, and above all controlled from Moscow. A central partisan headquarters coordinated local and regional operations. Partisans had to screen groups and individuals for loyalty as a matter of both ensuring operational effectiveness and maintaining a connection with Moscow that was increasingly crucial as a source of supplies and legitimacy. Soviet values and norms also proved useful to the partisans for coping with the psychological and social stresses of encirclement and isolation by an enemy who gave no quarter.

These problems were particularly salient in southern Russia, where the terrain offered limited opportunities for safe zones compared with the forests farther north, and where the German presence on the ground was proportionally larger in the run-up to Kursk. The region's partisans nevertheless effectively supported the long-range reconnaissance patrols that kept the German rear areas under observation. Civilians played an increasing role in intelligence operations. Local youths between eight and fourteen were particularly favored as agents, many of whom underwent four-week training programs. They showed remarkable talents for observation and espionage.

Since January, partisan operations against the railroads in the rear of German Army Group Center had been disrupting troop and supply movements. On June 14, Stavka initiated a comprehensive "rail war" focused on the lines into the Kursk sector. Raids destroyed bridges, disabled rolling stock, and diminished train crews' morale and effectiveness. They created traffic jams offering profitable targets to Red Air Force night bombers, who in turn were for practical purposes unopposed because night fighters, guns, and their supporting electronic systems were increasingly needed for the defense of the Reich itself.

Weapons and fortifications are nothing without fighting men. The Kursk salient was held by two entire Soviet fronts, the counterpart of Western army groups. The northern sector was the operational zone of the Central Front. From right to left—or base to tip—it deployed five rifle armies. Most of the heavy fighting would be done by the Forty-eighth, with seven divisions and 84,000 men; the Thirteenth, with twelve divisions and 114,000 men; and the Seventieth, with eight divisions and 96,000 men. The two armies wrapped around the salient's nose, the Sixtieth and Sixty-fifth, had fifteen rifle divisions between them. Facing infantrymen like themselves, they were projected to have an easier time than the other three, at least at first.

Front reserves were built around four tank corps plus a nearly uncountable number of smaller tank and artillery units. When all the figures are calculated and collated, the Central Front controlled eleven thousand guns and mortars and eighteen hundred tanks. Under its command and on call were the assets of the Sixteenth Air Army: 1,150 aircraft as of July 4. Almost a quarter of them were the formidable Ilyushin Il-2 Shturmoviks, one of the war's finest ground-attack aircraft. Another quarter were twin-engine bombers (including a number of Lend-Lease American Douglas Havocs), and the rest was a mixed bag of single-engine fighters. An indication of the Red Air Force's improved effectiveness was maintenance statistics showing almost 90 percent of the planes as serviceable.

Commanding this formidable instrument of war was General

Konstantin K. Rokossovsky. Born in what was then Russian Poland in 1896, he still spoke Russian with a marked Polish accent but had served the revolution and the Soviet Union since 1917 as a cavalryman. He was commanding a division in 1937 when he was arrested and charged not only with being a saboteur, but with spying simultaneously for Poland and Japan! He spent two and a half years as a guest of state security, returning to duty in 1940 with a mouthful of metal teeth—courtesy of his interrogators.

Beginning with Barbarossa, Rokossovsky established a reputation as one of the Red Army's rising stars. As hard a man as any in a system where any kind of vulnerability was a career killer, he got the best out of subordinates with strong wills and limited skills. This was particularly useful when handling the new generation of Red Army generals, still learning their craft on the job but expected to act as if they knew what they were doing. Rokossovsky had shone in front command during the Battle of Stalingrad and taken the final German surrender. One of his recent tasks had combined business with pleasure by getting rid of a large number of Seventieth Army's NKVD officers unable to make the transition from brutalizing their countrymen to fighting Germans. Kursk's northern sector could have been in no better hands.

Rokossovsky's counterpart in the south was more of an establishment figure. Nikolai Vatutin joined the Red Army as a private in 1920 and spent the next two decades developing an awareness of technological innovation and a reputation as a systematic planner not afraid to make decisions. Given the many top-level vacancies created by Stalin's purges of the senior officer corps, it was hardly surprising when Vatutin became the general staff's chief of operations in 1940 and its deputy chief a few months later.

Vatutin was one of the first to develop a sense of how comprehensive a disaster Barbarossa was and one of the few to inform Stalin of the blunt, unvarnished truth. He did well commanding the Southwestern Front in the Stalingrad counteroffensive. He was enough of a risk taker to overbet his hand against Manstein during the Kharkov operation of January–February 1943. But Vatutin was not the only Soviet general who had a similar experience. With Vasilevsky's support he survived, and in March he was given command of the Voronezh Front in the Kursk salient's southern half.

Vatutin initially advocated a preemptive attack as soon as possible. The longer the Germans delayed their own offensive, the more strongly Vatutin argued for "getting off our backsides." He telephoned Stalin himself, calling for an offensive no later than early July and by some accounts sufficiently reinforced Stalin's own anxieties that had Vatutin been on the spot instead of at the far end of a phone line, plans might have been changed even at that late date. Such aggressive determination made Nikolai Vatutin the kind of senior general both Zhukov and Stalin wanted at the sharp end: better to rein in the spirited stallion than try to inspire a mule, especially as Vatutin did not face a walk in the sun. His front would eventually commit more than 450,000 men: four rifle armies, a tank army, and two tank corps. The Thirty-eighth and Fortieth Armies, thirteen divisions and four tank brigades, covered the southern half of the salient's nose.

The Sixth and Seventh Guards Armies, which extended Vatutin's line to the salient's base, were expected to receive the first German assault. Each had seven rifle divisions, nearly seventeen hundred guns and mortars, and a number of armored fighting vehicles. They had been especially favored in the matter of minefields and antitank strongpoints and were expected to need both. The terrain in their sector was the most open on the salient's front and included the Kharkov–Kursk highway: the shortest paved distance between the two points. Both armies, moreover, had, at thirty-five to forty miles apiece, larger sectors than their Central Front counterparts.

Vatutin responded by concentrating his reserves behind the Sixth and Seventh Guards Armies: the Sixty-ninth Army's five divisions, the three divisions of the 35th Guards Rifle Corps, the First Tank Army, and two more Guards tank corps under his direct command. It was an impressive sector reserve in both numbers and quality, and First Tank Army's commander, Mikhail Katukov, was easily the best tank man in the salient. He had given Guderian a serious bloody nose during Barbarossa; he had helped rebuild the armored force in 1941–42; and he had come out of the fighting around Rzhev with a record of combining Soviet hardness with enough situational awareness not to insist on the impossible. He would prove a good man in the right spot.

III

As the ground pounders counted down the days, the battle for air supremacy over the salient took center stage. The Red Air Force had taken a brutal beating in the early weeks of Barbarossa. But enough aircraft were destroyed on the ground that their crews survived to man the new generations of aircraft and train the new generations that flew them. Designers and engineers, some released from the Gulag, produced state-of-the-art designs whose airframes, like that of the British Spitfire, had a capacity for improvement as opposed to needing replacement by entirely new models.

But by mid-1943, quality still lagged. Key to the air battle over Kursk were single-engine air superiority fighters. By mid-1943, the most common Soviet fighters, the Lavochkin La-5 and the Yakovlev Yak-1 and Yak-7, were still about a half generation behind the Messerschmitt Me-109Gs and Focke-Wulf Fw-190s that were their usual opponents. They were competitive—but it took a good pilot to make up the technical difference. There was the rub. Soviet fighter trainees were routinely assigned to frontline units after only eighteen flight hours, compared with seventy for their German counterparts. The quality gap was bridgeable by skilled, experienced squadron and group leaders, but they were still in short supply. The difference would be made up in blood.

Soviet air doctrine was geared to the ground war. Close support and interdiction were its foci. In the context of Kursk, that involved a campaign against German airfields and railroads in the salient's immediate rear by twin-engine bombers, as many as four hundred in a single raid. These were supplemented by the night light bomber regiments, composed of single-engine Polikarpov Po-2 biplane trainers—often flown by female military aviators (dubbed "night witches"). The planes' distinctive engine sounds won them the nickname "sewing machines" from *Landser* regularly awakened by their pinprick strikes.

Initially, German air offensives into Soviet rear areas were small-scale efforts, focused on train busting. These operations also diverted resources from a more relevant target: the Kursk rail yards, central to Soviet logistics in the salient. Major German raids on May 22 and June 2–3, the latter a round-the-clock operation, met bitter resistance from superior numbers of fighters. Losses were heavy enough and damage was so quickly repaired that the Luftwaffe decided to suspend daylight operations against Soviet rear areas for the balance of Citadel. Night operations continued at a nuisance level—though one midnight strike unknowingly hit Rokossovsky's command post. He escaped by "mere chance," or perhaps intuition. Both would be riding with the Red Army in the coming weeks.

During June, both sides concentrated primarily on building strength for the ground campaign. For the Germans, in that context air support had never been so crucial. The constrained nature of the fighting zone, the uniquely high force-to-space ratios on both sides, sharply restricted the ground forces' maneuver potential. No less significant was the absolute and relative decline of German artillery, particularly its medium and heavy elements, compared with that of the Red Army. Forbidden heavy metal by Versailles, the Germans had been playing catch-up since rearmament began.

Put plainly, the German artillery could not be counted on to neutralize the Soviet guns. That made airpower critical to provide not merely support, but the shock that would open the front and let the mobile divisions through. Citadel gave the Luftwaffe three synergized missions: Work with the tanks and infantry to break through the Soviet defenses, fix and weaken Soviet reserves, and maintain not merely control but supremacy in contested airspace.

That last point was vital, because a high proportion of the ground-attack aircraft were so highly specialized that they could not protect themselves in the air. The Luftwaffe's order of battle included only five ground-attack squadrons equipped with fighter-bombers in the Western style, modified Fw-190s. There were also five squadrons of specialized antitank aircraft: the Henschel Hs-129, whose twin engines, heavy armor, and 30 mm cannon made it the ancestor of the U.S. Air Force's well-known A-10. The legendary but lumbering Junkers Ju-87 Stuka was still the backbone of the close-air-support squadrons. Interdicting the battlefield was the responsibility of the medium bombers. Like the Stuka, the Heinkel He-111 and the Ju-88 were prewar designs, effective only in daylight, defended by a few rifle-caliber machine guns in single mounts.

By this stage of the war, the fighter squadrons were the Luftwaffe's elite, well trained, well led, widely experienced, and supremely confident. There is no such thing as a perfect fighter plane, but in the summer of 1943, the Fw-190A came close. Fast, well armed, and maneuverable, with a reliable engine, it would not be comprehensively challenged as an air superiority aircraft until a year later by the American P-51D Mustang.

Luftwaffe higher command for Citadel was flexible enough to be confusing. The Sixth Air Fleet cooperated with the Ninth Army and the Fourth Air Fleet with Army Group South. Their respective strike forces, the 1st Air Division and VIII Air Corps, incorporated most of the ground-support elements. Each also included four or five fighter groups, of around three dozen aircraft apiece. In practice, units were shifted from sector to sector as needed by a very efficient system of air liaison officers. Exact figures remain vague, but at Citadel's beginning, the Luftwaffe could call on approximately two thousand first-line fighters, medium bombers, Stukas, and other ground-attack planes. The first-rate maintenance system would turn them around as quickly as they could be refueled and rearmed and keep them in the air as long as there was enough airframe to repair.

The Soviet air force had paid a high tuition since 1941 but had learned the Luftwaffe's lessons of centralization and flexibility. Three air armies contributed directly to the defense of Kursk: the Sixteenth and the Second, attached, respectively, to the Central and Voronezh Fronts, and the Seventeenth from the Southwestern Front. The initial numbers totaled around 1,050 fighters, 950 ground-attack planes, and 900 bombers. Stavka had also assembled an impressive reserve force of three air armies with 2,750 planes. Intended to spearhead the attack projected to follow the German defeat, they soon joined in the fighting. Finally, more than 300 bombers from Long Range Aviation and 300 fighters from Air Defense Command were assigned for night raiding and point defense, respectively.

The air force possessed a counterpart to Zhukov in both ability and toughness. That Zhukov liked and trusted Alexander Novikov was significant—few on Zhukov's level could claim the same relationship. Novikov was also first-rate. As a junior infantry officer, in 1922 he won a fifteen-minute flight in a lottery. Twenty years later, he was the air force commanding general, with a burgeoning reputation as an innovator able to combine new ideas and equipment with overall Soviet doctrine. In the circumstances of the Eastern Front, that meant cooperating closely with the ground forces, concentrating on tactical and operational levels with independent missions of any kind having low priority. At Kursk, above all, it meant ground support.

The medium bombers would maintain pressure on the German rear areas, as they had been doing for months. But stage center went to the Shturmovik. The Ilyushin Il-2 first went into action on July 1, 1941. By 1943, it made up a third of Soviet-built frontline aircraft. Of mixed wood and metal construction, it carried an offensive armament of two 23 mm cannon and two machine guns in the wings, plus rockets and hundred-kilogram bombs. At Kursk they added shaped-charge antitank bomblets that could penetrate the rear-deck armor of any German tank and explode before they bounced off. The two-man crew compartment, the engine, and the fuel systems were protected by an armored "bathtub" up to half an inch thick.

Altogether, the "Ilyusha" was a formidable instrument of war. Its slow speed and limited maneuverability were disadvantages in single air combat. But their standard attack formation of a squadron-strength circle enabled the Shturmoviks to cover one another's tails against Luftwaffe fighters. That gave them a chance and decreased the burden of the Soviet fighter squadrons.

IV

Kursk's delays were not decided in a Hitlerian vacuum. The Oberkommando der Wehrmacht (OKW; Armed Forces High Command) was essentially responsible for directing the war everywhere except in Russia, which was the primary assignment of OKH. This divided command, ostensibly intended to facilitate focused planning, also reinforced Hitler's position as the Reich's ultimate decision maker. The OKW was increasingly concerned at the prospect of an imminent Allied landing in southern Europe—not only for operational reasons, but because of the opportunity the invasion would offer those Italian military and political figures who sought an exit from the war. On June 18, the OKW went so far as to recommend canceling Citadel and using the mobile divisions assigned to it to form two general reserves, one in Russia for theater purposes and the other in Germany.

Zeitzler too was having second thoughts. Intelligence reports on the metastasizing Soviet defensive system combined with continuing delays in the delivery not merely of new tanks, but of material of every kind, encouraged the chief of staff to question openly whether the series of delays had made Citadel an unacceptably dangerous risk. Then Model weighed in. A staff officer at

Army Group Center later suggested his original intention had been to convince Hitler not to delay Citadel, but to abandon it. That seems a bit subtle for someone who took pride in "serving uncut wine" by eschewing the byzantine, Machiavellian politics long associated with the general staff. Model was concerned at the growing Russian buildup on the Orel salient's northern face, in the rear of Model's concentration against Kursk. The prospects of a boot up the backside with no effective counterforce available to block it increased as Kursk's defenses grew more elaborate.

Using the panzers to make the breakthrough on Ninth Army's front risked not only getting them stuck—even if successful, the mobile formations might well be left able neither to exploit the situation on their front nor to shift sectors if that became necessary. However, using the infantry, the obvious alternative, meant relying on divisions whose strength and effectiveness were so low that only one was rated as capable of all operational missions. Seven more counted as suitable only "for limited attacks," and German staffs were extremely generous in those evaluations, at least before the shooting started.

Hitler's response was that Citadel would throw the Russians sufficiently off balance to prevent an independent offensive. He implied that Model would be reinforced by the Panthers that instead went to Hoth. And he finally set a last, unalterable date for the offensive: July 5, 1943. His mood varied. Nazi propaganda minister Joseph Goebbels noted that as the deadline approached, Hitler seemed increasingly optimistic about Citadel's prospects. But on July 1, the Führer summoned the senior generals and some of Citadel's key corps commanders to a final conference at Rastenburg. One participant described the meeting as a monologue, with nothing convincing, let alone inspiring, about the presentation. Hitler explained the repeated delays as necessary to make up troop shortages and increase production of Panthers and Tigers. He described the attack as a gamble, a *Wägnis*.

By then, that was one point on which "the greatest warlord of all time" and his generals were in near complete agreement. If, as

Kempf said after the war, Model believed the attack a poor idea, he was silent when it still might have counted. In his memoirs, Manstein concluded that it might have been a mistake not to have told Hitler bluntly that the attack no longer made sense. Writing more than a decade afterward, Mellenthin contributed a last word: "The German Supreme Command could think of nothing better than to fling our magnificent panzer divisions against Kursk, which had now become the strongest fortress in the world." Want of civil courage and military integrity? Perhaps. Or perhaps Hitler and his generals had in common the feeling a gambler knows when he has so much in the game: the easy decision is to call the hand.

It is a familiar axiom of modern war, expressed mathematically in something called the Lanchester equations, that an offensive requires a 3-to-1 superiority. Soviet doctrine optimistically reduced that to 3 to 2, assuming the Red Army's superior planning, staff work, and fighting power. But by the time the preparations for Kursk were complete, the Soviet defenders outnumbered the attackers in every category of men and equipment, in almost every sector. The average ratio was somewhere between 2.5 and 1.5 to 1 in favor of the Russians. Did that make Citadel a suicide run from the beginning? Given the respective rates of buildup, it nevertheless seems reasonable to argue that an early attack, mounted by the forces available in April or May, would have lacked the combat power to overcome the salient's defenses even in their early stages. The Germans' only chance was the steel-headed sledgehammer they eventually swung in July. And that highlights the essential paradox of Kursk. The factors that made the battle zone acceptable in operational terms also made it too restrictive to allow for the application of the force multipliers the German army's panzers had spent a decade cultivating. Kursk offered no opportunity for operational skill and little for tactical virtuosity. Militarily, the strength of the defensive system meant the German offensive had to depend on mass and momentum—which is another way to describe a battle of attrition, the one type of combat the German way of war was structured to avoid.

No less significant was the synergy between Kursk's geographic scale and the Red Army's command and control methods and capacities. Since Barbarossa, those had developed in contexts of top-down battle management, reflecting both the Soviet principle that war is a science and the fact that their senior commanders lost effectiveness operating independently. Previous German offensives had found no difficulty in getting inside Soviet decision loops, which generated increasingly random responses that frequently collapsed into chaos. Kursk enabled a timely response to German moves as the defense slowed those moves down. It enabled as well a degree of management absent in previous major battles—creating in turn a confidence at all levels of headquarters that a culture of competence had replaced a culture of desperation.

Those were significant force multipliers, in a situation arguably not needing them. But the panzers had a habit of defying odds, and Stalin took no chances. He dispatched Zhukov as Stavka's representative to the Central Front and Vasilevsky to the Voronezh Front. The marshals observed training, offered suggestions, and, not least, kept insisting on the importance of waiting for the German offensive instead of rushing the situation. "Time and patience"—Kutuzov's mantra from 1812—would be applied to another invader.

Chapter III

———

STRIKE

FOR THE SOVIET Central Front Citadel began in the early hours of July 5. Around 2:00 A.M., the Thirteenth Army reported to front HQ that one of its patrols had picked up a German pioneer, clearing minefields to prepare for an attack he said would come at 3:00 P.M. Zhukov immediately authorized Rokossovsky to turn his artillery loose—only then did he phone Stalin with the news that this was no drill.

I

Central Front's counterbarrage opened at 2:20 A.M. But Soviet gunners had not succeeded in registering German positions with complete accuracy. Imprecise targeting produced random firing and wasted ammunition—too much of it, given the intensity of the fire plan. Waiting until the German infantry were out of their dugouts and the tanks deployed in starting positions would have inflicted more damage for less ammunition. Mistakes on that scale were accountable to Stalin himself. But if specific results were episodic, the overall weight and intensity of the shelling was nevertheless so great that the German high command agreed to delay the attack for two and a half hours in Model's sector so that German artillery might reply.

The resulting disruption diminished the coordination so important to Model's plan. On the other hand, the Germans benefited from the Sixteenth Air Army's decision not to strike Luftwaffe airfields in coordination with the artillery, but to meet German air strikes as they came. The crewmen of Model's supporting 1st Air Division received a surprise in their final briefings on July 4. The original plan for a strike against the Soviet airfields had been abandoned as unworkable based on previous experience. Instead, the Luftwaffe was to act as literal flying artillery, concentrating on strongpoints and artillery positions in the forward battle zone. This was the first time in the war that a major offensive would be made without simultaneously attacking headquarters, airfields, and supply routes in the enemy's rear. It obviated any chance of reducing the odds by catching the Russians on the ground. It manifested as well the respect air and ground generals felt for the Red Army's defenses.

The first sorties were mounted at 3:25 A.M.. Medium bombers and Stukas repeatedly attacked the network of gun positions around Maloarkhangelsk. Soviet fighters, deployed piecemeal, took heavy losses at the hands of the Fw-190s of Jagdgeschwader (Fighter Wing; JG) 51. Stuka groups were correspondingly able to hammer the Russians until relieved by another group, then return to base, rearm, refuel, and rejoin the fight. After an hour of that, supplemented by an artillery barrage against the same targets, the infantry went forward.

Able to take initial advantage of the pioneers' night work clearing minefields, the *Landser* soon found the going heavy. On the far left, XXIII Corps was tasked with capturing Maloarkhangelsk and anchoring the armor's advance. The left and center divisions got a little over a mile into the defense system, then were driven out by local counterattacks. The main attack was made by the 78th Assault Division, with a battalion of forty-five Ferdinands attached. These began life as a competitor to the Tigers. When the design was rejected, the optimistically constructed prototypes were completed as 88 mm assault guns. Under heavy fire, the Germans successfully cleared a succession of strongpoints and trenches based on villages and low hill lines. But minefields slowed the Ferdinands, and the advance stalled in front of Hill 257.7.

Studded with bunkers supported by dug-in tanks, the Russian position was a nightmare version of the kinds of defenses Americans would encounter two years later on Okinawa. It quickly won the nickname "Panzer Hill"—but the Germans believed they had an armored counter. In 1940, German designers had begun work on a remote-controlled wire-guided mine-clearing vehicle carrying a thousand pounds of explosives. It had performed well enough in limited situations that three companies of the developed version had been assigned to the Ninth Army. Put to the test in front of Panzer Hill, they drew so much artillery fire that the resulting sympathetic detonations obscured the lane they cleared.

The Ferdinands went forward anyway. Enough of them reached the defenses, and enough infantry managed to follow, that the hill fell to close assault—a polite euphemism for a series of vicious fights in which bayonets were civilized weapons. But the "tank fright" that so often characterized Russian behavior in the war's earlier years had disappeared. The Ferdinands, built without machine guns for close defense, proved significantly vulnerable to infantrymen at close range. Grenades, mines—even antitank rifles took their toll. By day's end, only twelve of the original forty-five Ferdinands were still able to fight. The often-cited lack of hull-mounted machine guns was less a factor in the Ferdinands' discomfiture than the absence of their own infantry. Tank-infantry contact had been lost at the sharp end almost from the beginning—an unpromising portent. By the standards developing in the salient, Maloarkhangelsk was still a long way away.

Ninth Army's initial *Schwerpunkt* was its center: the six-mile front of XLI and XLVII Panzer Corps. Each had two divisions up front. Front left to right, the 292nd, 86th, and 6th Infantry and the 20th Panzer crossed their start lines around 6:30 under a massive air umbrella of He 111s and Stukas. Again the German fighters kept the skies against the best the Sixteenth Air Army could throw at them. Again the German infantry took heavy casualties from mines, small arms, and artillery fire. But the Ferdinands of Tank Destroyer Battalion 654 broke through the minefields, shrugged off armor-piercing rounds at point-blank range, and brought the infantry of the 292nd and 86th Divisions steadily forward. By evening, the 292nd was beginning its assault of the fortified village of Ponyri, albeit at the price of most of 18th Panzer Division's tanks being committed in support at an earlier stage than had been hoped.

The 6th Infantry Division had been built around one of the Reichswehr's original regiments. Recruited in Westphalia, it had a solid nucleus of old-timers and two years of hard experience fighting Russians. By 8:00 A.M., it had made enough progress to commit the temporarily attached 505th Tank Battalion, with its two companies of twenty-six Tigers and a company of a dozen mine clearers. Closely supported by Stukas and artillery, the Tigers crossed the Oka River and faced three hours of counterattacks spearheaded by waves of T-34s. Since the T-34's first appearances, the panzers had countered by maneuver. Now the Tigers halted, engaged their optic sights, and broke charge after charge at long range. Around noon, the big cats led elements of 6th Division's infantry into the village of Butyrki, leaving over forty burned-out T-34s in their wake. Three hours earlier, the 20th Panzer Division on the Westphalians' right had overrun a rifle regiment and gained three miles toward the fortified village of Bobrik.

For the 505th, this was the time to double down and commit the reserves, envelop the first lines of defense, and turn a breakthrough into a breakout. The 6th Division's commander later said that had the tanks been sent in, Kursk itself might have been reached the first day. Perhaps. But the Tigers were less of a surprise to the Russians, having been committed in small numbers on the Eastern Front since the previous August. The Russians had had corresponding opportunities to develop counters. Since Barbarossa, German tank armor had been vulnerable to Russian guns, but Tiger hunting required more refined skills: letting them close the range and then concentrating on the treads. Cool heads and steady aim were decisive. The Russians had both. In XLI Panzer Corps's sector, once the Ferdinands had passed through, the overrun Russians had emerged from their maze of trenches to tackle the mammoths with Molotov cocktails, satchel charges, and even antitank rifles, useful against thinner side and rear armor. The 20th Panzer Division was stopped around Bobrik by a similar combination of minefields, antitank guns, and close-assault teams. The 258th Infantry Division on Ninth Army's far right never got past the second defense line of the 280th Rifle Division in what amounted to a straight-up one-on-one fight. Were there enough Tigers anywhere to make a difference?

The Red Air Force was becoming a presence as well. Initially thrown off balance by Luftwaffe numbers and effectiveness, the Sixteenth Air Army found its equilibrium around noon. Shturmoviks challenged the German fighters and made effective use of the new shaped-charge bombs against tanks. One ground-attack group alone reported thirty-one tanks knocked out—an exaggerated figure, like similar claims in any war, but suggestive.

On the ground, Model committed over five hundred armored vehicles on July 5. About half were out of action by the end of the first day. Many of these could be repaired; the effect on crew morale was nevertheless significant. So were the consequences of occupying ground, shuttling back to relieve pinned-down or hung-up infantry, then repeating the entire performance a few hundred yards farther forward. The infantry too had suffered—not only in numerical terms, but because the nature of the fighting took a disproportionate toll on the aggressive and the leaders: those first around a trench traverse or across what seemed dead ground.

The often-cited criticism that Model failed to commit his armor on the first day is to a degree refuted by evidence that well over half of the Ninth Army's AFVs were in fact engaged on July 5. But the Tigers and the Ferdinands were organized in independent battalions, not as part of the combined-arms teams that were the real strength of the panzers. Their effectiveness most likely would have been maximized by using them to assist the infantry into and through the Soviet defenses. By early afternoon, the Germans had nevertheless gained more than a foothold in the Russian defenses. By the end of the day, the lodgment would be around nine miles broad and five miles deep. But it was a series of nibbles as opposed to a coordinated bite.

Walther Model was anything but a rear-echelon commando. He spent the first hours of the day with the two panzer corps and then returned briefly to his headquarters, where the reports were not all so optimistic. The Ninth Army's commander spent most of the afternoon visiting headquarters, shifting armor and artillery in response to what seemed crises or opportunities, and coming to the conclusion that the situation warranted committing his immediate reserves, the 2nd and 9th Panzer Divisions, the next day to exploit the gains in XLVII Panzer Corps's sector. That was arguably the consequence of a genuine miscalculation: underestimating the depth of Soviet defenses and the strength of Soviet resistance. But for Citadel to succeed, even if the Soviet threat to Army Group Center proved a chimera, Model had to break through and out, and quickly.

Whatever the fleeting prospects for an early-afternoon German breakthrough, they were insufficient to panic Rokossovsky. From the Soviet perspective, it was clear that the Germans were barely through the first defensive belt. Rokossovsky, freed of an immediate need to improvise, planned to reinforce the Second Tank Army and move it into position for a counterattack early on July 6. The barrage began at 2:50, followed by waves of medium bombers targeting positions and vehicles on the front line.

This was a major departure from the usual Soviet practice of using these planes to strike deeper into the rear. It was also an expedient. The previous evening, Stalin had phoned Rokossovsky. When the general began describing the day's events, Stalin interrupted: "Have we gained control of the air or not?" Rokossovsky temporized. Stalin repeated the question. When Rokossovsky said the problem would be solved the next day, Stalin asked whether the Sixteenth Air Army's commander was up to the job. A few minutes later, Zhukov arrived at Rokossovsky's headquarters to report a similar phone call with the same question.

For the Sixteenth Air Army's commander, Lieutenant General Sergei Rudenko, it was an underwear-changing moment. All too recently, such a question from the Vozhd had been a likely preliminary to dismissal or to a "nine-gram pension": the weight of a pistol bullet in the back of the neck. Rudenko quickly proposed mass attacks to saturate German air and ground defenses and to encourage the hard-pressed ground troops. Four successive waves of bombers literally caught the Germans napping: the commander of 1st Air Division had authorized his exhausted fighter pilots to rest that morning. But the Russian armor was slow getting into position in an already crowded battle zone. Their attacks were delivered piecemeal, the tanks and infantry poorly coordinated. The 20th Panzer gave ground, then held, then counterattacked successfully toward Bobrik. It seemed a good omen. And the Tigers were waiting.

The 505th Battalion's Tigers took out forty-six of a fifty-strong Soviet tank brigade, T-34s and light T-70s, the T-60's also obsolete successor, in a few minutes. The 2nd and 9th Panzer joined the fight by midmorning. With the 18th already on line, that brought the German AFV strength to around three hundred on a front of less than eight miles—as narrow as any major attack sector had been in the Great War and a correspondingly long distance from any concept of mechanized maneuver. The panzers' objective was a low ridgeline, the Olkhovatka heights, extending from Teploye on the left of the attack to Ponyri on its right and anchored by Hills 272 near Teploye, 274 at the village of Olkhovatka, and 253.5

east of Ponyri. Little more than high knolls, they nevertheless offered not only Tantalus's view of Kursk, but passage to relatively open terrain: ground favoring the Germans. And the only way out was through.

II

The day was so hot, in the high eighties, that some crews went into action with their hatches open. The fighting grew even hotter when what was intended as a breakthrough also became an encounter battle as the Second Tank Army entered the fight. The geographic objectives of the panzer divisions became unimportant; what mattered was getting forward. Model concentrated every available gun, rocket, and plane to blast the way for the panzers. The Russians responded in kind. Accounts from both sides describe a steadily intensifying kaleidoscope of shell bursts, screaming rockets, and exploding bombs, tanks bursting into flame or slewing to a stop, crews desperately seeking to escape and being machine-gunned when anyone on the other side had time to notice.

Model had tasked the Sixth Air Fleet with providing maximum support, and the Luftwaffe threw in every flyable plane. Elements of JG 51, scrambled in a hurry, caught a group of Shturmoviks and their fighter escort coming in at low altitude. The result: fifteen Il-2s downed in minutes. But when the next wave arrived, the fighters had returned to their bases to refuel. That made it the Shturmoviks' turn. With a temporarily clear attack zone, the "flying tanks" reported fourteen flamers and forty more put out of action in minutes. The Luftwaffe responded with formations of level bombers and Stukas as large as a hundred at a time—or so it seemed to the Soviet troops under the bombs. Sixteenth Air Army had several veteran fighter regiments, flying not only La-5s but some of the best of a new generation of fighters: La-7s and Yak-9s, which would serve the Red Air Force well even after 1945. But the

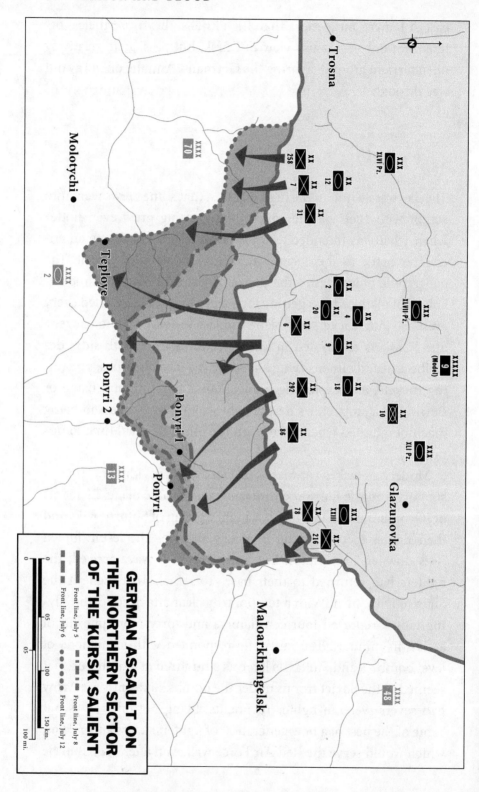

GERMAN ASSAULT ON
THE NORTHERN SECTOR
OF THE KURSK SALIENT

Germans took their measure and kept the ring as the panzers advanced.

That advance was by meters rather than kilometers and led the Germans only deeper into a defense system of dominating terrain devoid of natural cover, swept by some of the heaviest fire of the war. Infantry movement of any kind became near suicidal. It was not so much that the *Landser* immolated themselves trying vainly to advance. Langemarck was three decades past, and there were no innocents on the Russian front. Ordinary riflemen or panzer grenadiers constrained to fight that day on foot—it made no difference. Veterans and replacements alike went to ground and stayed there. The 6th Infantry Division had seven combat battalions. Their total combat strength was around 3,100 on July 4. By July 10, it was down to 1,600.

Forty percent frontline casualties in a week is no bagatelle, but neither was it uncommon under similar conditions in Russia or the West. The problem involved absolute numbers. A battalion of two hundred men was as much a group of survivors as a fighting force; its fighting power was likely to be even less than its reduced strength suggested. And as early as July 6, the Ninth Army divisions' replacement pools held no more than two hundred or three hundred men apiece.

It took at least a squad, preferably a platoon, but in any case a dozen or two foot soldiers to screen a tank effectively. In their absence, as on July 5, AFVs drove unwittingly into minefields, and were ambushed by antitank strongpoints and T-34s dug in to their turrets and enveloped by close-assault teams. At ranges of a hundred yards and less, even Tigers were vulnerable. Rokossovsky handled his reserves effectively, committing them as needed to hold the line or restore it, always with another rifle regiment or tank brigade as a hole card. A long afternoon of desperate fighting for the fortified village of Olkhovatka and the Olkhovatka heights ended with the Russians still in control of both.

The story was the same across the front. Model's 78th, 86th, and 292nd Infantry Divisions went into Ponyri at dawn, their surviving Ferdinands and mine-clearing vehicles reinforced by the 9th Panzer Division and what remained of the 18th Panzer. Ponyri was a railway station and a collection/distribution center for the region's collective farms. Its main buildings—the factory station, the school, the railroad station, the water tower—were solidly constructed: natural, heavily defended strongpoints that Rokossovsky initially supported with Katyushas and artillery as opposed to committing reinforcements directly. Germans described an intensity of shelling never before experienced and compared the seesaw fighting for buildings and houses with the worst Stalingrad had offered. The Germans captured and held Hill 253.5 but made no further progress when they tried to swing west and take the Olkhovatka heights in the flank and rear.

The XXIII Corps, lacking the kind of armor and air support concentrated in the center of Ninth Army's front, had even less success against Maloarkhangelsk. The day ended with the Germans everywhere still stuck—one might say trapped—in the second line of Russian defenses. Model had taken a chance. He believed that the 2nd and 9th Panzer Divisions would spearhead a breakthrough of the Soviet defenses but now accepted that they would be left too battered to develop the success. That left him a single division, the 4th Panzer, to lead the Ninth Army into Kursk.

Model's real gamble was not the attack itself. It was the belief he could use it to force Kluge's hand. At 5:40 in the morning, well before his own tanks were committed, Model phoned Army Group Center and asked for the 10th Panzer Grenadier and 12th Panzer Divisions. Kluge temporized. That would leave him with no strategic mobile reserve and increasing evidence of a Red Army buildup on his front. Kluge had another problem as well. Second Panzer Army's commander, General Rudolf Schmidt, had grown so openly acidic about the Führer and the party that he had been relieved on April 10, with the recommendation he be committed to a mental hospital. Kluge apparently offered a deal: The divisions now, with the condition that if the Russians did attack, Model would assume command of both armies.

Model's acceptance suggested that whatever his previous reservations, Citadel's success was the best counter to a massive strike at Army Group Center. Or perhaps he just had the bit between his teeth. *Fortiter in re,* not *suaviter in modo,* was Walther Model's trademark. He spent the day trying to drive the Ninth Army forward by willpower, dodging Shturmoviks in the morning as he moved among subordinate headquarters, then settling with 2nd Panzer Division for most of the afternoon. He might as well have been at a battalion command post. A division's communications facilities were insufficient to control an army-level battle—particularly when the division itself was heavily engaged.

Second-guessing and hindsight are staples of military history. Nevertheless, it should have been clear after the first day that Kursk in 1943 was not France in 1940 or Russia in 1941. This situation needed a battle manager rather than a battle captain. To develop a victory it was first necessary to win one, and that called for oversight rather than intervention. As the commander toured his front, fleeting opportunities went undeveloped; local gains went unsupported.

Not until 9:30 P.M. did Model finally return to his headquarters, to plan what became the next day's mistake. It amounted to using 9th and 18th Panzer plus what remained of the 86th and 292nd Infantry to take Ponyri and start south toward Olkhovatka. The 2nd and 20th Panzer and 6th Infantry, plus a dozen or so hastily repaired Tigers, and supported by 4th Panzer, would hit the Olkhovatka ridgeline and Hill 274, then break through to Teploye. By this time, Model was leading with tanks because the Ninth Army was running out of infantry. Nor was that the only problem. The Luftwaffe was running short of fuel. Domestic slowdowns in production had been exacerbated by partisan attacks on fuel trains—vulnerable targets that provided spectacularly gratifying results.

Calculating his resources, 1st Air Division's commander, Brigadier General Paul Deichmann, arguably more than Model, staked the game on a July 7 breakthrough. Beginning at 5:00 A.M., the 190s of JG 51 and 54 cleared Shturmoviks from the panzers' lines of advance. The level bombers went in behind them, then the Stukas. The Soviets had spent the night repairing wire entanglements, laying new minefields, deploying more guns and rockets, and bringing up tanks to reinforce the hard-pressed rifle formations. The air strikes were the signal for a massive barrage, heavier than anything unleashed anywhere to date during the entire war. The attack zones were so narrow that for the panzers, maneuver was virtually impossible. Tank after tank went up as heavy artillery shells fired at long range penetrated their thin rear deck and turret roof armor. The survivors emerged from the smoke and dust to find themselves in a fifteen-mile high-velocity killing zone of anti-tank guns supported by dug-in T-34s. Anything looking like dead ground was in fact a minefield, usually covered by close-attack teams.

The Russians saw Ponyri as the key to Central Front's position and believed the Germans were determined to capture it at all costs. The defenses were correspondingly reinforced as the fighting developed. The 307th Rifle Division was directly supported by three tank brigades and two more independent regiments, by enough antitank guns to provide a ratio of over 100 per mile, and by no fewer than 380 guns—a density never matched on the Russian front or anywhere else. The Germans hit Ponyri five times in the early morning of July 7. Each time, the 307th held its ground and counterattacked. Not until around noon did the Germans gain a permanent foothold in the town's outskirts, against ever-stiffening resistance reinforced from the air by medium bombers and Shturmoviks, which dropped over seventy-five hundred shaped-charge bombs across the fighting line that day.

At 3:30 P.M., the Germans came again, taking even heavier losses for almost no purpose. The town could be neither stormed nor enveloped. On what by now seemed to both sides a day that would never end, enough light remained at 7:00 P.M. for XLI Panzer Corps to make a final try. Its commander, Lieutenant General Josef Harpe, was an avowed Nazi sympathizer and as hard-boiled a tanker as any in the German army. He committed his last reserves. The 307th Rifle Division—what remained of it—finally abandoned its forward positions. For a few minutes around 7:30, a way into the Russian flank and rear appeared open. Then the anti-tank guns shut it once more, and the sorely tried Germans retreated to their blood-bought start lines, about halfway into Ponyri.

Model's intended *Schwerpunkt* for July 7 was, however, the sector of XLVII Panzer Corps's attack. The 2nd Panzer Division had almost two hundred tanks and assault guns under command, plus the 505th's two dozen Tigers. They went in using a new formation. The *Panzerkeil*, or armored wedge, replicated a tactic from the Middle Ages. At the tip of the wedge were the tanks with the heaviest frontal armor, the Tigers. The lighter tanks and assault guns extended outward on each flank; the soft vehicles, trucks and half-tracks, were in the middle. In contrast with German tactics in the war's early years, the wedge depended on depth and shock rather than breadth and mobility. Its assumptions were that anti-tank crews would be less effective because of having to adjust ranges constantly and that the guns would focus on the most heavily armored tanks. With a company of mine clearers to open paths through the minefields, Major General Vollrath Lübbe was reasonably confident as his tanks crossed the start line. But the supporting air strikes were limited in strength and time; after 7:00 A.M., the weight of available airpower shifted to Harpe's sector. Rokossovsky had committed two of Second Tank Army's corps in this sector, and they counterattacked constantly in formations of up to thirty at a time. The combination of superior numbers, the T-34's relatively high speed, and the cumulative effect of constant shelling was expected to throw off German aim long enough for the Russians to come to close quarters.

The Germans' optimal reply was to halt and take advantage of their quicker training guns and their superior sighting apparatus. But the achieved kills were bought at the price of momentum. An initial steady pace became a series of stops and starts that gave the Russians time to breathe and recover. Soviet accounts have the

140th Rifle Division, which was in the thick of the fighting, repulsing no fewer than thirteen attacks before finally giving ground. It was noon before the panzers broke through in the center. Teploye was less than three miles away, Olkhovatka a mile farther, and the ground seemed open and rolling all the way. But again the Soviet rifle divisions on the flanks held and counterattacked, cutting off tank and infantry spearheads caught in unseen minefields and halted by camouflaged strongpoints on the right. Shturmoviks, supported by modified Yak-9s with fuselage-mounted 37 mm cannon, saturated a German defense whose fighters were heavily outnumbered. The 1st Air Division managed only 307 sorties against 731 for the Russians, flown by men whose skills had improved through experience in the learn-or-die battles of the previous days. By July 7, in the Olkhovatka sector, the Shturmovik groups claimed thirty-four kills for no losses. The German frontline flak could be reinforced only at the expense of leaving the Ninth Army's rear areas uncovered to Soviet attacks that grew in numbers and effectiveness each day.

Lack of numbers was critical in another area as well. A panzer division had only four infantry battalions, one mounted on armored half-tracks and three in ordinary trucks. These "panzer grenadiers," as they had been retitled in 1942, were intended to work with the tanks, attacking alongside or ahead of them against fortified positions or minefields. To facilitate taking out strongpoints quickly, the battalions included a formidable array of supporting weapons: mortars, light infantry guns, half-track-mounted short 75 mm cannon. The trucks and half-tracks enabled the infantry to move deeper into the battle zone before dismounting and catch up quickly with the tanks once the defensive lines had been breached and the remaining pockets of resistance eliminated or contained. On the Ninth Army's front, however, the strength of the defenses forced the panzer grenadiers onto their feet almost from the beginning of any advance. From then on, their additional firepower became a literal burden: carry it forward or resort to bayonets, grenades, and sharpened entrenching tools against the omnipresent strongpoints. Tanks that stayed to help the infantry became easy targets. So did tanks that moved forward independently. There was nothing intrinsically wrong with the panzers' tactics. It was rather that the forces applying them were too weak for the specific situation. The combination of the rifle divisions' defense and the massive air and armored counterattacks brought the panzers to a halt before nightfall.

In most cases, the tanks and infantry set up perimeter defenses on the ground they had gained—a reflection not only of a determination to hang on, but of a recognition that they would have to fight their way back, as they had fought forward. Better to scratch foxholes and slit trenches, keep alert for the ubiquitous Red Army patrols, and curse the no less ubiquitous "sewing machines" with their flares and bombs.

In principle, the Germans' significantly superior tactical skill outweighed the advantages inherent to the defense. In practice, the Ninth Army had taken more than thirteen thousand casualties in two days, an overwhelming number of them in the infantry and correspondingly irreplaceable even by warm-body cannon fodder. Actual tank losses at this stage are difficult to determine accurately. On the German side, no one was counting; across the fighting line, so many weapons engaged each target that the Soviets were counting triple. Since the start of the offensive, German mechanics were repairing tanks and replenishing ammunition supplies depleted enough that Model had phoned Berlin for an emergency shipment of a hundred thousand rounds. Total write-offs in tanks—around fifty—were strikingly modest. But how long the field repair jobs would last was anyone's guess. The crews were suffering not merely from combat stress but from sheer fatigue. Three days without sleep was not unusual among the tankers. The Luftwaffe's shortfalls in fuel and general overexertion had also grown worse.

Attrition on the wrong side of the balance sheet? Perhaps. But German intelligence calculated that the Russians had lost more than sixty thousand men, three hundred tanks, and even more aircraft. Model, who had again spent the day traveling among his headquarters, was not stupid, but neither was he reflective. It would have been against his character to take a detached, critical approach to the intelligence reports—or, indeed, to the events of the past seventy-two hours. The Ninth Army's hard fighting had to have eroded the Soviet reserves in front of it. And if the Russians were planning something massive on Army Group Center's front, the best way to deter that was to divert it. Manstein was making solid progress in the south. Apart from any sense of competition with a colleague so different in background and temperament, continuing the attack in Ninth Army's sector clearly seemed to Model the most promising and least worst option available.

IV

Manstein and Model had little in common as commanders, but their initial orders were almost exact duplicates: two strong corps going down the center, covered on each flank by weaker elements. Army Group South was to attack with concentrated force from the line Belgorod–Tomarovka, break through the Soviet defenses, and meet Model somewhere east of Kursk.

Nikolai Popel, chief political officer of the opposing First Tank Army, later compared the Fourth Panzer Army's attack to a knight's move in chess. The metaphor was mistaken. Army commander Hermann Hoth's plan had nothing in common with the freewheeling spontaneity associated with chessboard knights. It was a straight force-on-force exercise. Hoth's main attack, toward Oboyan, was assigned a sector only fifteen miles across, and his geographic objective, the town of Oboyan, was thirty miles away—a long distance for a narrow front.

Should a hammer blow fail, one option was to send for a bigger hammer. But the Fourth Panzer Army already had the heaviest hammer Germany could provide. The XLVIII Panzer Corps and the Waffen SS had almost eleven hundred tanks and assault guns between them. The Fourth Air Fleet counted almost 1,100 aircraft, and 966 of those were concentrated in VIII Air Corps, which specialized in direct ground support. Almost 250 were Stukas; 75 more were tank-busting He-129s—and Manstein expected to need every one of them from the beginning.

On May 10, Manstein met with Hoth and the senior commanders of XLVIII Panzer Corps. Manstein had by then decided that a straight line was the shortest distance between two points. Given his sector's geography, the best option was a massive frontal armored attack, using the limited infantry forces to provide flank protection. The initial objective was to cross the Psel River, then to capture the road-junction town of Oboyan. Kursk would be the next stop. In the course of a freewheeling discussion on how best to make that work, Manstein reinforced that it was going to be not only a hard fight but a long one. The main battle would begin only once the first defense lines had been penetrated. That alone would require detailed, precise planning based on the combined-arms tactics that were the essence of panzer doctrine. Lead with heavy tanks. Use artillery to take out antitank positions. Expect major Soviet air attacks from the beginning. The next day, Manstein communicated the same urgency to the SS at corps headquarters: Take nothing for granted. Assume strong defenses continually developed. Prepare thoroughly—this was no time for heroic improvisation.

Manstein may have been conveying doubts. He may also have been emphasizing the importance of an early breakthrough. In either case, in the weeks before the attack he honored the established German principle of delegation, allowing subordinates to plan the details and listening to their specific proposals. The panzer divisions rehearsed down to small-unit levels, emphasizing cooperation with the Luftwaffe and the tactics of overcoming antitank defenses in depth. And Hermann Hoth cogitated.

Hoth was what Germans call *ein alter Hase*—"an old hare." Unlike the fox—even the Desert Fox—who outwits danger, the hare stays alive by anticipating it. As early as March, Hoth had expressed doubts about Hitler's projected preliminaries to Kursk. He questioned whether the panzer divisions' losses would or could be replaced. He was even more concerned about the armored reserves the Red Army could mobilize around the Kursk salient. As preparations for Citadel proper increased, so did Hoth's worries about the latter point. Well aware of the strong Soviet reserves moving into position just outside the theater of operations, he became convinced they posed too great a risk to his right flank to ignore—especially should the German advance be slower than expected.

And delay in turn, Hoth reasoned, was virtually guaranteed, because as configured, XLVIII Panzer Corps was unlikely to reach its objectives and secure its left flank as well in the same time frame. Hoth addressed part of the problem by convincing Manstein to add the 3rd Panzer Division to the corps's order of battle, allowing its commitment from Citadel's beginning. The other, larger element was beyond his control. To rest the tankers and panzer grenadiers, Fourth Panzer Army's riflemen had been required to hold the front for days and weeks longer than doctrine or common sense recommended. The infantry divisions were rated "satisfactory," but the evaluation was at best overly generous, at worst recklessly optimistic. Manstein understood the problem. On June 1, he warned Zeitzler that not only could the attack not succeed with the forces currently allotted, but the concentration of strength around Kursk opened wide opportunities for the Red Army to create crises elsewhere.

"If it were done when 'tis done, then 'twere well it were done quickly." To that end, Manstein put everything on Front Street, leaving no significant sector reserves. Hoth also reinforced Manstein's conviction that breaking directly through the Russian defenses would be a long, absolutely expensive process. At Manstein's May 10–11 visit to the Fourth Panzer Army, Hoth suggested that a straight line was not necessarily the shortest distance between two operational points. The terrain in front of the Psel River, and the course and configuration of the river itself, suggested that an opposed crossing would prove time-consuming. If his corps had to fight for bridgeheads, they would be wide open to a flank attack by Soviet strategic reserves, mounted from the northeast, through the passage between the Psel and the Donets.

Hoth recommended that instead of advancing straight ahead in tandem with XLVIII Panzer Corps, II SS Panzer Corps should swing northeast short of the Psel and draw the Russians onto their guns around the village of Prokhorovka. The III Panzer Corps in turn would shift its axis of advance northeast and strike the right flank of the Soviets attacking the SS. The XLVIII Panzer Corps, with Grossdeutschland doing the heavy lifting, would keep abreast of the SS, changing direction to correspond with its movements, and reinforce the expected decisive engagement as necessary. From there, the Fourth Panzer Army could advance in any appropriate direction: north to a direct junction with Model, northeast into the left rear of the Russians in the Orel salient—perhaps even due east, for another time-buying "forehand stroke." A series of map exercises held by Kempf, Hoth, and their corps commanders beginning on May 29 developed the concept. On June 3–5, Army Group South conducted a final war game. Later that month, Hoth ran a command post exercise for the Fourth Panzer Army, testing the intended course of Citadel's first days. By June 2, Fourth Panzer Army's war diary was presenting the "Hoth variant" as settled.

The decision was minimally reassuring. Shifting the panzers' axes of advance would still leave the right flank of Army Group South wide open. Addressing that by turning III Panzer Corps north left Army Detachment Kempf's infantry divisions to secure with their own limited resources sectors that in one case extended ninety miles. This was a substantial risk, especially should the main advance be delayed.

Like many senior German generals, Manstein was horsey in a way only George Patton matched on the Allied side. To relax, he rode an hour or so each day—until Hitler exploded. Manstein's aide responded to the Führer's expressed fear of partisans by arranging for a motorized escort. That, however, defeated the purpose of the exercise in both senses of the noun. Manstein condignly and unhappily dismounted. The field marshal embraced high tech, on the other hand, with the train he adopted as his mobile headquarters. Its half-dozen cars supported antiaircraft and ground security, maintained an elaborate communications system, and above all provided stable working and living conditions. Any fool can be uncomfortable, and while Manstein was not decrepit, at fifty-eight he was well past his youth. The train also enabled him to visit subordinate headquarters by day, then travel to the next destination by night and arrive rested and breakfasted.

Army Group South's attack began in the late afternoon of July 4. In XLVIII Panzer Corps's sector, the panzer grenadier battalions of Grossdeutschland and 11th Panzer Division went forward in a driving rain against the Soviet outpost zone and its network of fortified villages. Grossdeutschland had begun the war as an elite infantry regiment, and it prided itself on maintaining traditional infantry skills. But mines, small arms, and artillery turned what was expected to be a shock attack into a stop-and-go operation extending into the late evening. The fighting was hard enough and the casualties high enough that division and corps assumed the defenses had been breached and ordered the main armored force to move into attack positions.

Dawn broke around 3:00 A.M., with the promise of clear, hot weather. During the night, there had been more heavy thunderstorms in Manstein's sector, and much of the ground would remain frustratingly soft for most of the day. A more immediate concern was the Soviet bombardment that delayed the initial attack until around 4:10 A.M., when artillery and rocket fire pounded Voronezh Front's forward positions for fifty minutes. The Stukas and the medium bombers of VIII Air Corps appeared as the barrage ended, hammering Kursk's railway station and Russian gun positions in the rear zones, then shifting to the visible strongpoints of the forward defenses.

Luftwaffe airfields in this sector were closely concentrated. For two months, the Red Air Force had left them relatively undisturbed, hoping to take them out in a surprise attack. As the Russian barrage began, the Second and Seventeenth Air Armies sent 150 Shturmoviks, plus fighters and level bombers, across the front line to the German airfields, where 800 German planes sat waiting to take off, wingtip to wingtip. It might have been the Red Air Force's chance to collect payback for the first day of Barbarossa, when it was caught by surprise on the ground and suffered catastrophic losses.

But German signal intelligence noted the sudden surge in communications among the Russian air units, and German radar picked up the incoming aircraft. The Germans were launching their own attack earlier than expected, to deal with the Soviet guns. Even so, the next few minutes were chaotic as bombers, scheduled to take off first, scrambled to clear the runways for the fighters, then sought to take off themselves. By now, the Luftwaffe specialized in emergencies. By the time the Soviet aircraft appeared, not only were the targeted airfields empty, but the German fighters had the advantage of height.

Their Me-109Gs technically were no more than an even match for the Red Air Force Yaks and LaGGs. But the pilots of JG 3 and 52 were among the Luftwaffe's best. A number of the Shturmovik crews by contrast were flying their first missions with the Il-2. The Soviet fighter groups, also largely inexperienced, flew close escort, matching the Shturmoviks in speed and altitude. When they did break off to engage the German fighters, they too often lost contact. Russian attack routes were marked by shot-down Shturmoviks. The targeted airfields escaped significant damage. And VIII Air Corps had a free hand in its initial attack.

The impact was multiplied by the Germans' highly effective air–ground liaison system. Luftwaffe radio teams accompanied corps and division headquarters into action, reporting the situation regularly to their headquarters, contacting formations, and vectoring strikes onto targets as they emerged. In the first hour, over four hundred aircraft appeared in a sector only twenty miles wide. One rifle division reported formations of eighty at a time. Another was hit by five Stuka groups in succession—on a front two miles wide and less than five yards deep! These demonstrations of precision bombing were more necessary than XLVIII Panzer Corps expected or wanted. It advanced three divisions abreast: 3rd Panzer, Grossdeutschland, and 11th Panzer, over 450 tanks and assault guns. More than 350 of those were in Grossdeutschland's two-mile sector of the front. Two hundred were Panthers, combined with Grossdeutschland's two tank battalions into a provisional 10th Panzer Brigade that seemed formidable enough to break through defenses weakened the day before in raids made by GD's panzer grenadiers.

Hoth's decision to attack without any reserve has been questioned cogently. A two-division front, with the 3rd or 11th Panzer held ready to exploit any tactical success, was one alternative. Another was to use the Panthers as the nucleus of a reserve force in a sector where arguably too many tanks were committed on too narrow a front. Hoth and his chief of staff, Major General Friedrich Fangohr, discussed both options and rejected them on the grounds that Grossdeutschland would need strong armored support on both flanks in order to force an immediate breakthrough. Hoth was nevertheless confident enough to set XLVIII Corps's objective for July 6 as the Psel River—thirty miles away. But that meant cracking the nut of Cherkassoye, a village three miles behind the panzers' start line, whose elaborately camouflaged defenses were manned by an entire Guards rifle division, the 67th, the one hit by five Stuka attacks just before the Germans appeared.

A year or two earlier, that might have been enough. This time the 67th's positions and their supporting echelons responded with the heaviest fire GD had experienced. The Panthers had reached Army Group South on July 1: too late for field-testing the tanks, much less attempts at training. Even their radio equipment remained untested for the sake of communications security. Tension between the commanders of the Panthers and GD's tanks further complicated planning.

The improvised panzer brigade went in around 9:00 A.M. The

Panthers were slowed by wet ground, then drove into a minefield. Some lost treads. Others spun tread-deep in muck trying to extricate themselves. The battalion of GD infantrymen the Panthers were supposed to be escorting and supporting pushed forward but was pinned down and shot to pieces. It took ten hours for Grossdeutschland's pioneers to clear paths through the minefield and for the maintenance crews to replace damaged tracks.

That was only one sector. Grossdeutschland's tank commander, who rejoiced in the name of Hyazinth Graf Strachwitz von Gross-Zauche und Camminetz—his men called him "Panzer Count" and "Panzer Lion"— was a member (apparently nominal) of the Allgemeine (General) SS, courtesy of Heinrich Himmler. He had also won the Knight's Cross of the Iron Cross during Barbarossa for taking his tank across a bridge and single-handedly annihilating a Soviet convoy. When he saw the Panthers halted, he shifted his own tanks, including GD's organic Tiger company, to support 11th Panzer.

The Russian defenses were the usual maze of entrenchments, minefields, and strongpoints, strengthened further by wet ground that slowed the armor. The ideal result for a German attack was a more or less simultaneous penetration of a defense sector, then a swing right and left, attacking bunkers and strongpoints from the flank. Like Japanese positions in the Pacific theater, Red Army defenses depended on an interlocking chain of enfilade fire. The more bunkers taken out, the more gaps opened in the firewall, the more vulnerable became the entire system to coordinated attack from front and flank.

That was the theory. In practice, the heavily built bunkers often resisted anything but armor-piercing rounds. For two years, the panzers had usually been able to generate "tank fright" as they came to close quarters. Around Cherkassoye, Guardsmen took on the Mark IVs hand to hand with near suicidal determination, jumping onto the vehicles to blow off turrets with mines. Tankers responded by rediscovering the Great War tactic of straddling a trench, then turning to collapse it and bury the defenders alive. In contrast with events in Model's sector, the panzer grenadiers were able to maintain contact and supplement the mutual covering fire of the tanks' machine guns.

But Cherkassoye held even after the surviving Panthers and their panzer grenadiers finally escaped their personal bog and came up in support of GD. The 11th Panzer was able to bring up in its sector a number of Mark IIIs converted to flamethrowers and burn out defenders who at times served their guns until roasted alive. Even then the Soviet survivors of the 67th and the antitank regiments that stood with them maintained a foothold in the village outskirts, falling back to the second line only with the end of daylight, and only under orders.

The 3rd Panzer Division, on GD's left, had easier going. With its left effectively covered by the 332nd Infantry Division, the 3rd's panzer grenadiers took the strongpoint of Korovino by day's end, and a tank battalion took advantage of the transfer there of local reserves to break through the 71st Rifle Division's forward defenses and drive a narrow salient three miles into the Soviet rear.

IV

Hoth's final attack orders to the SS panzers, replicated in the corps order of July 1, were to break through the first two Russian defense lines, then advance in force to the Psel River in the area of Prokhorovka. The II SS Panzer Corps thus had the most demanding assignment on Manstein's sector—and expected it. The identity of the Waffen SS was constructed around its panzer divisions. From unpromising military beginnings, they established a deserved reputation as some of the most formidable combat formations in the brief history of armored war. The Waffen SS began life in 1925 as a security force to protect Nazi meetings and officials. From its beginnings, the force was a party instrument. Its personal loyalty to Hitler was manifested in the regiment-sized Leibstandarte (Bodyguard) established in 1933. The Totenkopf (Death's-

Head) units were created the same year as concentration camp guards. In 1935, a number of local "Emergency Readiness Formations" were grouped into three regiments of Special Service Troops (Verfügungstruppen). All three were expanded to motorized divisions; Leibstandarte was the last to be reconfigured in May 1941.

Ideologically, the SS was projected as a new human type, able to serve as a model and an instrument for revitalizing the Nordic race. Militarily, the SS way was headlong energy and ruthless, never-say-die aggressiveness, emphasizing speed and ferocity. SS training stressed physical toughness and incorporated risk to an extent far surpassing the army's training. Operationally, the results were initially mixed. Not until Barbarossa did the Waffen SS come into its own. Not until after Stalingrad did it join the first team. Only at Kursk did it begin defining combat on the Eastern Front.

From the Leibstandarte, the Waffen SS drew an identity as the Führer's personal elite. The Verfügungstruppe, which had become the Das Reich Division, contributed a willingness to learn soldiering from the professionals. Totenkopf emphasized ferocity as a norm. All three qualities attracted attention. An army report singles out the SS riflemen of Das Reich for "fearlessness and bravery" during the drive for Moscow; on one occasion they swarmed over heavy tanks to set them afire with gasoline when antitank guns proved useless. A Leibstandarte rifle company set up the victory at Rostov by seizing a vital railway bridge before it could be blown. Totenkopf was the heart and soul of the defense of the Demyansk Pocket, created by the Soviet Northwest Front's massive offensive of February 1942. The SS men held nothing back; their spirit of "no quarter, no surrender" left four-fifths of the division as casualties by the time the pocket was relieved in April 1942.

The chosen three of the Waffen SS spent most of 1942 in France, being rebuilt, reconfigured, and upgraded to panzer grenadier status. In fact, all three had two-battalion tank regiments, at least one of their six panzer grenadier battalions in armored half-tracks, generous allowances of supporting weapons, and by Citadel, a company of Tigers. Authorized strength was more than twenty thousand. The newly created SS Panzer Corps was supremely confident that it was the instrument needed to restore the situation and turn the tide in the East. Redeployed in January 1943, the SS panzers played a crucial role in Manstein's offensive, paying for Kharkov's recapture with more than twelve thousand casualties. Leibstandarte's fighting strength was reduced by almost half, the city square was renamed in its honor, and its men were accused postwar of clearing a hospital by the simple expedient of shooting its seven hundred patients. When Manstein received the Oak Leaves to the Knight's Cross of the Iron Cross, he owed a good deal of the award to the men in SS black.

Left to right, the alignment for Citadel was Leibstandarte, Das Reich, and Totenkopf: another five hundred AFVs on a front of less than eight miles. *Schwerpunkt* of the attack was the junction of Leibstandarte and Das Reich, their Tiger companies operating side by side: the apex of a massive formation twice the size of anything deployed in Model's sector.

Manstein and Hausser believed that mass and fighting spirit, plus Luftwaffe support, would carry the SS through any defense the Soviets might put up. Front and army commands were aware of whom they faced in this sector: "Hitler's guard." The position had been entrusted to a Soviet counterpart, the heavily reinforced 52nd Guards Rifle Division. The panzers rolled out at 4:00 A.M. and from the beginning encountered determined compound resistance—staff-speak for everything the Red Army could throw at them.

The advance was across relatively open ground, through grain fields and across steppe grass. As the tanks moved forward and the Soviet positions opened fire, the Tigers took on the bunkers while the lighter tanks covered the infantry, who began clearing the trenches, and the pioneers, who blew up the antitank ditches to create ramps for the tanks to advance. The tanks would repeat the performance as the pioneers and infantry "reduced" surviving bunkers with grenades, demolition charges, and flamethrowers.

It reads like a staff exercise but played like a never-ending scene from Dante. A war correspondent rhapsodized about "the hour of the tank." An SS officer described—from a safe distance—tanks charging "like knights in combat with horse and lance." Reality was Soviet crews countering with Katyusha rocket launchers fired horizontally over open sights and Soviet tank crews charging forward to engage at ranges nullifying the long-range advantage of the German high-velocity 75s and 88s. Each antitank gun had to be silenced individually, each trench cleared from traverse to traverse, each bunker taken in close combat. A flamethrower crewman from Das Reich wrote of the "strange feeling to serve this destructive weapon and it was terrifying to see the flames eat their way forward and envelop the Russian defenders." A more matter-of-fact veteran of the day mentioned to the author in passing that ever since then he had been unable to tolerate the smell of roast pork.

There was nothing to choose between the adversaries in terms of courage and determination. Tactical skill was at a discount in the close-quarters fighting. But the Germans had three things in their favor. One was their tank armament—not only its long range, but the excellent sighting equipment that enabled precise targeting of the Russian positions once they revealed themselves. The second advantage, this one sector-specific, was the third infantry battalion in each of the SS panzer grenadier regiments and the increased strength and flexibility it provided. The third German trump card was the Luftwaffe. The 52nd Rifle Division took fifteen hours of virtually uninterrupted, unopposed air attack by as many as eighty aircraft at a time. These wreaked havoc not so much on forward positions, but in the second-line trenches, the mortar, gun, and rocket positions constructed to resist shelling but vulnerable to direct air strikes.

By 9:00 A.M., the Germans were through the first defense line. But every report reaching higher headquarters confirmed resistance of an unprecedented nature and scale despite the relative ineffectiveness of Soviet air attacks. A Russian tank commander described the intensity and scale of the battle as challenging human comprehension. The sun itself was obscured by dust and smoke. But the Russians held on and fought back. Not until 4:00 P.M. did the key strongpoint of Bytkova fall to Leibstandarte, and by then a third of the 52nd Guards's original eight thousand men were dead or wounded. Thirty minutes later, the SS panzers were ordered forward: Break through the next defense system and throw a bridgehead across the Psel. It took ninety more minutes to organize the attack, which promptly ran into an antitank "front"—an integrated system of gun positions that checked the Tiger spearhead to a point where division command ordered a halt.

Das Reich had kept pace on Leibstandarte's right despite initial problems, caused by wet ground, of maintaining tank-infantry contact. During the night assault, parties of the 3rd SS Panzer Grenadier Regiment had infiltrated the outpost line and cleared part of the way before the main attack went in around 6:00 A.M. By around 8:15, Das Reich had reached its major initial objective, the strongpoint village of Berezov, and the panzer grenadiers were clearing it with flamethrowers. Not until 4:00 P.M., however, did the division's final objective fall to a hastily committed reserve battalion. Totenkopf had also done well initially in a supporting role, pushing the opposing 155th Guards Rifle Regiment back and out of its way, but then was stopped by a tank brigade that blocked the road to Oboyan. Nevertheless, Hausser, his division commanders, and Hoth saw the next day's prospects for the SS as favorable.

The same could not be said for Army Detachment Kempf. Its first assignment involved crossing the Donets. No aircraft were available. The artillery was so weak that three Luftwaffe flak regiments were temporarily assigned as substitutes: an indirect-fire role ill-suited to the high-velocity 88s. Kempf and his corps commanders correspondingly agreed on a broad-front crossing spearheaded by their three panzer divisions. German armor had been leading river crossings since 1940, and the multiple attack sites were expected to throw the Soviets into predictable confusion. But at the end of Manstein's post-Stalingrad counterattack, the Germans had established a bridgehead at Mikhailovka, across from Belgorod. Steadily reinforced during the run-up to Kursk, it represented enough of an immediate threat that the Seventh Guards Army was on local alert all along its front.

Around 2:30 A.M. on July 5, the Russians opened a full-scale barrage. Katyushas took out one of the pontoon bridges connecting Mikhailovka to the main German positions. Another was blocked when an assault gun and a pontoon truck collided. That meant 6th Panzer Division had to improvise—and the 81st Guards Rifle Division spent the day demonstrating that tactical flexibility was not inevitably a substitute for determination backed by firepower. By 4:00 P.M., the 6th Panzer Division had captured a couple of dots on the map, but its commander acknowledged that "considering the sacrifices . . . you can't call this a victory."

In Army Detachment Kempf's center, the 19th Panzer Pioneer Battalion spent the night building a pontoon bridge and the early dawn clearing minefields—with bayonets, since the wooden box mines were invisible to metal detectors—and cutting wire. The Russians observed and waited. Minutes before 19th Panzer's attack went in, guns, mortars, and Katyushas flogged the assembly areas and the crossing site. With no reports from forward observers, the division's artillery remained silent or fired blindly into the dust and smoke. Their Russian opponents had observation points on high ground and a communications system that the Germans failed to disrupt. Kempf had divided the Tiger battalion he had been assigned: one company to each panzer division. The 19th's Tigers lost thirteen of fourteen before noon, mostly to mines. Thanks to the panzer grenadiers' success in exploiting the boundary between two Russian rifle divisions, 19th Panzer made enough gains to consolidate a bridgehead. But the division's artillery had used so much ammunition that at 4:15 it reported that is was likely to need resupply to support the next day's operation. Part of that resupply capacity was provided by literal horsepower— demodernization in practice. The bridgehead was more a foothold. As the division commander summarized events, "The whole thing was almost a failure."

In Kempf's southern sector, the 7th Panzer Division's lead elements crossed the Donets at first light on a pontoon bridge placed by the division's pioneers. A textbook operation—until Soviet artillery took out the bridge and left the 7th's advance battle group isolated under increasing air strikes and artillery fire. The 7th's attached Tigers were too heavy to cross the first bridge and bogged down when they tried to ford the river. Not until 2:00 in the afternoon were the pioneers able to construct a bridge that could bear the Tigers' weight. Until then, the most they could do was bunker busting for the sorely tried panzer grenadiers on the far bank.

Here, as in every sector the Tigers attacked, Russian infantry initially let them pass and concentrated on the infantry following them. The Tigers in turn sought desperately for concealed antitank guns that scored hits that may not have penetrated armor but disconcerted crews. The Seventeenth Air Army weighed in with a continuing series of air strikes that around 3:00 P.M. had the German air liaison officers calling urgently for fighters. The 109s responded; the Russians increased the ante; and by 6:00 P.M. what began as a series of small-scale fights turned into what World War I pilots called a "furball." Shturmoviks and Messerschmitts mixed it up for more than an hour in one of Citadel's more one-sided aerial engagements. One German pilot claimed four kills, another six. The Seventeenth Air Army recorded a loss of no fewer than fifty-five Shturmoviks in the sector. By day's end, the German bridgehead was secure. That, however, was a long way from a breakthrough.

The study of Operation Citadel has been dominated, arguably overshadowed, by statistics. That does not make them irrelevant. In Manstein's sector, the Luftwaffe owned the air, scoring more than 150 Soviet kills for a loss of two dozen. On the ground, Army Group South had suffered more than 6,000 casualties for no more than limited tactical gains on narrow fronts. Given the nearly empty replacement pipeline and the distance between the fighting zone and its base areas, 6,000 men arguably meant more than the relatively few tanks and assault guns—no more than forty or fifty—permanently written off on July 5. The raw number, however, hardly compared with the first day of Verdun or July 1, 1916, day one of the First Battle of the Somme. The Panthers' combat debut had been a fiasco. But only two of them had been destroyed by gunfire: a tribute to their survivability. The balance of attrition by itself, in short, was not discouraging.

In comparing the first day's fighting in Model's, Hoth's, and Kempf's sectors, three points nevertheless stand out. First is the Soviet ability at all levels to conceal their strength and their dispositions even as the battle developed; *maskirovka* did not stop at zero hour. Second is the Soviet ability to disrupt German timetables. Since the start of the war, the Germans had been able to set the timing and force the pace of any attack they initiated. Manstein's successes at the turn of the year made it possible for the Germans to interpret the disaster of Stalingrad as an exception, if not an accident. Now, in the initial stages of a long-projected, long-prepared offensive, the Russians were controlling the agenda to a unexpected degree. Finally, Kempf's experiences in particular suggested that the Germans' ability to work inside what today is called the Red Army's "observe, orient, decide, and act" loop was a diminishing, when not a wasting, asset. The Germans were expert players of military thimblerig: getting the Soviet yokel to bet on which shell contained the pea. Facing Kempf, and Hoth and Model, the Red Army was demonstrating the most effective counter: refusing to play the game by trying to stay ahead of it.

A senior staff officer with a bit of time to reflect on the maps and the strength reports might have put the pieces together. But under the Third Reich, the Wehrmacht had adjusted to Adolf Hitler's five-minutes-to-midnight pace and to a pattern of so much multitasking and overstressing that this kind of calculation, once a general staff trademark, had become outmoded, retrograde. There was tomorrow's action to prepare. That morning, a Leibstandarte tanker had shouted, "Lunch in Kursk!" as the attack went in. Bravado must become reality—and soon.

Chapter IV

_____

GRAPPLE

FROM THE RUSSIAN PERSPECTIVE, the Germans were doing all too well for comfort. Lieutenant General Ivan Chistiakov, commanding the Sixth Guards Army, managed his reserves carefully enough that he was able to deploy two fresh divisions in his second-echelon defenses in the afternoon and evening of July 5. Vatutin ordered his armor forward to block the German penetration and restore Sixth Guards Army's front. Two corps of the First Tank Army would confront XLVIII Panzer Corps, while two independent Guards tank corps took the SS in front and flank.

I

On paper, that raised the total number of Russian tanks committed against the Fourth Panzer Army to around a thousand. On the ground, the First Tank Army's commander, Lieutenant General Mikhail Katukov, was receiving alarming reports on the performance of the Tigers. The riflemen of the Sixth Guards Army were holding on by their fingertips but did not offer a stable base for a full-scale counterattack. Katukov, working in his undershirt in the July heat, recommended his armor go over to the defensive until the next day. Vatutin agreed, authorizing his subordinate to resume the attack only when the German advance was halted. The air armies too needed time to count their losses and regroup for the next day.

Whether or not Vatutin had been shaken by the force of the German attack, he estimated his situation as unlikely to benefit from desperation and improvisation—at least at the operational level. Tactically, it was another story. Over the objections of his armor officers, Vatutin ordered his forward units to dig their tanks in—not just throw up berms, but bury the T-34s sometimes up to their turrets, converting them into pillboxes. The reasoning behind Vatutin's high-risk decision was that based on initial reports of what Tigers and Panthers could do in the open, staging more than local, spoiling counterattacks invited the destruction of Voronezh Front's armor to no purpose. The best chance of defeating Citadel was to use operational reserves defensively, a breakwater against which the panzer waves would dash themselves until Stavka's grand plan unfolded and the Red Army's strategic reserves inverted the battle's dynamic.

Zhukov's angry reaction was that Vatutin's order violated armor doctrine, common sense, and Stalin's wishes. Nikita Khrushchev threw his weight behind Vatutin. A political officer he might be, but he had garnered enough frontline experience at Stalingrad to appreciate Vatutin's points—and the front commander's personal and professional qualities. The orders went out: Dig them in. The simple command cannot convey the blind, stumbling exhaustion of the tankers, infantrymen, and engineers who shoveled during the night.

By "flying light" on July 6, the Soviet Second Air Army was able to mount large-scale, wing-strength fighter sweeps in temporarily empty air. A storm front had shut down VIII Air Corps's fields, but when Hoth resumed his attack around 9:00 A.M., the Stukas were overhead. They proved less effective at ground support than the day before. Since 6:00 A.M., the Seventeenth Air Army had resumed sending its remaining Shturmoviks against Army Detachment Kempf's bridges and bridgeheads. Experience indicated fighters were best employed in masses, and VIII Air Corps commander Brigadier General Hans Seidemann responded by dispatching his Messerschmitts to support Kempf. That left the Stukas and the ground-attack 190s in Hoth's sector as unexpected but welcome meat on the table for the La-5 pilots. JG 77 alone had 10 of its 120 Stukas shot down or badly damaged. The dive-bombers kept coming. The 6th Tank Corps alone reported four strikes of sixty to seventy planes each day. The XLVIII Panzer Corps was nevertheless forced to depend on its own ground resources. The 3rd Panzer Division's war diary noted laconically, "Fewer fighters today."

The attack began with a ninety-minute artillery barrage that the Russians countered with their own guns and with repeated air strikes that inflicted heavy losses on the advancing tanks. In the center of the panzer corps's front, Grossdeutschland sent its panzer grenadiers closely supported by tanks against the high ground north of Cherkassoye—and into the 250 AFVs of Katukov's 3rd Mechanized Corps. Originally intended as part of an armored counterattack, the corps found itself in an infantry support role intermingled with the 90th Guards Rifle Division and what remained of the 67th. Almost immediately, Vatutin's improvised tank pillboxes proved their worth. Each of them was a strongpoint in itself that had to be fought for individually. Turrets posed small targets, and their 76 mm guns were too dangerous to ignore. The Tigers and Panzer IVs had to close the range, sacrificing the advantage of their high-velocity guns. Given the heavy, well-sloped armor of a T-34 turret, a direct hit was no guarantee of a kill. And the dug-in tanks were only half the panzers' problem. Soviet commanders deployed other tanks in concealed positions in front of the immobilized ones. Panzers concentrating on the entrenched AFVs often overlooked the mobile ones—until taken under fire from the flanks or rear.

Tanks concealed in ambush seldom survived long once they revealed their positions. Their crews were dead men from the start. But they earned the thanks of the Soviet Union: their lives had a purpose. And the tankers' sacrifice had an unexpected secondary effect. The Russians' adjusted armor deployment tended to separate the panzers from the panzer grenadiers. When the tanks engaged, the infantry kept moving, and without the direct, immediate support of the tanks, infantry losses were heavy against the formidable trench and bunker networks of the Russian second line. Army and Luftwaffe antiaircraft guns kept the constant Russian air attacks distracted but could not generate enough firepower to choke them off.

Grossdeutschland made steady progress up the Oboyan road. But after as many as eight separate attacks, a breakthrough still eluded this elite formation when its forward elements "leaguered" for the night. It had begun Citadel with more than three hundred AFVs, attached and organic. Eighty remained operational.

On GD's left flank, 3rd Panzer Division fought its way by midafternoon to the Pena River—a river by name, more of a stream in fact. But its banks were marshy enough to daunt even the Mark IIIs and IVs. High ground on its far side, while low by measurement, gave Soviet tanks and antitank guns enough of an advantage to block the panzers' advance. With some tank help from GD and infantry from the 167th Division, the 11th Panzer got into Olkhovatka (a village with the same name as the one so hotly contested in Central Front's sector), but advanced no farther against the 1st Mechanized Brigade and its supporting antitank guns and riflemen. Hoth was not pleased with the slow progress in Knobelsdorff's sector. Otto von Knobelsdorff, however, was an old-time infantryman who did not expect miracles. His corps might be running late, but it would get through the second defense line. It would catch up with the SS: it needed just "one day more!"

On July 5, the men of the lightning runes had approached what had been expected from Citadel from the beginning. Repair crews had reduced the long-term armor losses to around fifteen, bringing the panzer regiments back to near authorized strength. On July 6, Hausser deployed them on an even narrower front. Leibstandarte and Das Reich again went in side by side on a front of a little over six miles, with a shallow river and soft ground on both flanks. Their first objective was a network of fortified heights, the core of the second Russian line in the sector. Leibstandarte jumped off at around 7:30 and took fire and losses from elements of the First Tank Army, but by midmorning pushed through the remnants of the 51st Guards Rifle Division, bypassed the strongpoint village of Yakovolevo, and shouldered the Soviet defenders westward. While the panzer grenadiers kept the Russians in check, an armored battle group drove as far as eight miles into the Soviet defenses before encountering the next zone of minefields, bunkers, and antitank guns.

The panzers had already refueled and rearmed in the forward zone once that afternoon. Now they were falling victim to mines scattered openly on the roads and trails—and occasionally delivered by specially trained dogs. The air support coordinator's radio vehicle was destroyed: no small loss to a spearhead now beyond its own artillery's effective range. The approaching darkness amply justified closing down and closing up.

Das Reich faced tougher going in the early stages. Its leading panzer grenadier regiment was halted in front of Hill 243 by knee-deep mud, minefields, dug-in tanks, and artillery and small-arms fire. The division's Tigers stopped an armored counterattack, but not until Das Reich's headquarters could coordinate a ninety-minute air and artillery strike on the hill were the infantry able to storm and clear the bunker-trench complex. It was the kind of technologically based flexibility at which the Germans excelled, enabling Das Reich's tanks to keep pace with Leibstandarte in the course of the afternoon.

By the end of the day, the SS had breached the defense system's second line. But the Soviet strongpoints on the flanks held on and held out. Around noon on July 5, Leibstandarte had reported a "general impression that the Russians were running." By evening, its reports spoke of "tough and determined resistance" with "strong" air support. The corps reported a total of 552 prisoners for the first day. Only 15 were turned in by Leibstandarte. It was enough for interrogation purposes. The fresh-caught POWs said the rifle companies were well supplied with weapons and ammunition. Rations were good, thanks in part to Lend-Lease. Decades later, Red Army veterans remembered their surprise and amusement at cartons that contained packets of salt, factory-made cigarettes, and toilet paper sometimes used to write letters home. Morale was generally described as "good." But that the SS already knew. For all the superheated postbattle narratives of participants and correspondents, the ground gained by Leibstandarte and Das Reich on July 5–6 was no more than a narrow salient, on a map resembling nothing so much as an upthrust middle finger.

Whether more could be made of it remained an open question. Leibstandarte proposed to establish a bridgehead over the Psel on the next day, but its Tigers were still engaging T-34s at midnight. Corps headquarters, moreover, had other concerns. Totenkopf's dual mission as offensive force and flank guard involved at best a dispersion of effort. With the Tiger company leading the way, armored battle groups made gains of up to twenty miles, crossing the Oboyan–Belgorod road and reaching the Belgorod–Kursk railway before halting. So far, so good. But the success of the division's advance left its right flank—and that of the corps— increasingly exposed. By the panzer handbook, security was the task of the infantry, but the division assigned had already been committed elsewhere. Manstein had been aware of the potential problem and had stressed his need for at least two more infantry divisions, but he had been refused. Meantime, Totenkopf was or-

dered to find flank guards from its own resources—at the expense
of being able to develop opportunities in the main sector.

Smoke, mirrors, and shows of force worked well enough during
the afternoon. But the Soviets continued first harassing, then
counterattacking, the lengthening right flank of the SS panzers.
Hoth's orders for the next day praised the corps's "unstoppable
forward storming" and recognized the problem by ordering Totenkopf to attack east-northeast early and often the next day,
thereby securing the corps flank and supporting III Panzer Corps's
advance.

II

Unlike Model and Rommel, Hermann Hoth did not make a
practice of trying to command an army from the front. But since
Citadel's beginning, he had been visiting corps and division headquarters, seeing for himself and making recommendations. Hoth
had expected a breakthrough of the Russian second line of defense
on July 6. Muddy ground and Russian resistance had prevented
that, but the Fourth Panzer Army's commander felt comfortable
describing the day as "a complete success." Manstein, though, was
sufficiently concerned at the general lack of progress that on July 6
he asked the Army high command to release XXIV Panzer Corps.
When Zeitzler refused, Manstein responded by ordering Hoth to
keep hammering forward. But both generals understood too well
that Fourth Panzer Army's further success depended on Kempf
and III Panzer Corps securing Hoth's increasingly exposed right
flank.

Like everything else about Citadel, that was easier stated than
achieved. For July 6, Breith had ordered 19th Panzer Division to
move north along the Donets, while 6th and 7th Panzer were to
advance northeast in the dual role of flank guard and strike force.
It took 6th Panzer the entire morning to concentrate and cross the
heavy pontoon bridge in 7th Panzer's sector. The other two divi-

sions were in action before dawn. The 19th Panzer lost eighteen tanks to mines before successfully shifting its axis of advance, taking the 81st Guards Rifle Division in the flank and rear, and capturing the strongpoint village of Razumnoye and its environs. But casualties in the panzer grenadier regiments were high; the Russian defense was comprehensive and stubborn, and the fierce counterattacks shook the division's many green replacements.

The 7th Panzer, Erwin Rommel's old Ghost Division, led with its 25th Panzer Regiment and an attached Tiger company and reached Krutoi Log before encountering a blocking position established the previous night by a division committed from the Seventh Guards Army's reserve. The 73rd Guards Rifles answered the doubts about the Red Army's ability to fight outside of prepared positions. "Step on it!" (*"Mit Vollgas heran!"*) was the order of one tank battalion commander. Instead, naturally broken ground utilized by antitank guns and rifles in the hands of determined men blocked the Germans through the heart of the day. Rarely had the experienced panzer grenadiers encountered such levels of firepower; even the Tigers were checked. Not until 6th Panzer, on the principle of better late than never, came up on 7th's left was the division able to resume an advance that—as so often in so many sectors—was stopped at nightfall at the foot of a nameless hill, thickly wooded and ranged in by what seemed to be hundreds of Russian guns.

Vatutin had spent almost as much time on July 6 arguing with his superiors as fighting the Germans. It was increasingly apparent that the armored counterattacks of Voronezh Front's tank corps were too small to have a serious effect on the massed German armor. Vatutin responded by requesting the prompt commitment of four additional tank corps from Stavka reserve. This formidable force would enable a counterattack with enough weight to at least shift the balance in his sector.

Vasilevsky concurred, recommending two tank corps as direct reinforcements and moving the Fifth Guards Tank Army closer to the combat zone. Stalin telephoned his reply. Vatutin would receive the two tank corps, hold his ground, and wear the Germans down. Steppe Front would move the Fifth Guards Tank Army toward Kursk. All these decisions were aimed at keeping the enemy fixed until the projected multifront offensive was ready.

Vatutin's response for July 7 was to reinforce his forward positions: pin the German center in place and wear it down. This would give the newly committed tank corps time to move up and turn stalemate to victory. The 2nd and 5th Tank Corps would hold the SS while the 31st Tank Corps moved against their right flank. The 6th Tank and 3rd Mechanized Corps would block Knobelsdorff's advance toward Oboyan. Two air armies would provide all-out support. Local Soviet counterattacks continued across the front through the night of July 6–7 until mist forced a general breaking of contact. The mist prefigured a weather change: rain and clouds, which would slow the German tanks and hinder their Stukas. Manstein's weathermen could also read charts. For July 7, Knobelsdorff's corps was ordered to drive toward Oboyan and cover Hausser's left flank as the SS drove into and through the Soviet defense system. The unspoken demand on both generals was "Pick up the pace!"

The Luftwaffe promised Hoth the bulk of its assets as well, and when the Fourth Panzer Army crossed its start lines around 4:00 A.M., the Stukas were overhead, hammering Soviet positions. Sixty to eighty aircraft every five or ten minutes concentrated on anything resembling an artillery or antitank position. The 11th Panzer and Grossdeutschland, the center and right-flank formations, broke through around Dubrova in the early morning—only a few miles from the open country the panzers had sought for three brutal days.

It was then, around 5:00 A.M., that 6th Tank and 3rd Mechanized Corps counterattacked: more than a hundred T-34s covered by Shturmoviks, with the usual massive gun and rocket support. Grossdeutschland was stopped in its tracks for three hours in front of the village of Syrzevo when its attached Panthers ran into an unmarked minefield. By late afternoon, only 40 of the 184 that began the battle were still operational. That did nothing for the morale of even an elite unit. Questions were arising about whether the Tigers were being wrongly employed as a spearhead, whether they were not more effective using their long guns at ranges the T-34s could not match rather than be caught at close quarters by superior numbers. But on this day, any idea of using the Mark IIIs and IVs as the land-warfare counterpart of destroyers screening the Tiger battleships was abandoned when the lighter AFVs regularly had to be withdrawn to reverse slopes to escape the plunging fire of the Russian heavy howitzers. In back-and-forth close-quarters fighting that took the rest of the day, Grossdeutschland managed about three miles, finally reaching Syrzevo, the last major strongpoint before Oboyan. The 11th Panzer matched that gain, but no more, against equally strong resistance.

Every time it seemed the Russians were entering panic mode, they rallied and counterattacked. Vatutin shifted reinforcements from relatively quiet sectors and funneled them down the Oboyan road by brigades and battalions. The 6th Tank and 3rd Mechanized Corps stabilized the line around Syrzevo. Shturmoviks broke up advances Grossdeutschland's history describes as "slow and laborious." Grossdeutschland's panzer grenadiers took heavy losses from artillery and mortar fire, and the last of the division's Tigers was disabled during a Russian counterattack. The artillery duel continued even after dark, with guns and rocket launchers firing blindly or at previously located target sites now often abandoned.

It was slow; it was expensive. But it was progress—from the Russian perspective, dangerously steady progress. The problem was that Hoth had set the corps's objectives up to three times farther than the actual advance. One bright spot was the capture of Hill 230 east of Syrzevo in a surprise attack delivered by Grossdeutschland's reconnaissance battalion supported by the division's assault guns. It was Citadel's first success won by finesse and maneuver. It was correspondingly featured in the reports and the histories as a valuable starting point for the next day's operations.

This was putting the best possible face on circumstances, and it was cold comfort to the pioneers who spent another night marking and clearing minefields around Syrzevo to enable the panzers' morning advance.

The Waffen SS did better—a good deal better. Hoth had reiterated to Hausser that the corps's ultimate objective was Prokhorovka, and he "hoped" it could be achieved by day's end. Leibstandarte and Das Reich moved out around 2:30 A.M. and crossed their start lines three hours later. Despite constant counterattacks, their forward armored elements, deployed in wedges with Tigers at the apex, pushed back what remained of the 5th Guards Tank Corps far enough during the morning to be into the Soviet third defensive line by the end of the day. The Luftwaffe controlled the air, keeping Soviet fighters off the backs of the Stukas and Henschels. Battle groups from Leibstandarte and Das Reich drove up the Prokhorovka road, leaving a trail of knocked-out vehicles, dazed prisoners, and dead men behind them. Leibstandarte claimed the destruction of 75 tanks and the capture of 123 more. The air crews responded that it was impossible to tell who was responsible for what in the growing tank graveyard.

But the SS spearheads faced seemingly endless counterattacks by tank forces between thirty and sixty strong. Without the "excellent Luftwaffe support" Das Reich described and corps headquarters affirmed, prospects would have been dim. As it was, the tankers were punching holes as opposed to opening fronts, getting forward as best they might, and letting the flanks take care of themselves.

A panzer division's reconnaissance battalion was not configured to "sneak and peek." Eighteen months in Russia had demonstrated that any information worth acquiring had to be fought for, and the panzer reconnaissance battalion had become a formidable instrument of war, with armored cars, light half-tracks, and a panoply of heavy weapons. Leibstandarte's reconnaissance battalion joined a few still-operable tanks on a late-afternoon final drive to the Psel River, then ran into a minefield large enough and fire heavy enough to make discretion the best part of valor, at least for that night.

The drive to the Psel fit the SS self-image of brio and bravado. It was also a temporary option. Vatutin had ordered the 2nd Guards Tank Corps to strike the SS Corps's right flank, and the attacks began around daybreak. Where Totenkopf's guns were able to reach, they hit. The panzers' maid of all work, the Mark IVs, proved almost as effective as the Tigers in taking out Russian tanks at long range from hull-down positions. By noon, enough T-34s were out of action to blunt the counterattack. But the farther the other two divisions advanced, the more exposed their forward units became. Confederate general James Longstreet once described new troops as being "as sensitive about the flanks as a virgin." But neither could veterans ignore constant groping. Both Leibstandarte's and Das Reich's commanders were increasingly forced to detail their panzer grenadiers to expand a corridor the Russians were determined to shut.

The mission was no bagatelle. The heavy fighting that continued into the night was epitomized by the experience of an SS rifle company pinned down in front of a railway embankment. The company commander was wounded; a young second lieutenant took over for six hours' worth of close-quarters combat. Twice wounded, he appeared to be everywhere things seemed worst. When a T-34 hit the Germans from a flank, he attacked it single-handed. Then a stray bullet touched off a smoke grenade in his trousers pocket. Without hesitating, the lieutenant tore off trousers and underwear and continued to lead from the front, naked from shirttail to boots. The anecdote invites jokes about "risking all for the Führer," but it also evokes the part of the Waffen SS ethos that appealed, and continues to appeal, to males brought up in societies equating the progress of civilization with the elimination of challenge. Lieutenant Joachim Krüger's luck ran out a week later. Not until June 1944 did he receive a posthumous Knight's Cross, the Reich's highest award for courage and leadership in combat.

Hausser submitted his report to Hoth at 10:40 P.M. It described a Russian "offensive defense" characterized by advances, flank attacks, and counterattacks, heavily supported by small-scale air strikes. The forward elements of Leibstandarte and Das Reich were still engaged too closely to provide details. Totenkopf, supported by an army infantry regiment, had made gains despite heavy air attack and artillery fire. But the weather was "sunny, dry, warm." The roads were "passable for all vehicles." And the corps was moving in the right direction.

That was unwittingly affirmed by a German-intercepted radio message Vatutin sent his subordinates that evening, stating that the Germans must on no account break through to Kursk. It was inspired by a pithy and unmistakable order to Vatutin from Stalin himself, eloquently reinforced by Khrushchev, that the Fourth Panzer Army must be stopped. It was plain that the USSR's entire system of motivation and management stood behind the directive. The First Tank Army was still combat-capable, but Vatutin was deploying Stavka reinforcements behind its reorganizing forward units. Nikolai Popel, a battle-experienced armor officer as well as Katukov's chief political officer, described July 7 as one of the hardest days in the Battle of Kursk, leaving First Tank Army with its strength substantially diminished. First Tank's commander had previously called sober attention to the Germans' "larger units" and "heavier tanks," whose guns far outranged the 76 mm of his T-34s. And German ground-attack planes were inflicting heavy losses even before armored units reached the front.

The Red Army of 1943 was not kind to senior officers who saw ghosts and shadows. Vatutin and his subordinates were seasoned combat veterans. To speak of shaken nerves is to overstate the case. Yet the question simmered: What would it take to stop these Hitlerites? Since June 1941, they had won their victories through finesse: smoke, mirrors, and maneuver. Stalingrad had suggested they were vulnerable to hard pounding. Now, army and SS alike, they were taking what the Soviet Union had to give and they kept coming, as inexorable, as pitiless, and as nonhuman as Russian weather—or, perhaps, the Soviet system.

Such thoughts owed something to what seemed the Germans' inexhaustible supply of Tigers. Soviet infantry, antitank crews, and tankers were reporting kills into the dozens—yet every day the Tigers led the attack. In part that reflected the effects of adrenaline, of fear, of distorted time frames, of smoke and dust, all of which tends to enhance a universal tendency to exaggerate the material number and the formidable nature of opponents. To aircrews in the Pacific, destroyers became battleships. The Allies on Normandy's front lines reported every tank a Panther or a Tiger. In Kursk's specific context, moreover, a Tiger and a Mark IV looked sufficiently alike at battle ranges that left no time for close verification.

Realities were substantially different. Army Group South's Tigers were assigned by companies to the panzer divisions, which provided an initial maximum strength of fifteen or sixteen. Two or three days of combat would reduce a company to half that, another two or three days to a quarter. Then the numbers stabilized thanks to the maintenance crews.

Nor did all of the disabled vehicles drop out due to battle damage. Some suffered from new-vehicle teething troubles. Others needed routine maintenance—particularly the Tiger. But neither condition was likely to take a vehicle off the line for more than a day. Combat damage as well was often superficial even for the Mark IIIs and IVs. Hits from antitank guns, especially the smaller ones, were by no means always fatal. Barring a fuel or ammunition explosion sufficient to burn out or blow apart a vehicle, damage could be repaired, interiors cleaned of body parts, and casualties replaced, in days or hours.

Crews could often repair track damage themselves, and the risks from exposure were far outweighed by those involved in remaining a large stationary target. Maintenance under fire, while not exactly common, was familiar: some damaged tanks were re-

paired three times in a day and sent back in for a fourth round.
On-site repairs, however, were more often made after dark, accepting the risks of showing light from welding torches and flash-
lights. As the Russian tankers had warned, armor dug in could not
be dug out in a hurry. When the Germans held the ground at day's
end, they kept control of the disabled or abandoned tanks of both
armies, making Russian losses permanent.

When the numbers were tallied and cross-checked, the SS Panzer Corps had ten more AFVs at the end of July 7 than at the day's
beginning. Given fuel, water, and ammunition and a few hours of
bomb-interrupted and adrenaline-disturbed sleep, the tankers of
Leibstandarte and Das Reich might yet fulfill their next day's mission and in cooperation with XLVII Panzer Corps destroy the
Russians to their front.

III

Manstein was increasingly disturbed by III Panzer Corps's failure
to advance. He gently reminded Breith that success depended on
coordinating his divisions. But on July 7, the Russians had other
ideas. On the corps's left flank, held by the 19th Panzer Division,
the 73rd Panzer Grenadiers captured the railroad station and the
village of Kreida, then, closely supported by a tank battalion, took
Blishnaya Yigumwenka and the high ground around and beyond
it. Meaningless names; barely discernible spots on a map. But the
Russian 81st Rifle Division held its ground until literally overrun
by the panzers. The 73rd Panzer Grenadiers lost their colonel,
leading from the front in approved German fashion. One of the
regiment's companies was down to ten men at day's end. At the
end of the day, the German battle group commander declared
there were no reserves and there would be no relief: "All that's left
for you is to dig yourselves in where you are."

The 6th Panzer Division, in the corps center, moved out at
7:30 A.M. under Stuka cover, its four operational Tigers in the lead.

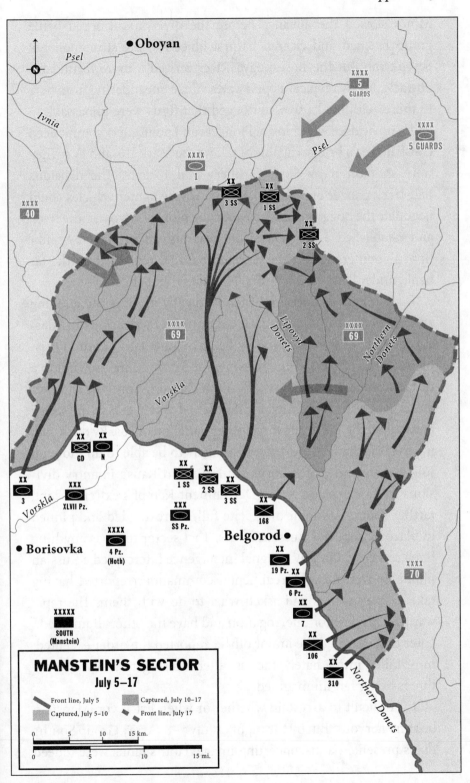

●Oboyan

Psel

Ivnia

XXXX
5
GUARDS

Psel

XXXX
5 GUARDS

XXXX
1

XX
3 SS

XX
1 SS

XXXX
40

XX
2 SS

XXXX
69

Lipovyl Donets

XXXX
69

Northern Donets

Vorskla

XX
GD

XX
N

XX
1 SS

XX
2 SS

XX
3 SS

XX
3

XXX
XLVII Pz.

Vorskla

XXX
SS Pz.

XX
168

● Borisovka

XXXX
4 Pz.
(Hoth)

Belgorod ●

XXXX
70

XX
19 Pz.

XX
6 Pz.

XX
7

XXXXX
SOUTH
(Manstein)

XX
106

XX
310

Northern Donets

MANSTEIN'S SECTOR
July 5–17

Front line, July 5   Captured, July 10–17

Captured, July 5–10   Front line, July 17

0   5   10   15 km.

0   5   10   15 mi.

Mines slowed the advance before the division's armored battle group reached and cleared its first objective, the strongpoint of Sevrukova. But the Rasumnaya River proved a more formidable obstacle. It was a typical steppe watercourse: meandering from here to there, with banks so waterlogged that fords were impassable—and both bridges were blown. Pioneers and pontoniers commenced constructing a bridge capable of taking the Mark IIIs and IVs. They were shot off it by Soviet artillery and rockets. The division's half-track panzer grenadier battalion, whose lighter vehicles could negotiate the boggy ground, covered the pioneers, crossed the river, and established a bridgehead but was pinned in place by tank-tipped counterattacks. The German panzers remained on the far bank, under heavy artillery fire. Not mate—but check.

The 7th Panzer Division began its day by driving into a killing zone of 76 mm antitank guns. It continued it by clearing the Miassoyedovo strongpoint house by house, taking two hundred prisoners in the process. The division ended it by being drawn into a de facto ambush set up by the Seventh Guards Army. The counterattacks were strong enough for Breith to divert Tigers to the sector and call on the Luftwaffe for another battalion of 88s. By day's end, it was clear that 7th Panzer was unlikely to be able to do more on July 8 than protect the corps flank. Erhard Raus's infantry divisions in XI Corps on Army Detachment Kempf's extreme right, farther south, had their own plate full, overextended and pinned in place by superior Russian forces. That sector too was anything but a rest cure. On July 5, signal intelligence intercepted a Russian phone conversation. A regimental commander reported having taken 150 prisoners and asked what to do with them. The reply was, "Keep a few for interrogation and have the others liquidated." Later that evening, the junior officer reported the order executed: most killed immediately, the rest after interrogation—whose nature is better left unimagined.

It is difficult to ascertain whether or when Erich von Manstein became nervous. But by the night of July 7–8, Army Group South's maps presented a disconcerting image. Hoth's tanks were indeed working through the defenses—the SS had advanced more than twelve miles—but they were still creating salients rather than sectors. The resulting flanks were under growing pressure as they grew longer. The attacking divisions were diverting increasing forces, tanks as well as infantry, to shore them up. Neither the army group nor the Fourth Panzer Army had any effective disposable reserves left. Hoth's headquarters reported two fresh tank corps moving into the Oboyan road sector and increasing truck activity on the panzer army's eastern flank. Again Manstein made his case to the high command for committing XXIV Panzer Corps. But that corps represented the hole card of the entire southern sector, even though its two understrength panzer divisions made it more a five-spot than a face card in Citadel's contexts.

Had Manstein's recreational reading included Joel Chandler Harris, he might have recalled the image of a tar baby and the experience of Brer Rabbit. Instead he ordered XLVIII Panzer Corps and the SS to advance north on July 8 as rapidly as possible, envelop the Russian armored forces to their front, and destroy them. Simultaneously, the SS were to secure their own right flank against any threat from the northeast. The plan was a necessary departure from Hoth's proposal to turn the entire SS corps northeast. Fourth Panzer Army's two salients had to be consolidated in order to secure the army's flanks. And the best way out was through—or at least forward. With the salients converted to a sector, Knobelsdorff could drive forward toward Kursk and a junction with Model. Hausser would cover the advance and take care of whatever emerged from Steppe Front's sector on the projected killing ground of Prokhorovka.

Vatutin had originally intended to use the still largely intact Thirty-eighth and Fortieth Armies from his right flank to attack Knobelsdorff's left in force. Instead, implementing Stalin's order, he transferred the bulk of their respective mobile forces to confront the German advance directly. That essentially took his counterattack off the board. The reinforcements, however, gave the hard-pressed front line a combination of tank and motorized battalions strong enough to require Grossdeutschland to swing west and support 3rd Panzer more closely than either division commander intended.

In any case, XLVIII Panzer Corps was going nowhere until it took Syrzevo. The 3rd Panzer and Grossdeutschland hit the strongpoint again at dawn. Grossdeutschland's Tigers and Mark IVs repeatedly broke up tank attacks that amounted to berserker headlong charges, hoping to bring at least some T-34s to killing range. But Syrzevo itself held out, its garrison exhorted by the political officers to fight to the death. They came close. It was well into the afternoon before Grossdeutschland's panzer grenadiers and elements of 3rd Panzer Division's tank regiment cleared a village that by then resembled a cross between a wrecking yard and a slaughterhouse. Katukov and Popel witnessed the final scene, Katukov reporting as he looked through his binoculars: "They're regrouping . . . advancing . . . I think we have had it."

What the First Tank Army saw was Grossdeutschland's tanks assembling to continue the advance north. They had anything but an easy time of it.

Earlier in the morning, one of the division's panzer grenadier battalions reported that it had captured Verkhopenye—a village far enough north of Syrzevo to suggest that Russian defenses were finally beginning to unravel. The division commander committed his immediate reserves, the reconnaissance battalion and the assault gun battalion, to push north, go around Verkhopenye itself, and occupy Hill 260.8, across the Oboyan road.

The half-tracks, armored cars, and assault guns advanced, only to find that the panzer grenadiers had misread their maps. They were on the Oboyan road, right enough—but in another village several miles away from Verkhopenye. XLVIII Panzer Corps chief of staff Friedrich von Mellenthin opined later that such mistakes are in the nature of war. But lofty Clausewitzian aphorisms were no help to troops a long way out on a shaky limb. Advancing up the road was impossible: it was bisected by a tributary of the Pena River, and the bridge was not designed for armored vehicles. Division ordered the battle group to hold its ground while headquarters thought of something. The battle group sent the assault guns across the bridge one by one, set up a perimeter on the far bank, and began passing the recon battalion across the by now very shaky bridge. While that enterprise was under way, the Russians began a sequence of armored counterattacks. Shifting from position to position, the outnumbered German assault guns managed more than fifty kills during an extremely long afternoon. The bridgehead held until relieved by a second Grossdeutschland battle group, accompanied by bridging equipment.

The column reached Verkhopenye by twilight, thanks in good part to the Stukas. SG 2 and 77 flew seven hundred sorties between them on July 8, in formations up to fifty strong, and paid the heaviest price of the fighting to date. The Russian fighter pilots were learning on the job: dividing their forces tactically with one element first engaging the covering Luftwaffe fighters, then a second one going for the suddenly unprotected Stukas. The resulting losses were unsustainable over any length of time—especially when only in the wake of these attacks was Grossdeutschland's column able to "claw" its way into a town the division's history calls a "hard nut to crack."

Verkhopenye, whose buildings straggled along both sides of the Pena River, was critical for its bridge, which could support Mark IVs. Also able to support T-34s, the bridge was too important to the Soviet defense network to be condignly demolished. The result was a bitter fight, with the Germans taking heavy losses from artillery and antitank guns massed on the river's far side. A single Russian tank brigade sustained no fewer than twelve attacks before withdrawing behind the Pena and digging in as part of what the Germans hoped would be a last stand the next morning.

Their immediate opponents were reeling. The 3rd Mechanized Corps had borne the brunt of the fighting in the Oboyan-Syrzevo sector for three blazing days. The commander of its 1st Mechanized Brigade duly noted that by the evening of July 8, his tank regiment could no longer hold its position. His radio communications were out. His supply of armor-piercing shells was almost exhausted. The wounded were piling up. The neighboring brigade had retreated; 1st Mechanized seemed to be "on an island in the midst of a sea of fire. It was senseless to stay in this sector any longer."

Grossdeutschland were the army's glamour boys: first in line for new weapons and trained replacements—with a postwar status in the Federal Republic that enabled the publication of a three-volume divisional history. But the 11th Panzer Division's warriors for the working day kept pace on Grossdeutschland's right. It was no easy task. Vatutin's continuing shift of his reserves to Oboyan created a situation where once a line was penetrated, the attackers faced fresh troops in even greater numbers. Nevertheless, without matching its neighbor's advance to the Pena, 11th Panzer protected Grossdeutschland's flank and pushed forward toward the advance units of the SS Corps, which was simultaneously shifting its axis and redeploying its assets.

IV

For July 8, Hausser proposed to send the combined armored strength of Leibstandarte and Das Reich northwest toward the Psel. Das Reich's panzer grenadiers would continue toward Prokhorovka—whether as spearhead or mobile flank guard was still an open question. Totenkopf was to turn over its flank-security mission to the 167th Infantry Division, currently deployed between Das Reich and 11th Panzer, and move northwest to Leibstandarte's left flank. This maneuver, if it succeeded, would establish firm contact with 11th Panzer, get the SS across the Psel, and open a clear way north for the SS and XLVIII Panzer Corps in tandem, as opposed to the existing parallel salients.

The "if" was a big one. Totenkopf's relief began at 2:15 A.M. but took most of the day to complete—at that a remarkable piece of staff work by an SS often described as indifferent to such details.

The corps reported a "quiet" night—at least by Citadel standards—but by 8:00 A.M., patrols and troop movements were visible all along the front. The SS tanks and assault guns pushed forward in stops and starts, scoring heavily against the outranged T-34s in the relatively open terrain. Repeated counterattacks by T-34s that seemed to find every gap in the German front gave way during the day to increasingly formidable air-armor-infantry strikes, built around as many as a hundred tanks. Leibstandarte gained about twelve miles at the price of losing contact with the 11th Panzer Division, stopped three miles west of the Oboyan road. Das Reich made about eight miles, cutting westward behind the Soviet defenders and coming within a few miles of Voronezh Front's third line and ten miles of Prokhorovka itself.

The way into the First Tank Army's rear seemed open. The 31st Tank Corps reported defenses broken and men fleeing in panic. A shaken Khrushchev contacted Vatutin. The front commander promised an immediate counterattack. He also ordered what was left of 31st Tank and 3rd Mechanized Corps to fall back to new positions north of Verkhopenye, across the Oboyan road, and along the Solotinka River to the Psel. Vatutin hoped that Katukov could hold on until his blow from the northeast had time to develop.

The First Tank Army's survival already owed much to the increasing pressure on the SS right flank. Das Reich, in particular, beginning around 11:00 A.M., reported having to divert forces to secure the immediate right flank of its armored battle group and to take some pressure off the division's hard-pressed panzer grenadiers. The reconnaissance battalion, the assault gun battalion, and finally the panzer regiment itself turned to meet armored counterattacks. Toward evening, the Luftwaffe appeared in force. Its Stukas and medium bombers were welcome sights to men left on their own most of the day.

The SS Panzer Corps reported 290 Soviet AFVs destroyed—a third of them by infantrymen using "close combat means." That meant grenades, explosive charges, Molotov cocktails. It also meant fighting power. One of Das Reich's panzer grenadier regiments had "organized" an intelligence section of half a dozen Russian "auxiliaries," prisoners of war who for many reasons chose working for their captors over life as a POW. Part of its job was to monitor radio traffic—often in plain Russian rather than code, for the sake of haste or as a consequence of fatigue. When two higher headquarters began exchanging threats over the nonappearance of reserves, an SS company infiltrated Russian lines, made its way to the command post of a rifle brigade, and returned with the commander, his staff, and the whole headquarters company. The stunt was facilitated by the area's lack of the built-up defenses characteristic of main combat zones. But call it a "hussar trick," as in the German idiom, or a "John Wayne," in Vietnam-era argot—either way it remains the sort of performance the Waffen SS expected of itself. They may have been willing servants of a criminal regime, but the men of SS Panzer Corps were also men of war.

Following his communication with Stalin during the evening of July 7, Vatutin reoriented the focal point of his intended major counterattack. Front orders issued at 11:00 P.M. sent the fresh II SS Panzer Corps southwest down the road from Prokhorovka in the direction of Teterivino. To the left, 5th Tank Corps would attack directly west. The 2nd Guards Tank Corps, deployed on the 5th's left, would move against the right flank and rear of the SS while covering the front's counterattack against a III Panzer Corps assumed to be too busy in its own sector to have much impact elsewhere.

The combined strength of the four corps amounted to around four hundred AFVs. The attack would be supported by thirty minutes of artillery preparation, making up in intensity what it lacked in duration, and by a maximum effort from the Second Air Army. Things began going wrong when Leibstandarte and Das Reich crossed their start lines ahead of 10th Tank Corps's projected dawn attack. The corps, one of the two just assigned to Vatutin by Stavka, was getting its first taste of armored war Citadel-style. Its brigades were caught off balance; its commander reacted by initiating the attacks mentioned above, delaying the Germans without stopping them.

The 2nd Guards Tank Corps, Stavka's other contribution, provided—unwittingly and unwillingly—the most spectacular initial results of Vatutin's counterattack. It too had deployed slowly, going in only around noon, and was essentially uncommitted when Vatutin ordered it forward in response to Khrushchev's report. The somewhat disorganized advance was promptly spotted by a patrolling Hs-129 piloted by the tank busters' commander.

The Hs-129B was a defining artifact of the later Third Reich. It was a promising, indeed futuristic, design, whose main armament also redefined state of the art. The 30 mm MK-101 automatic cannon was accurate, hard-hitting, and able to fire nine kinds of ammunition, from conventional high explosives to tungsten-cored armor-piercing rounds. But tungsten was in short supply, and the MK-101 had teething troubles. The aircraft itself was powered by two Gnome-Rhône engines looted from France, whose low horsepower further reduced an already limited airworthiness. To date, the Henschels had been held back. Their large size and limited maneuverability rendered them disproportionately vulnerable to fighters and antiaircraft guns, especially when compared with the Stukas. But on July 6 they had shown—against the same 2nd Guards Tank Corps—what even small numbers of them could do in the right conditions. Four squadrons of them came in at carefully timed intervals: one attacking, one on the way, one taking off, and one returning to refuel and rearm. A participant described the formula for success: a low-level run and a carefully timed, well-aimed shot at just the right time. "I would say that it was a real art," he concluded. Its practice required ignoring the small-arms fire returned by the desperate tankers. It required as well the kind of battle-space control achieved by Luftwaffe fighters vectored in from everywhere in the sector, which gave the Henschels an entirely free hand.

After two hours, despite missed signals, jammed cannon, and similar examples of fog and friction, more than fifty T-34s were burning or immobile. The rest of the corps was in one of the few disorderly retreats made by either side during Citadel. It was a tour de force the SS Panzer Corps acknowledged wholeheartedly: "good cooperation with the Luftwaffe" had made the day's "full defensive success" possible. It was also an unpleasant jolt to the tank crews and the armor generals of Voronezh Front. Unlike the bombs dropped by the Stukas, which might do only superficial damage even by a direct hit, a tungsten-cored 30 mm high-velocity round through a T-34's rear deck was a certain kill and an almost certain flameout. For the first time in history, a large armored force had been destroyed entirely from the air. How many of the cursed planes did the Fritzes have? And where were the vaunted Red Falcons?

The most obvious direct response was to make no more large-scale moves of armor in the daylight. That in turn slowed the movements of local reserves to block German penetrations—a key to Vatutin's conduct of the battle. And if that were not enough, the Germans seemed on the point of developing a new, potentially decisive surge in an unexpected sector of the front: that held by III Panzer Corps. The corps's advance of July 7 had actually extended the gap between it and II SS Panzer Corps to about twenty miles. Breith's response depended on the infantry division assigned to his corps. The 168th had been holding the Donets line on the left of the corps's three panzer divisions since Citadel's beginning. The 19th Panzer Division was ordered to swing hard left, take the Russians in the rear, and clear that sector. In by now predictable fashion, the attack made initial gains, then was halted by minefields and an untouched second line of defense.

Things were little better in the rest of the 19th's sector, where the two panzer grenadier regiments were reduced during the morning to the combined strength of a battalion. Breith had to commit the 168th Infantry Division to restore the situation. In III Panzer Corps's center, the 6th Panzer Division was delayed an hour when the scheduled artillery barrage failed to materialize. The armored battle group went in on 19th Panzer's flank, was stopped by the same minefield, and was targeted by a massive artillery and Katyu-sha barrage. The pioneers cleared a path. A few minutes later, the panzers encountered an antitank ditch. It took three hours for the pioneers to blow in the sides. It was 4:00 P.M. by the time 6th Panzer, by now with Tiger support and covered by the division's artillery and a flak battalion, reached Melikhovo. It took heavy losses from T-34s dug in to their turrets, from Russian infantry who seemed to have to be killed twice, and from antitank guns. One Tiger crewman recalled, "There were so many of them that they gave me permanent diarrhea." Every thirty minutes "I squatted down at the rear of the tank without the enemy noticing me."

Another victory for a regimental war diary; another day that led nowhere in particular, only creating another salient needing protection. The 7th Panzer Division spent its day covering the 6th Panzer's right when the 106th Infantry Division was unable to fulfill its assignment and take over the screening role. Indeed, the 106th was pushed so hard that 7th Panzer had to send tanks to its support.

Raus, among the best German armor commanders, was not easily shaken—one reason for giving him the unglamorous but vital job of commanding the army group's flank guard. But the 106th was sufficiently overextended that on the previous day a Soviet tank reached its command post. Raus himself led the counterattack that restored the line. He also requested reinforcements: the Red Army's spare change was taking his XI Corps to its limits. At that point, Napoleon's rejoinder to Ney at Waterloo may have crossed Manstein's mind: "Troops? Do you think I can make them?" The army group commander consulted Zeitzler, only to be told in effect to do more with less: Germany and its Führer were watching.

V

A commander's best friend is an obliging enemy. An obliging enemy is not one who merely makes mistakes, but one who acts as though his orders had been written by his opponent. In Walther Model, Rokossovsky had found—or rather, his soldiers had created—an obliging enemy. For July 9, Model concentrated five panzer divisions on a ten-mile front: more than three hundred AFVs, the Ninth Army's last resources. Central to the effort was the fresh 4th Panzer Division, including a hundred tanks, most of them the new models of Mark IV with long-barreled 75 mm guns. It had suffered from a night of unremitting air attacks as it deployed. The weather had broken as well, meaning saturated ground, reduced visibility, and limited air support. But all that seemed needed was one more push.

Rokossovsky for his part had used the time bought by his forward units to transfer everything that could be spared from quiet sectors to Teploye-Olkhovatka-Ponyri: two rifle divisions, an artillery division, a mixed bag of smaller units. Rokossovsky too was reaching the bottom of Central Front's barrel. Specifically, morale in the Second Tank Army was also fraying at the edges. Soviet, and now Russian, treatments of World War II state or imply that almost all the comrades were valiant in defense of the motherland, communism, and Stalin. In fact, the T-34 crews were in much the same situation their Sherman-riding U.S. and British counterparts would face in Normandy. For a year, the T-34s had been the technical masters of the armored battlefield. Now they were being picked off at ranges from which they could make no reply. Charging forward only brought them closer to German AFVs that seemed able to adjust their fire automatically against tanks on the move and zero in on them when they halted to use their own guns. Rokossovsky responded by detaching two fresh brigades from the tanks corps he had left covering Kursk as a final defense against a massive German breakthrough. Those tanks were his last hope, he declared in his memoirs. As Wellington said at Waterloo, it was hard pounding. The question was who could pound the longest.

At 8:00 A.M. on July 8, 2nd Panzer Division went forward against Olkhovatka. The 4th and 20th followed a new axis, on XLVII Panzer Corps's right toward the village of Samodurovka, seeking to realize a breach that so far had proven a mirage by developing a gap between the Thirteenth and Seventieth Armies. Luftwaffe radio intelligence scored the first points by picking up the Sixteenth Air Army's order for a major Shturmovik strike at dawn, supporting a counterattack against German positions at Ponyri. A group of 190s was waiting at altitude and scattered the attackers. By the time the ground attack began, the weather had closed in and closed down. For three hours, the 307th Rifle Division grappled with German infantry in mud that matched that of Passchendaele, with fog and rain reducing the fighting to hand-to-hand flounderings in the mire that left the Red Army riflemen in possession of part of Ponyri—how much depends on which report one reads.

Artillery on both sides was firing nearly blind, but the Soviets had far more guns in action and were more used to area barrages. On the German right, 20th Panzer Division's grenadiers led the way toward Samodurovka. Companies reduced to platoon strength were being commanded by sergeants in the first hour of a daylong series of attacks that pinned the Russians in place but otherwise made little progress against the 17th Guards Rifle Corps. An observer called El Alamein a modest operation by comparison and declared that even Stalingrad took second place. The 20th Panzer Division had only one tank battalion, and its war diary describes a day of being shuttled from place to place, supporting the infantry, checking Russian counterattacks, dodging close-attack teams, and running into minefields. The battalion had gone into action on July 5 with seventy-five tanks. Thirty-nine remained operational when the unit took up positions for the night.

The 4th Panzer Division's prospects might have improved had not XLVII Panzer Corps commander Joachim Lemelsen detached the division's panzer regiment to form part of a provisional tank brigade, replacing it with an assault gun battalion that left the 4th with just about half its standard number of AFVs. As it was, a battle group of the division fought through to Teploye and moved toward the high ground south of the village. When the panzer grenadiers could go no farther into Russian fire, the armor continued alone. A platoon, well led or simply lucky, took out enough of the first-line gun positions to give the infantry a chance to move forward against the high ground south of the village. Tank-supported Russian reserves threw the Germans back repeatedly. Russian antitank guns held their fire to as near as four hundred yards. In a single battalion, one battery was reduced to a single gun and three crewmen. Another gun, its carriage shattered, was propped up on ammunition boxes and aimed by sighting down the barrel. The antitank riflemen evoked German praise for the "courage and coolness" that cost one company 70 percent casualties. But by the end of the day, the panzer grenadier companies too were reduced to fifteen or twenty men. With the division commander and one of the regimental commanders wounded, a breakthrough in the sector seemed impossible.

Lemelsen had not "borrowed" 4th Panzer's tanks on a whim. An artilleryman by trade, he was highly rated by Kluge as a corps commander. He had had three days to experience the limits of tank-infantry cooperation following currently accepted German armor doctrine. And it is worth remembering that the Wehrmacht's original panzer divisions were armor-centric and armor-heavy even though equipped with light tanks. It was not prima facie chimerical to reason that a large, concentrated force of AFVs—around two hundred when the panzer regiments from 2nd and 4th Divisions, the Tigers, and some stray assault guns were added together—could break through what *had* to be the final Soviet positions. Instead, the 6th Infantry Division—what remained of it—was stopped on the slopes of Hill 274 outside Ol-khovatka, the key point of the defense in that sector and manned by the Seventeenth Army. The panzers went forward repeatedly and were repeatedly thrown back. At the end of the day's fighting, around 5:00 P.M., only three Tigers remained in action. And the high ground remained in Soviet hands.

Model's first reaction to another futile day was to consider relieving a number of his subordinate commanders. His second was to order the panzer regiments returned to their proper divisions. His third was to plan for a renewed attack the next morning. Then the Ninth Army's staff weighed in. Over thirty-two hundred men had been sacrificed for gains at best measured in hundreds of yards. Half the panzer grenadiers in 2nd, 4th, and 9th Divisions were casualties. Hundreds of tanks were undergoing major repairs. Fuel and ammunition reserves were low. The only plentiful commodity was fatigue, with four sleepless days the norm in the infantry divisions. Model responded by using July 9 to rest and reorganize—everywhere except around Ponyri, where elements of the 292nd Division finally took and held Hill 239 east of the village. On a map, the success offered a chance of a breakthrough. On the ground, it presented another fortified hill, 253, on the new German right flank. The 292nd was fought out. And by now it is almost redundant to say that the Russians literally crowded Hill 253 and its environs with every weapon that could find a position, from T-34s to light machine guns.

Model's decision to suspend operations led Kluge to call a senior officers' conference for the morning. He met Model, Harpe, and Lemelsen at XLVII Panzer Corps headquarters and opened the discussion with an implied "What now?" Harpe said he was running out of infantry; Lemelsen said he was running out of tanks. When Kluge offered three more mobile divisions as reinforcements, Model responded that the best to be expected was a *rollenden Material-abnutzungsschlacht,* a "rolling battle of material attrition." The World War I subtext of this Teutonic circumlocution was not lost on men who had been junior officers in 1914–18. Were Kluge and Model, recognizing that the northern half of Citadel had failed, seeking to provide a smoke screen against Hitler's expressed insistence to continue? Certainly both men were concerned with the developing risk of a major attack in the central sector. Certainly as well, Army Group Center's headquarters, physically isolated and responsible for a static front, had become a focal point for anti-Hitler plotting. But there was no sign of a smoke screen in the attack XLVII Panzer Corps sent in on July 10.

Once again, the initial objectives were the high ground south and southwest of Olkhovatka and the much-contested village of Teploye. The 1st Air Division, somewhat revitalized by its weather-assisted stand-down on July 9—only about four hundred bomber and attack sorties were flown—mounted almost seven hundred sorties against the gun positions that had scourged the attacks two days earlier. Its fighters took the action to Sixteenth Army's airfields, effectively controlling the sky most of the morning. On the ground, Model replicated Lemelsen's action of July 8, combining tanks from 2nd, 4th, and 20th Panzer Divisions into an improvised brigade. It got as far as Teploye, which was finally cleared by 4th Panzer Division's infantry. Rokossovsky had reinforced the defense with a fresh rifle division from Seventieth Army. On the night of July 7–8, he committed his last immediate armored reserve, the 9th Tank Corps. It proved to be enough, and once again the Germans were held or thrown back along the front of Seventeenth Rifle Army, sacrificing some of their small earlier gains. The previous day's success at Ponyri had led Model to relieve the 298th with one of Kluge's fresh divisions and make one more try in that sector as well. The 10th Panzer Grenadier Division came on line slowly, handicapped by high wind and rain, and despite close support from the surviving Ferdinands, its late-afternoon attacks foundered like all the rest on Soviet determination and Soviet firepower.

The Central Front on July 11 mounted a series of counterattacks all along its sector. Retrospectively, these were local operations—or at least held to local gains by Germans whose resistance was no less determined than their Red Army counterparts. But the gains were serious enough to tired men and tired generals. Initially optimistic notions of wearing down and breaking through were giving way to a nearly visceral sense that the Russian reserves might, after all, well be inexhaustible.

By the end of the day, Model had nothing left with which to change the situation. The Ninth Army's immediate rear zones were by this time a combination wasteland, junkyard, and butcher shop. Disabled vehicles, destroyed weapons, and abandoned gear littered an area overrun by stragglers and *Versprengten*—men literally knocked loose from their units by the intense, uninterrupted combat. Kursk was an early instance of a phenomenon that fully manifested itself two years later on Okinawa. High-end industrial war, with tanks and aircraft added to artillery and machine guns, the whole combined with an extreme environment, could break men in a matter not of weeks or months, but of days. It was not a case of systemic demoralization, as in the German rear echelons when the Russians enveloped Stalingrad. The Russians were not immune. As defenders, Rokossovsky's men had stable positions whose abandonment often entailed more risks than sticking it out. Perceived shirkers or fugitives were likely to get even shorter shrift from the Soviet military police and the NKVD than from the legitimately feared "chain dogs" of the Wehrmacht. On July 10, the Sixteenth Air Army's commander responded to reports that his fighters were defensively minded, patrolling at a safe distance behind the front line, by threatening "cowards" with transfer to a penal battalion or execution on the ground.

The OKW (Armed Forces High Command) reacted to the impasse by noting the necessity of reversing the balance of attrition. Model responded with a revised plan. Kluge had previously promised Model the 12th Panzer and 36th Infantry Divisions. Now he offered as well, once they arrived, the 5th and 8th Panzer Divisions, freshly refitted and assigned to Army Group Center. Model's intention was to reinforce the as yet unengaged XLVI Panzer Corps and use it to envelop the Olkhovatka heights on their left flank. Its four infantry divisions were the last relatively fresh troops of the Ninth Army's original order of battle. But only a battle group of 12th Panzer Division reached Ninth Army's sector, and it was too late in the day to be of any use. A limited night attack in XLVI Panzer Corps's sector went nowhere; by then, the Red Army owned the night all along Model's front. The Ninth Army had lost only about seventy-five AFVs. The 1st Air Division held control of the skies as the Soviet Sixteenth Air Army cut back activity to rest its crews, but without some major change in the overall situation, the rational prospects of a renewed attack seemed no more than adding to a casualty list already exceeding twenty-two thousand.

That major change would soon be provided by the Red Army. Rokossovsky's Central Front had stopped the Germans almost in their tracks. The Thirteenth Army and Second Tank Army had chewed up half a dozen panzer divisions. Nowhere had the Tigers and the Ferdinands contributed to anything but limited tactical victories. The price had been high—almost half the front's tanks, and almost half of those were evaluated as write-offs. Human costs remain debatable. The former Soviet archives lists thirty-four thousand casualties between July 5 and 11—almost half killed. But strength figures for the Central Front during the same period show a reduction of almost ninety-three thousand with no major changes to the order of battle. A discrepancy of fifty-nine thousand cannot be overlooked but as yet remains unexplained.

Rokossovsky noted that the Germans' fighting power and tactical skill had forced him to commit reserves earlier than he intended and to hold sectors as opposed to mounting a general counterattack. He dismissed the supply situation as chaotic. What was nevertheless important was Rokossovsky's confidence that the Central Front had won its battle. What was even more important was Zhukov's agreement.

Early on July 9, Stalin had phoned Zhukov to express his opinion that the offensive in the Orel sector was ripe for launching. Zhukov agreed. The Germans, he declared, no longer had the resources to achieve a breakthrough against the Central Front. That, however, would not stop them from continuing to try. Let the Germans bleed themselves for another day or two while the inevitable loose ends of what had been titled Operation Kutuzov were tightened. Timing was everything. If Kutuzov started too soon by even a day, the Ninth Army might still be able to pull one of the almost patented German rabbit-out-of-the-helmet shifts and hit the Russian left flank. It does no disrespect to Rokossovsky and his men to say that the Central Front would at best face extreme difficulty mounting an attack strong enough to hold the Germans in place.

Stalin concurred. Not until the night of July 11 did normal patrolling in Kutuzov's designated sectors give way to battalion-level probes and initiatives that provided information for a final readjusting of attack formations and artillery targets. Not until July 12 would the Red Army begin changing the parameters of Operation Citadel and the Russo-German War.

Chapter V

DECISIONS

ERICH VON MANSTEIN'S FORTE was the maneuver battle: mass multiplied by impulsion. To date, Army Group South's impulsion had been episodic. The mass had been provided by the Russians. On the night of July 8, Vatutin and Vasilevsky had one mission: Hold the Germans in place for the coming counteroffensives on either side of the Kursk salient. That meant hold the center, from Prokhorovka to the Oboyan road, and keep hitting Knobelsdorff and Breith as they attacked into the defenses on their front.

I

That in turn required shuffling. Vatutin took advantage of the night, and a diminishing German air effort, to order 5th Guards Tank Corps to move west to the Oboyan road and join the First Tank Army. The 10th Tank Corps would also shift to the Oboyan sector, while 2nd Tank Corps took over on the Prokhorovka road. The 31st Mechanized and 3rd Tank Corps would fall back to a new line from the Oboyan road to the Psel River. Reinforcements— rifle divisions; tank, artillery, and antitank regiments from Stavka reserve; and replacement tanks—were lavishly distributed as they arrived. The Soviet high command ordered Sixty-ninth Army to move between Sixth Guards and Seventh Guards Armies on Vatutin's left, increasing the general pressure on the Germans. It also ordered Fifth Guards Army, seven first-class divisions, from the Steppe Front to the Oboyan-Prokhorovka sector.

That reinforcement was no less welcome for requiring several days' march. Fifth Guards Army had fought in Stalingrad as the Sixty-sixth Army, retaining four of the divisions tempered in that cauldron, and adding three new ones: two airborne and one rifle, all Guards, and fully equipped. It was a sign of the shifting balance of the Eastern Front that Stavka had this kind of an elite infantry force available for a near routine commitment, while the Germans were scrambling to man their "quiet" sectors with anyone able to sight a rifle and walk unassisted. Stavka's major initiative, how- ever, was to transfer Fifth Guards Tank Army from the Steppe Front to Vatutin's command. Fifth Guards Tank was a high card. It had been formed on February 10, 1942, and its 5th Guards Mecha- nized and 18th and 29th Tank Corps were considered to be well trained, well equipped, and well officered. Its commander, Lieu- tenant General Pavel Rotmistrov, was a colorful figure by the rela- tively anonymous standards of the post-purge Red Army. He had worn the Soviet uniform since 1919 and carried himself with somewhat the air of Tolstoy's Vaska Denisov, or Denisov's real-life counterpart, Denis Davydov. A combat-experienced tanker, he had done well commanding a brigade and a corps. It remained to be seen whether he could walk the walk as head of an army.

On the other side of the line, Hoth too was testing the wind. Fourth Panzer Army was down to six hundred AFVs ready for ac- tion on the morning of July 9—a 40-percent loss. The army's spearheads were still fifty miles from Kursk, almost a hundred from Model's bogged-down front, and three days short of the initial objective of a two-corps bridgehead over the Psel.

Hoth had not lost confidence in the prospects of an eventual breakthrough and a victory. But XLVIII Panzer Corps was still under such heavy pressure on its left flank that it could not deploy its full strength frontally. Breith's panzers remained enmeshed in the Soviet defenses on the Donets's east bank. Luftwaffe reconnaissance was reporting large and increasing Soviet armored forces moving west and south, toward the Psel.

Official doctrine and common sense alike called for an all-out effort to interdict the movement. The Luftwaffe had been originally configured for just that type of mission. But the need for direct ground support had so intensified that no aircraft could be spared from the front lines. The counterattacks engaging the SS from the northeast thus could only be expected to increase in strength and fighting power—until they matched and overmatched the panzers. Hoth's original concept for this contingency had been to draw the Soviets into a fight on ground of German choosing: open terrain, where their tank guns' longer range and excellent optics would give them the kind of technical advantage denied in the earlier fighting at close quarters. The burden of the plan rested squarely on the Waffen SS. Hoth would not admit it willingly, but ideology, experience, and armament made the SS more suited than the army's panzers to force a breakthrough in a frontal attack. As party troops in an army war, moreover, they were more readily expendable.

Hoth had originally expected the army and the SS to keep pace and be in a position to act in tandem as they approached the Psel. Instead, XLVIII Panzer Corps was lagging behind: a function of the resistance to its front and the continuing threat to its left flank. Fourth Panzer Army's Order No. 4 for July 9 was ambiguous. The XLVIII Panzer Corps would push a strong right flank up the Oboyan road, throw the Russians over the Psel, and simultaneously secure its left flank for good—all by attacking and enveloping the 6th Tank Corps. The II SS Panzer Corps would drive northeast with "all available force" while simultaneously maintaining a strong flank guard against any attacks from the direction of Prokhorovka. On July 10, Hausser was expected to be ready to shift its axis of advance toward Prokhorovka itself—should the movement become necessary as Soviet reinforcements arrived.

Manstein backed Hoth's play directly by giving Hausser priority for air support. More consequential was Manstein's continued pressure on Kempf and Breith to get III Panzer Corps moving north, toward Prokhorovka, broadening and integrating his front, covering the SS by intercepting the Fifth Guards Tank Army. But first Breith had to clear his own sector. The 19th Panzer Division spent a long, hot, frustrating July 8 in a series of back-and-forth engagements with counterattacking Russians who nearly broke through the overextended lines of the 168th Infantry Division, making heavy weather of its advance up the Donets from Belgorod. It took the last four operable Mark VIs of a Tiger company, plus half a dozen flamethrowing tanks, before the 19th could even consider breaking out and moving forward on any scale. On the other flank of III Panzer Corps, the 7th Panzer Division remained committed to its flank guard role: "No changes planned for today . . . I had slept well," in the words of one Tiger company commander. But an infantry division, the 106th, was being rushed into position to relieve the panzers, making the 7th available to support what seemed the first real tactical opportunity Breith's corps had created since the fighting started.

That was the work of 6th Panzer Division, whose day began when two of its tank companies were shot up while resupplying in a forward area and continued when a green and ambitious lieutenant took his tank platoon in a head-down charge to the top of a hill, only to find himself pinned down by the usual heavy Soviet defensive fire. But matters improved as the division's armored advance guards found enough exploitable points in the 92nd Guards Rifle's defenses to reach and capture the high ground north of Melikhovo, a dozen miles northeast of Belgorod, before running into impassable belts of minefields, guns, and antitank ditches. As yet, it was just another salient, another extended middle finger. But if 19th and 7th Panzer could manage to close on the 6th, the result might be a paralyzing closed-finger karate strike.

Might be—the mantra of Citadel on the German side. Knobelsdorff initially responded to Hoth's revised orders by redeploying a battle group of Grossdeutschland; two panzer grenadier battalions, and more than fifty tanks and assault guns, including a Tiger company, turning them west to cooperate with 3rd Panzer and the 332nd Infantry in finishing off 6th Tank Corps. Knobelsdorff believed the diversion would be temporary. But despite "outstanding" Stuka support, the advance took ninety minutes to reach the last houses in the north part of Verkhopenye against the tank-supported 67th Guards Rifle Division. That, moreover, was nowhere near the same thing as having the village cleared and secured. The battle group was also coming under heavy artillery and Katyusha fire from the west: a clear indication that 3rd Panzer Division was still not out of the woods.

Grossdeutschland's other panzer grenadier regiment and the reconnaissance battalion, with the rest of the division's armor, resumed the advance on Oboyan around 6:00 A.M. The grenadiers ran into an antitank screen; the reconnaissance battalion sidestepped it and kept moving under Stuka cover. So far, so good—good enough that Grossdeutschland's commander moved the tanks at Verkhopenye to reinforce what he considered the *Schwerpunkt* of his attack. The panzers passed through the half-tracks and assault guns of the reconnaissance battle group and engaged the fresh 86th Tank Brigade at ranges long enough to allow the Panthers and Tigers to keep the advance moving up the Oboyan road until higher orders brought it to a halt during the afternoon around the village of Novoselovka.

The 3rd Panzer Division was another warrior for the working day. It had no claim on Tigers or Panthers. Half the eighty-odd tanks the division took into the battle were Mark IIIs with 50 mm guns. But thus far its losses in men and tanks had not been particularly crippling, especially compared with other sectors of Citadel. From Major General Franz Westhoven down to the battalions and companies, its commanders were solid. The division made a dozen tactically successful attacks during the day. The problem was that antitank guns and dug-in T-34s, supported by the mobile armor of 6th Tank Corps, kept 3rd Panzer from forming a functioning *Schwerpunkt*. Instead, a sequence of opportunistic advances brought its forward elements to the Pena River but produced and confirmed a westward shift of the division's overall front—almost a right angle to XLVIII Panzer Corps's intended route toward Oboyan. The 332nd Infantry Division on 3rd Panzer's left forced a crossing of the Pena against the 71st Guards Rifle Division and elements of the 6th Tank Corps. In terms of facilitating a breakthrough by the 3rd Panzer Division, however, the 332nd was a knife in a gunfight. In their own sector, the panzers reached the Pena and began constructing a bridge strong enough to carry Mark IIIs and IVs, although Soviet artillery, rockets, and mortars made it an overnight job.

Grossdeutschland responded to 3rd Panzer's situation by leaving most of its panzer grenadiers to hold the Oboyan sector and turning its tanks and the reconnaissance battalion west again, to clear 3rd Panzer's front. It may not have been too little, but it was definitely too late—at least too late in the day. Not until 10:00 P.M. did Grossdeutschland's spearheads make contact with Soviet tanks around Verkhopenye. After fifteen hours of combat and maneuver, only one order made sense: Hold in place for the night; refuel, rearm, repair, and rest. The 11th Panzer Division, on Grossdeutschland's right, initially either achieved a degree of tactical surprise or was drawn along in its partner's wake, depending on the reports and narratives. Whatever the reason, it made good progress astride the Oboyan road early in the day—only to create another small salient, its forward elements ahead of Grossdeutschland on one flank and the SS on the other.

As previously stated, Hoth's orders gave II SS Panzer Corps as many as four potential missions: Break through the Soviets in their immediate front; disrupt the looming counterattacks by the Red Army's reserves; draw along with them the army panzers on their left; and open an alternate route to Kursk. Any one was a major assignment. Hausser's orders, issued at 11:00 P.M. on July 8, were correspondingly ambitious. The general intention was for the corps to establish contact with the 11th Panzer Division, destroy Soviet forces south of the Psel, and throw bridgeheads across the river in preparation for a further advance on a broad front, direction northeast. Das Reich would develop its present position as a main battle line (*Hauptkampflinie*). Totenkopf would advance west-northwest, contact 11th Panzer, and force a crossing of the Psel. Leibstandarte would clear its front, then begin shifting position, moving between Totenkopf and Das Reich to become the center division of the corps. As soon and as far as possible, the tank regiments of Leibstandarte and Das Reich were to be taken out of the line for maintenance and to rest the exhausted crews.

Leibstandarte advanced around 10:00 A.M. on July 9, its four remaining Tigers leading the way. The division had taken fifteen hundred casualties in four days, most of them in the combat regiments, but morale was high—and it improved when a company of Mark IVs scattered the counterattack of a regiment of T-34s. By noon, the SS had crossed the Solotinka River and made contact with the 11th Panzer Division's vanguard. Elements of both divisions made it to the village of Kochetovka, Sixth Guards Army's headquarters, before being stopped by a reorganized 10th Tank Corps that proved to have a good deal of fight left, and by heavy rocket and artillery fire.

As the day waned, Leibstandarte began turning over the corps left wing to Totenkopf. The relatively fresh Death's-Head Division lost no time mounting a head-down frontal attack toward the Psel. Despite strong resistance from the rear guards and the survivors of the 3rd Mechanized and 31st Tank Corps and the 51st and 52nd Guards Rifle Divisions, the SS gained as much as ten miles. The division's artillery and tank guns literally blew the Guards headquarters out of Kochetovka before the panzer grenadiers took the

town by close assault. Totenkopf's main attack then turned northwest, to high ground a mile or two outside Kochetovka that overlooked the approaches to the Psel. There for the first time
Death's-Head encountered the shield-and-sword tactics of dug-in
tanks and fixed defenses fighting to the finish while mobile T-34s
launched repeated counterattacks. Totenkopf was held in place;
not until darkness did its pioneers and panzer grenadiers succeed
in bridging the Psel and establishing a foothold on its far bank.

Das Reich also spent the day in place, blocking with Citadel-
relative ease a series of attacks along the Prokhorovka road by 2nd
Tank and 5th Guards Tank Corps. But by evening, II SS Panzer
Corps received ground and air reconnaissance confirming major
armor movements to the northeast, against the corps's right flank,
along with heavy air activity. One column with 250 trucks and as
many as 80 tanks had already passed through Prokhorovka. Soviet
strength was such that German forces probing in the opposite direction had been pulled back. The further introduction of armor
reserves from outside Citadel's sector was probable.

July 9 was a long day at the higher headquarters of Voronezh
Front. By its end, Sixth Guards and First Tank Armies had sacrificed any but the most basic tactical maneuverability, their original formations ground down, the successive reinforcements in no
better shape. Katukov could assemble a hundred AFVs, more or
less, and rather less than more. Both commanders had spent much
of the day requesting immediate support and asking when Fifth
Guards Tank Army would arrive.

Vatutin responded during the night of July 9–10 by sorting out
his front. Katukov's sector from right to left was now held by 6th
Tank Corps along the Pena River; 3rd Mechanized Corps, or what
remained of it, across the Oboyan road; and 31st Mechanized
Corps extending the line to the Psel. Three fresh rifle divisions
were taking position in the army's rear. More significant, Vatutin
placed 10th and 5th Tank Corps under Katukov's direct command.
Those were Voronezh Front's last blue chips. Now it depended on
Katukov's ability to hold his sector and the ability of Fifth Guards

and Fifth Guards Tank Armies to arrive in time to turn the battle around. It depended as well on the front's ability to stop a developing shift of Fourth Panzer Army's focus in the direction of Prokhorovka. The Soviet field communications system's redundancy had proved its value repeatedly since Citadel's beginning. By midafternoon, reports were coming in by radio, phone, and messenger that the SS was in effect replacing Leibstandarte with Totenkopf, thereby shoving the entire corps rightward, away from the Oboyan road. There was only one direction it could go: toward Prokhorovka.

Thus far, Lieutenant General Vasily Kriuchenkin had been a virtual spectator. Now his Sixty-ninth Army was bolstered by the 2nd Tank Corps and the usual smorgasbord of independent brigades and regiments, and he had been ordered to hold Voronezh Front's northeast shoulder and its artery, the road to Prokhorovka. Lest the point be missed, Vatutin personally phoned 2nd Tank Corps just before midnight and warned its commander to expect a major attack the next day.

Vatutin would later describe July 9 as the turning point in his sector. The front commander may have been confident by day's end, but too many things had gone too wrong too often since June 22, 1941, to allow any complacency. Apart from the Germans to his front, Vatutin and Vasilevsky were still a step behind the Rokossovsky-Zhukov team on the salient's northern half. Model's offensive had come to a dead stop. Manstein's had reached the Psel, the last prepared defense system before the open steppe. The Prokhorovka sector was as yet defended by bits and pieces. Even if a German breakout was contained and defeated by Stavka's reserves, Stalin would remember the general who buried tanks turret-deep and exhausted reserves in a vain defense. And should the Vozhd forget, Zhukov would be there to remind him.

In making and implementing decisions for July 10, Manstein and Hoth had to take into consideration another set of statistics. The Fourth Panzer Army had received a maximum effort from VIII Air Corps. But that term meant something different after four intense days. The Luftwaffe flew over fifteen hundred sorties—twice the number managed by the Red Air Force on July 9. The Stukas, the Heinkels, and the Ju-88s hammered Russian defenses, but against a steadily improving air-ground defense. JG 52's III Group lost an entire four-plane flight on an early-morning weather reconnaissance mission, bringing its total of shot-down and written-off aircraft to sixteen out of forty-two since July 5. An initial fuel shortage had expanded to tools and spare parts. A tank jury-rigged by exhausted mechanics could be abandoned if it broke down again. For aircraft, that option was too risky.

More serious was the loss of eleven of the group's pilots. The German ability to maintain an edge in the air depended on the quality of their aircrew, and Luftwaffe kill ratios were declining with each sortie. Two or three Shturmoviks for one or two fighters was an unsustainable rate of exchange. The five planes lost by VIII Air Corps's 2nd Stuka Wing was a reminder of the fate of these lumbering aircraft in other theaters, earlier in the war, when used en masse in daylight. The advantage enjoyed by any dive-bomber was its ability to convince everyone under the dive that he personally was the attack's focal point. In fact, once committed to a dive, the Stuka and any of its relatives were hanging targets. The best chance an antiaircraft crew had was to stick to its guns; the best survival mechanism was to put out rounds. By July 9, the Russians had had enough experience to be convinced, and the Stukas were paying the price.

In the air as well, Russian fighter pilots described their opponents as less willing to take risks and more committed to close escort of the bombers than to the independent sweeps that had proved so costly in Citadel's early days. In part that reflected increasing fatigue and orders to bring the bombers through. But it also reflected the effective, albeit expensive, crash course in aerial tactics the Luftwaffe had provided the Red Air Force since July 5. Lieutenant Ivan Kozhedub was as yet no match one-on-one for the German *Experten*. But he scored two victories on July 9 to add to his single kills on July 6 and 7. He would finish the war as the

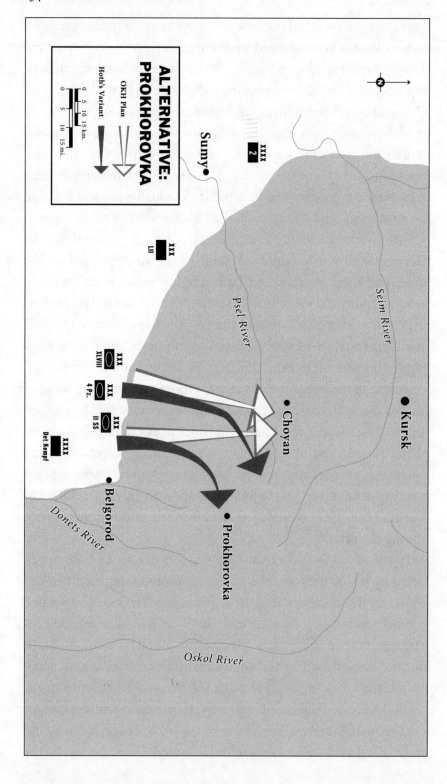

top-scoring Soviet ace with 64 victories. Not every fighter pilot was a Kozhedub-in-waiting. But the careless, the slow learners, and the plain unlucky were gone. The survivors were learning—in particular, how to escort the Shturmovik strikes that harassed and delayed German armor movements all across the southern sector. Air support, so vital to even the limited advances to date, was a diminishing (when not a wasting) asset. As early as July 7, almost half of VIII Air Corps's combat planes had been assigned to Model's sector. For July 10, all the medium bombers were also assigned to Model, and a large number of fighters were sent to conduct sweeps over the Soviet airfields supporting the Central Front. That meant that after five days, Manstein and Hoth could count on only a third of the air support originally available—and that was assuming Model's situation did not suddenly become desperate.

On the ground, Hoth had originally expected XLVIII Panzer Corps to by now be across the Psel and III Panzer Corps to be closing on the right flank of the SS. Instead, both were still fighting their own battles. Pressure against the Fourth Panzer Army's flanks had increased exponentially as the advance progressed. Hoth was optimistic enough to believe that XLVIII Panzer Corps could in a day or two clear its flank and get across the Psel. He believed Breith was capable of breaking free to support Hausser as intended. But both events were still "Citadel conditional." Neither Knobelsdorff nor Breith seemed able in practice to get out of his own way. Hoth decided the time had come to throw the switch.

II

That involved persuading Manstein, who still wanted Hoth's corps to cross the Psel, even if on narrow fronts in separate sectors. That, Manstein asserted, would gain the favorable tank country north of the river and—probably—drive an exploitable wedge between the river line's defenders and any oncoming reinforcements. Hoth proved persuasive. Sometime between noon and 1:30, Army Order No. 5 was composed and distributed. It described the enemy on the army's front as making a fighting retreat northward while seeking to hold the line of the Pena River. Fresh motorized forces (the Fifth Guards Tank Army) were advancing west from the Oskol River. For July 10, the Fourth Panzer Army would expand its sector on one flank by driving northeast, on the other by encircling the Russian forces in the bend of the Pena: 3rd Panzer Division's sector. Specifically, XLVIII Panzer Corps would ("finally!" was strongly implied) finish 6th Guards Tank Corps in the Pena sector while continuing reconnaissance to its north, toward the Psel. The SS mission took only one sentence: Drive the Russians southwest of Prokhorovka eastward, and take the high ground northwest of the town on both sides of the Psel. It did not refer specifically to any new threat from Soviet reserves, but Hausser was already moving in the direction Hoth intended.

An indication of how seriously Hoth took his approach came when at midnight he received an order from Army Group South to support Breith directly by sending a division across the northern Donets. Hoth replied that his orders had been given and it was too late to change them. This was no time to debate details with the commander on the spot, so Manstein let it stand.

It is with these orders that evaluations of German command decisions diverge beyond obvious reconciliation. Historians David Glantz and Jonathan House describe Hoth as "fatally" altering his plans because of the unexpected effectiveness of the Red Army's defense of the Oboyan sector, compounded by the continuing pressure on Fourth Panzer Army's flanks. Their supporting data goes back as far as Vatutin's statement on July 10, making the same point. Soviet staff studies, official histories, and general accounts—not that there was much difference among them in conceptualization and construction—offer the same explanation. It was repeated uncritically in corresponding East German accounts. The interpretation is credible, and it is flattering—a solid combination for official and semiofficial military history in any culture. Its drama can be enhanced by suggesting or implying that the men holding the Oboyan line were at the last ditch, that one more push would have taken the panzers "through mud and blood to the green fields beyond" and put them into the salient's rear and on the direct route to Kursk. Instead, Hoth and Manstein flinched from the decisive encounter and sought an easier way—which led them onto the killing ground of Prokhorovka and the final ruination of the Third Reich's hopes.

Exactly what happened at Prokhorovka is the subject of a later chapter. The present importance of the conventional Russian thesis is that it presents the German decision as reactive rather than proactive. But the staff and field officers who discussed the subject in postwar analyses commissioned by the U.S. Army, or in later memoirs and histories, spoke with a common voice in insisting the "Prokhorovka variant" was not an on-the-fly improvisation, and certainly not a consequence of unexpected Soviet fighting power.

Documentary evidence supports the basic German position that the shift in the SS axis of advance manifested forethought. But was Hoth's timing only a higher-level reaction to the growing mass of Soviet reserves concentrating to the northeast? Were there immediate advantages, any exploitation of "fog and friction," to be gained by the decision? Neither Hoth nor Manstein discussed the subject in detail—which warrants careful speculation.

To this point, Hoth and Manstein had left the primary conduct of operations to their respective subordinates. But "mission tactics," to the extent the concept actually existed in the German army, was not a euphemism for command passivity. Neither Fourth Panzer Army nor Army Group South had achieved anything like effective maneuvering room. On the material side, reports from Hoth's subordinates combined optimism in principle with specific frustration at the effectiveness of the defense and the slow pace of the advance. Fourth Panzer Army's loss/recovery/repair figures for armored fighting vehicles by July 11 were favorable on the surface. Over 450 remained operational. As of July 11, total losses amounted to only 116. The balance, another 450, were in varying stages of repair. But the cumulative statistics also indicated that a good number of tanks and assault guns had been damaged more than once—and this was only the initial stage of the battle.

In the matter of reinforcements, on July 9 Manstein again asked Zeitzler to inform Hitler that Citadel's outcome depended on using XXIV Panzer Corps. Hitler agreed to the formation's concentration near Kharkov, but it remained a high command reserve under the Führer's direct control. By this time, the corps contained three divisions: SS Wiking, and 17th and 23rd Panzer. Its commander, Walther Nehring, was first-rate; the corps included almost two hundred AFVs and, no less important in Citadel's context, thirteen battalions of panzer grenadiers.

Whether the corps could have arrived in time or if it would have made a difference if it had remains debatable. On the one hand, its presence might have enabled resting exhausted units and supporting a final drive, whether from Oboyan or Prokhorovka. On the other hand, given the Red Army's potential for reinforcing Vatutin, committing XXIV Panzer Corps might merely have shoveled coal on a fire. In either case, the question was moot on July 9—certainly as far as Hoth was concerned.

The Fourth Panzer Army's commander had the maps on his side. And of the two possible solutions, his came closest to enabling a meaningful breakout. Geographically, Prokhorovka was in the middle of the land bridge between the Psel and the Donets Rivers. West and south of the town, relatively high ground overlooked open steppe. Control of that terrain was operationally and tactically a major element in Hoth's projected economy-of-force defense against odds. That success, however, would be only stage one. Prokhorovka was also a major road and rail junction on the Belgorod–Kursk axis. By the time the SS had seen off the Russians from the northeast, Hoth expected that at least Grossdeutschland would have completed the secondary mission of securing its corps's left flank and resumed its position on the Oboyan road.

Along with 11th Panzer, and perhaps 3rd Panzer as well, it would then either support the SS directly or be part of a two-pronged drive toward Kursk from Prokhorovka and Oboyan. Either alternative was a chance to move Citadel from the level of minor tactics to at least the lower rung of operational art.

Both Hoth and Manstein were masters of maneuver warfare in the context of modern technology. Manstein had demonstrated as well his understanding of positional warfare during his 1941–42 conquest of the Crimea. That operation had been executed against fixed defenses in a limited geographic area, with forces far less formidable than those available for Citadel. Even in those circumstances, Manstein had sought with some success to avoid a simple battle of attrition, and Citadel was coming too close to that model for his comfort. Manstein was also an accomplished bridge and chess player. One of his gifts as planner and commander was an ability to think several moves ahead. Another, less often demonstrated because Manstein's talent gave it fewer opportunities, was to recognize when a subordinate thought even a step further. Focusing on a frontal assault was to risk tunnel vision for limited results. Hoth had made the bid. Manstein said, "Make the contract."

III

Fourth Panzer Army's frustrations on July 10 began on its always troublesome left flank. From Citadel's beginning and before, Grossdeutschland had been Hoth's trump card, with more expected from it than from the SS. Even with the remaining Panthers of the attached 10th Panzer Brigade, the division counted fewer than ninety AFVs at 3:30 A.M., when its armored battle group went forward against the high ground across the road south to Berezovka and 3rd Panzer Division. That road—little more than a country track by Western standards—was also the main north-south artery in the sector and the defenders' major link to the So-

viet supply base at Kruglik. Cut it permanently and XLVIII Panzer
Corps's flank problems would take a long step toward resolution.

Grossdeutschland secured enough of a tactical surprise to overrun 6th Tank Corps's 200th Tank Brigade and draw two more brigades into a swirling encounter battle in which the Germans had
a combined-arms advantage. Grossdeutschland's artillery and the
attached rocket batteries were complemented, when the rain and
thunderstorms permitted, by massive level-bomber and Stuka
strikes. A battalion war diary commented on the "wonderful precision" of the dive-bomber attacks, which seemed able to target
and destroy T-34s almost at will. In a model example of battle
group tactics, Grossdeutschland's reconnaissance battalion, its
mechanized panzer grenadiers, and the assault guns seized Hill
247. After three hard hours, the panzer regiment led truck-riding
panzer grenadiers onto neighboring Hill 243. The 6th Tank Corps
fought desperately to reopen the route north, but desperation
evoked improvisation—still not a Red Army strongpoint. Attacks
ordered in brigade strength devolved to battalion- and company-
level strikes, further disrupted and misdirected by the woods,
small forests, and ravines that dotted the fighting zone. Meanwhile, 3rd Panzer Division finished its bridge and crossed the Pena
in a short left hook that flanked stubborn Russian rear guards and
brought the division's armored battle group into line with Grossdeutschland. During the afternoon, the two German divisions
caught the Russians in a vise that by nightfall put the front line on
the Berezovka heights and reduced 6th Tank Corps to fewer than
fifty AFVs, and half of those were light T-70 tanks, little more than
panzer fodder.

But again the Russians bent without breaking. Some encircled
units made their way out across the same kind of terrain that had
disrupted their attacks and that now obstructed the Germans.
Others fought to the finish, using Katyushas against AFVs until
the panzers found the range. But the corps commanding officer,
Major General A. L. Getman, formed a new, shorter line around

the village of Novoselovka. Katukov backed it with reinforcements, including the 10th Tank Corps. The panzer grenadier regiment that Grossdeutschland left facing the Psel came under repeated attacks from units that even by Eastern Front standards should have been considered ineffective. But Citadel was different. The Germans committed anything on tracks or with a high muzzle velocity. Thinly armored, open-topped, self-propelled antitank guns took the places of assault guns otherwise employed. The 88 mm antiaircraft guns anchored improvised ground positions, their crews grateful that the weather inhibited Soviet air strikes. And at nightfall, exhausted Germans stood in place—still a long way from where Hoth and Knobelsdorff had expected them to be.

The 11th Panzer Division reached high ground to its front but then stalled. From there it was literally downhill into the Psel valley and twelve or thirteen miles to Oboyan. The town's buildings were visible through binoculars. But the Russians held Hill 244.8, on the Oboyan road itself, against anything 11th Panzer committed. The division commander called in vain for Stuka support. As a result, the 11th Panzer Division spent July 11 consolidating its positions and patrolling forward toward the Psel. It seemed military housekeeping. But the prospects of a single division attacking into even a disrupted Citadel-style defensive system were close to zero. Most of Grossdeutschland, along with 3rd Panzer, was still engaged in clearing XLVIII Panzer Corps's left flank of Soviet fragments, probing the new defense lines in that sector, and regrouping.

As if Knobelsdorff did not have enough problems, at 11:30 A.M. on July 10, his headquarters welcomed a visitor. Heinz Guderian, in exile since Barbarossa's failure, had been recalled as inspector general of armored troops on March 1, 1943. The Army High Command had tasked him with finding out why the Panthers seemed to be performing so badly.

The German army had a word for such visitors: *Schlachtenbummler* (battle bums). But Guderian was no voyeur. He concluded that a major problem was training. The Panther battalions committed to Citadel had been unable to get used to their new vehicles, which meant a high level of minor technical problems and an escalating pressure on field maintenance units. Even the radios had not been tested and set to the correct frequencies before the offensive began. Knobelsdorff and his staff could not be held responsible for decisions made far above their level of authority.

That absolution did not solve Knobelsdorff's tactical dilemma. To understand what may seem to be limited activity by XLVIII Panzer Corps on July 11, it is worth noting that clearing sectors, reorganizing units, and carrying out resupply and maintenance all took time. Moreover, the corps's newly gained rear area had not even a developed network of trails, much less roads. As combat units and supporting echelons began shifting positions, traffic control was a major challenge. A week's worth of combat of a kind that pushed endurance to its outer limits had human consequences as well, ranging from misunderstood orders to temper outbursts to simple physical mistakes made by men exhausted or traumatized. German personal memoirs and unit histories dealing with the Eastern Front encourage overlooking such factors. They are commonly infused with a kind of heroic vitalism implying that fear and fatigue were weaknesses to be acknowledged but overcome. Otto von Knobelsdorff was no Erwin Rommel or Erhard Raus when it came to inspiring—or compelling—supreme efforts. But he kept control of his sector and was confident that his system could stay far enough ahead of its Russian counterpart to give him the edge on July 12. There was material reason for optimism as well. The provisional Panther regiment, still attached to Grossdeutschland, had gone into action on July 10 with only ten runners. During July 11, twenty more were returned to service from workshops whose personnel were beginning to get abreast of the tank's mechanical quirks. By day's end, the regiment's commander reported thirty-eight Panthers operational. Properly played, their long 75s might yet prove a trump card.

IV

Nikolai Vatutin did not survive the war. He was mortally wounded in February 1944—ironically by a band of anti-Soviet Ukrainian partisans. He left no systematic reflections on his handling of the Voronezh Front during Citadel. But on the evening of July 9, he did some serious thinking. The German spearheads were still a good distance from Oboyan and Prokhorovka. In the past two days, however, they had advanced at a much faster and steadier pace than at Citadel's beginning. Logic—and the Red Army approached war making as a scientific, rational exercise—suggested that losses should have been slowing them down. Vatutin had been committing his own reserves by corps, divisions, regiments, and battalions, for five days. Ten of his antitank regiments had lost all their guns; twenty more were at less than half strength. Logic suggested either that the Germans were bringing in reserves—or that their shock power and fighting prowess were proving a match and more for Vatutin's men. Front intelligence, moreover, had been asserting the arrival and commitment of fresh German forces since the night of July 5.

Vatutin considered his front's tactics. In Citadel's early stages, they had featured an active defense. Short, sharp, tank-heavy counterattacks had bloodied German noses and retarded their progress. On July 8 and 9, casualties and material losses combined with fog and friction to impose a passive approach. What were the prospects of shifting back to an aggressive mode?

Reevaluating the intelligence, Vatutin and his staff noticed reports overlooked in the previous days' intensive fighting. As early as 7:00 A.M. on July 8, the Germans were described as constructing trenches on their steadily lengthening left flank. By July 9, trenches were emerging on both flanks of the salient, supplemented by mines and barbed wire, suggesting long-term occupation. A disgruntled German prisoner said he was one of thirty men from a veterinary company condignly transferred to a flank-guard infantry regiment: a sign the Germans were scraping the manpower barrel.

Were these straws in the wind? Perhaps. For Vatutin, they were sufficient to conclude that the recent German progress had been achieved by concentrating their mechanized forces at the expense of their flanks. That in turn meant the panzers were thrusting their own heads into a noose: a salient within a salient. How best to take advantage of the developing situation? In a map exercise, the answer was clear—strike the overextensions. But Voronezh Front's realities made that option a nonstarter. The Germans had Vatutin's main forces no less pinned in place than they were themselves. A counterattack in force would require the just released Stavka reserves. And Fifth Guards and Fifth Guards Tank Armies were concentrating at the salient's tip: around Prokhorovka. Even had Vatutin considered redeploying them, there was no time. He and his front were the balance point for the entire sequence of strategic offensives from Leningrad to the Ukraine, projected to end the Russo-German War by the turn of the year. The first—or next— phase, Operation Kutuzov, was planned to begin against Army Group Center on July 12.

Operation Kutuzov is best described as Citadel in reverse. Its genesis becomes obvious by even a casual look at the monadic shape of the post-Stalingrad, post-Kharkov front in south Russia, with its two salients matching each other. Preliminary planning began in April. By mid-May, the operation was on the board. By early June, forces had been allocated and details established. Directly, Kutuzov was a counterpoint to the plans for a defensive battle around Kursk. Indirectly, it was part of another in Stavka's war-long series of coordinated strategic offensives. Once the Orel blow had taken effect, Voronezh and Steppe Fronts would finish off Manstein's army group. Stavka expected that this task would be easier because the II SS Panzer Corps would have been sent north to stem the tide in the Orel sector. Even before Stalingrad, this had become an almost automatic German reaction: seeking to restore a breakthrough with minimum force promptly applied. This time it would be too little and too late. Once the Germans were stopped and pinned at Kursk and Orel, Southwestern and Southern Fronts would begin diversionary, sector-level offensives, to fix German forces in that area and deprive Manstein of reinforcements. The final stage was expected when Soviet forces around Leningrad and the two southern fronts launched full-scale offensives against anything remaining in their sectors.

Although Vatutin was hardly a careerist, his prospects were unlikely to be improved were he to be viewed by Stalin as dancing with the Germans rather than hammering them. The Vozhd indeed was already commenting acidly on who would bear the responsibility if the Germans broke into Voronezh Front's rear areas. Nor could Vatutin forget about the Germans. Even if they were unaware of the magnitude of the strategic campaign confronting them—which could not be assumed—the concentration and deployment of their forces indicated a final try to break Voronezh Front's defensive system. Manstein had demonstrated in the Crimea that he feared neither frontal offensives nor heavy casualties. Add up intelligence reports of increasing concentrations of AFVs in the Psel region, connect them to Totenkopf's determined attack in the river bend, and the deciding question became which adversary would be first off the mark.

Almost by default, Vatutin's decision was to make his main effort around Prokhorovka. Its preparation involved readjusting deployments, resupplying frontline formations, providing detailed orders, and supervising their implementation. That last point reflected less a doctrinally based Red Army mania for control than it did the very large number of independent, regiment- or battalion-sized formations that had been shuffled from armies to corps to divisions almost at random. Just determining their locations was a demanding task after the past week. Above all, it was necessary to inform Stavka and secure permission. On the night of July 10, Voronezh Front reported that the Germans had suffered

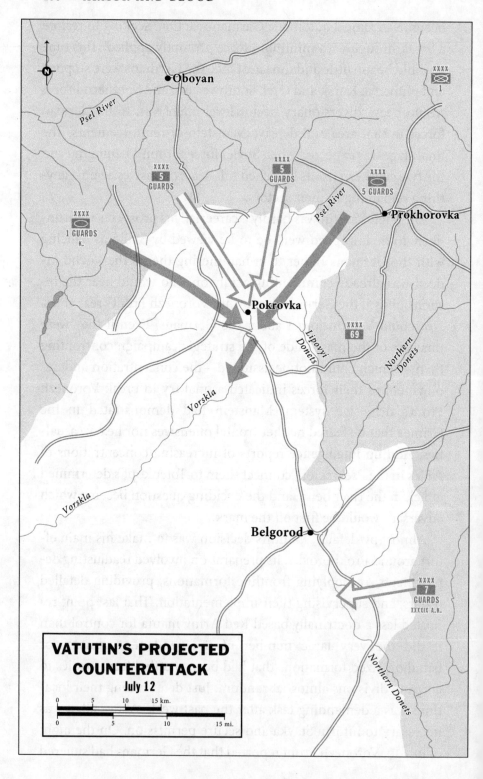

VATUTIN'S PROJECTED COUNTERATTACK

July 12

heavy casualties, had exhausted their reserves, and were concentrating in the Prokhorovka sector. The front proposed to attack with all available force on the morning of July 12. The main thrust would be delivered by the Fifth Guards Tank Army: four tank and one mechanized corps, more than seven hundred tanks, reinforced by three additional rifle corps. In the front's left sector, two tank corps and supporting elements of the First Tank Army, plus two rifle corps of the Sixth Guards Army, would hit XLVIII Panzer's overextended flank. The intended result was encirclement and annihilation of a half dozen of the Wehrmacht's best armored divisions: a perfect counterpoint to the simultaneous attack in the Orel salient.

Rotmistrov's Guardsmen were the key. On July 10, he met with Vatutin at front headquarters in Oboyan. Vatutin explained the situation and the mission and told Rotmistrov he would have two additional tank corps. Then Vasilevsky interjected. The Germans, he said, were deploying new heavy tanks, Tigers and Ferdinands, that had been very effective against Katukov. How did Rotmistrov feel about taking them on? Rotmistrov replied confidently. Steppe Front, he declared, had provided tactical and technical information on the new German tanks. Rotmistrov and his staff had considered ways to combat the German heavies. The Tigers' thick frontal armor and long-range guns meant that T-34s could succeed only at close quarters, using their superior mobility to engage the weaker side armor. "In other words," Vatutin observed, "engage in hand-to-hand combat and board them."

Perhaps the front commander was being sarcastic. Since he was aware that a large number of Rotmistrov's tanks were the light T-70s, he may also have been indicating his awareness that the Fifth Guards Tank Army could expect heavy losses whatever its tactics. Further indication of his concern came later on July 10, when he and Khrushchev met with Rotmistrov's corps commanders and their political officers. Khrushchev insisted on the importance of moral preparation. Get the men ready to fight, he said. Explain our goals. Remind them of the suffering of their countrymen under German occupation. Tell them that victory is near, and that it will begin here, in the Kursk salient. Vatutin emphasized that the Guardsmen should not expect easy success. Stubbornness, decisive action, and skillful maneuvering were essential. In conclusion, aware that the SS were likely to press their offensive the next day, he emphasized that the start lines must be held. His facial expression reinforced the subtext: Hold, whatever the cost.

Voronezh Front's staff worked through the night and into the next morning on the attack's details. Vatutin ordered all preliminary measures to be undertaken in a twenty-four-hour time frame: on July 11 and during the following morning. This was a nearly blitzkrieg-level standard, impossible to implement without mistakes, misunderstandings, and missed connections. Subordinate armies received their orders at varying times between 9:00 A.M. and 5:00 P.M. Not until midnight on July 11 did they percolate to some of the brigades and independent regiments.

Simultaneously, Vatutin and Rotmistrov considered the launch point for the Fifth Guards Tank Army. Vatutin initially favored concentrating on the right, against the Psel sector. The combination of seriously inundated ground, few favorable crossing points, and going directly through even a weakened Totenkopf marginalized that option. Rotmistrov and his staff favorably considered going in on Fifth Guards Tank's opposite, left flank. A breakthrough there would put the Russians directly in SS Panzer Corps's rear and in good field position to turn toward Oboyan. The German front was held by an overextended infantry division: easier pickings than the Waffen SS. Here, however, broken terrain and the steep, heavily mined railroad embankment gave pause.

Finally decisive for the next day's *Schwerpunkt* was Rotmistrov's conviction that the flat, open ground east of the Psel and opposite Fifth Guards Tank Army's center offered the best opportunity for the kind of attack he had sketched to Vatutin on his arrival: a charge supported with every gun, Katyusha, and plane the front could muster. Made at full throttle, it would come to close quarters before the Germans had time to react. It might mean taking a week's losses in a few hours if necessary, but superior numbers would enable Fifth Guards Tank to break in, break through, and break out.

Vatutin approved; Rotmistrov's preparations continued. With the time for reflection denied formations struggling to get into position while topping up fuel tanks and ammunition racks and maintaining camouflage discipline, one point becomes clear. The Fifth Guards Tank Army was expected to implement both the breakthrough and the immediate exploitation with its own resources, but a tank army lacked organic heavy artillery. The two tank corps Vatutin attached, when maintenance and straggling are calculated, gave the Fifth Guards Tank Army more than eight hundred AFVs available on the morning of July 12. This was almost a hundred tanks per mile of front, a concentration unprecedented in armored war. But forgetting the Germans, or underestimating them, could change any prognosis in a hurry.

V

It was 10:00 P.M. on July 9 before Hausser's final orders for the next day were ready. Synthesized, they described a full-scale turn northeast, with security on both flanks left to isolated strongpoints unless a major threat emerged. Totenkopf, now on the corps's left, would get its assault gun battalion back from the 167th Division, cross the Psel in force, turn right, and be ready to mount a division-strength attack by 10:00 A.M. in support of Leibstandarte. That division, led by a panzer grenadier regiment accompanied by Tigers and assault guns, would advance at 6:30, then capture and hold Prokhorovka. Das Reich would keep pace en echelon on Leibstandarte's right and occupy the high ground southwest of the town.

What that amounted to in distance was an average advance of around seven or eight miles. In the context of the previous two days, the expectation was not unreasonable. Leibstandarte's commander, with the advantage of an actual paved road on his axis of advance, expected to be in Prokhorovka by nightfall. But the division's armored battle group had only forty tanks, four of them Tigers. Its progress correspondingly depended on Totenkopf's ability to throw bridgeheads across the Psel, then swing right to come in on Leibstandarte's left flank. The high ground northeast of the Psel was stiff with guns, heavy mortars, and rocket launchers. The terrain on Leibstandarte's front was open—good tank country, but providing very little cover and presenting a potential killing ground. The Stukas and fighter-bombers of VIII Air Corps were expected to compensate by bombing the attack forward. But at 8:45 A.M., Hausser was informed that visibility was too poor for the forward air controllers to direct close-support strikes. That same bad weather, plus heavy artillery fire, was delaying Totenkopf. Leibstandarte's supporting rocket launchers were also stuck in the mud, and its artillery observers were no better off than their Luftwaffe counterparts.

That placed the burden on the panzer grenadiers—nothing exactly new in Citadel. Jumping off at 10:45 A.M., they endured artillery fire, engaged tanks with hand grenades and explosive charges, and by 1:00 P.M. had fought their way into the Komsomolets State Farm on the Prokhorovka road. Russian resistance was no less determined. It was grenades and entrenching tools and pistols, and sometimes knives and bayonets, for the close work as the SS struggled up the slopes of their next objective: Hill 241.6. Then came the Tigers: four of them, moving slowly forward as bullets and shell fragments struck sparks on their armor. Leibstandarte's attack struck the 183rd Rifle Division. This was one of the Red Army's anonymous formations that histories of the Eastern Front usually consign to tables of organization and indexes. It put up a fierce fight despite the appearance in force of Stukas as the weather cleared. The dive-bombers and the tanks worked forward, taking out dug-in T-34s while accompanying pioneers cleared minefields. It took the Germans two hours to reach the crest of Hill 241.6 and two hours more to secure it.

An area the Germans were never expected to reach did not have the elaborate defensive system of more exposed sectors. Elements of Leibstandarte, some of the riflemen riding tanks Red Army style, pushed along the railway leading to Prokhorovka Station until checked by a Guards heavy tank regiment equipped, of all possible anomalies, with British Lend-Lease Mark IV Churchills. Their six-pounder guns were no match for a Tiger, but their relatively thick armor helped enough to blunt the attack. Nevertheless, only one of the twelve Churchills remained operational at the finish as Leibstandarte buttoned up and dug in to resume its advance next morning.

For most of the day, Leibstandarte had been slowed by heavy, albeit intermittent, artillery and antitank fire from the Psel sector. Totenkopf spent a long, difficult night moving its heavy equipment through the boggy ground on its side of the river. Its orders were to force a crossing, establish a bridgehead, and turn northeast to secure Leibstandarte's flank by taking the high ground along the riverbank, especially Hill 226.6. Then the division's tanks were to cut the Oboyan–Prokhorovka road, severing Soviet supply lines and communications, and setting the stage for a final attack on Prokhorovka itself.

The weather and the Russians had something to say about all three objectives. The rain grew heavier before dawn—so heavy that the Luftwaffe was unable to support the river crossing. Soviet aircraft had no difficulty, however, harassing German deployments consistently and effectively. The core of the defense was Sixth Guards Army's 52nd Guards Rifle Division. Well supported by artillery, it repelled initial German attempts to cross the Psel in rubber boats. A foothold established around 11:00 A.M. was more of a toehold as Russian fighters strafed the riverbank continuously, without Luftwaffe interference. Another temporary bridgehead had to be withdrawn under heavy fire. Then during the afternoon the skies cleared. German artillery and rocket launchers engaged their Soviet counterparts. Stukas made a welcome appearance. Russian guns fell silent; Russian infantry began falling back. More and more rubber boats reached the Psel's far bank and made return trips. German pioneers had earlier seized a small, undamaged bridge. Now it became simultaneously a funnel and a choke point for a small, precarious bridgehead less than a thousand yards wide and foxhole-shallow in many places. Not until 4:00 P.M. was division headquarters sufficiently satisfied with the situation to report success after "bitter fighting." And that success was highly contingent on the ability of specialist pioneers to throw stable bridges over the Psel during the night.

Das Reich spent most of July 10 holding its positions as ordered. Initiative was limited by a tank battalion reduced to fifty-six effectives, including a single Tiger and seven captured and refurbished T-34s. Das Reich also reported constant tank and troop movements across the line, but its outposts were unable to determine whether they involved reinforcements or position shifts. The best response seemed to be to give the mechanics time to build up the division's armor resources and await developments, especially since the Russians mounted numerous small-scale attacks on the division's right flank, where the 167th Infantry Division was relieving a regiment of SS panzer grenadiers for the next day's operations. More significant from the corps perspective were the similar spoiling attacks in Das Reich's left sector. The battalion assigned to support Leibstandarte was unable to move forward until 1:45 P.M.—too late to do any good—and at nightfall remained over a mile behind its neighbor's spearhead. Was the SS Panzer Corps in a state of high-risk overextension or in potential position to initiate the breakthrough of Citadel's original vision?

At 7:45 P.M., Hausser reported to Hoth that the weather was cloudy with occasional rain, the roads partly bad, but on the whole drivable. The enemy was resisting strongly to the north and northeast and seemed to be deploying tanks and motorized infantry on his corps's right flank. He complained about the absence of air support and reported the successes of Leibstandarte and Totenkopf.

The SS general stuck closely to the facts. Although his report was hardly spectacular, it seems to have encouraged Hoth. His comprehensive army report, issued at 8:30 P.M., mentioned without particular alarm that reserves from "areas distant from the front," specifically the Fifth Guards Army, were deploying in the Psel sector. Nothing was said about the Fifth Guards Tank Army because neither air reconnaissance nor signal intelligence had as yet delivered word of its transfer, much less its arrival. What army group intelligence did report were high Soviet tank losses and corresponding evidence that Soviet armored and mechanized formations were either redeploying to shore up weak points or withdrawing altogether, ground down and burned out by the German attack. The XLVIII Panzer Corps and the SS were therefore to continue their advance: the former toward Oboyan, the latter to Prokhorovka.

Hausser's intention on July 11 was to move forward at daylight. But the rain in Totenkopf's sector, combined with vehicle traffic, had turned the Psel's banks into a five-hundred-yard mudflat, virtually impassable even for tanks. At 3:00 A.M., Totenkopf radioed that the bridges would be ready by 7:00. From 3:20 A.M., the division also reported at frequent intervals of increasingly heavy Soviet attacks, growing shortages of artillery ammunition, and worsening road conditions. Then came news that the heavy bridging equipment, under artillery fire, had taken cover in a deep gully, become stuck, and would be delayed indefinitely. The pioneers were improvising a corduroy road out of whatever timber they could scrounge. The tanks, instead of preparing for battle, were straining their transmissions hauling bridging equipment through the morass. Totenkopf, in short, was going nowhere in a hurry.

Once again, Leibstandarte was on its own. Its forward elements moved out in the aftermath of overnight heavy rains in a south Russian summer. Mud made cross-country movement almost impossible; fog and mist did the same for air support; and muggy humidity wore down men doing stressful physical work. The road Leibstandarte expected to take into Prokhorovka was the central feature of a terrain corridor bordered on the north by the Psel

River and on the south by a railroad embankment, built unusually high because of the frequent floods. Small satellite villages along the Psel offered concealment to tanks and antitank guns. The focal points of the Russian position, however, were the unusually large October State Farm and the neighboring hill 252.6. Both had been transformed into formidable strongpoints featuring minefields, antitank barriers, and barbed-wire entanglements. Prokhorovka was unlikely to prove a walk in the sun—assuming the defenders matched their positions. The front line was initially held by remnants of the 52nd Guards Rifle and 183rd Rifle Divisions. Backing them up was the 2nd Tank Corps. This was an improvisation. A Russian tank corps was armor-heavy, tailored for breakthroughs and exploitiations, and 2nd Tank Corps had taken heavy losses in the past two days. It was able to issue detailed deployment orders to its component units only around midnight on July 10–11, and these emphasized establishing strongpoints for defense rather than preparing for counterattacks.

The Russian situation brightened around dawn. Since Citadel's beginning, Voronezh Front had been focused on the situation in the Oboyan sector. Vatutin's decision to shift two tank corps and supporting elements from Prokhorovka to Katukov's front had been a gamble, contingent on the imminent arrival of reinforcements from Stavka reserve. On July 10, Vasilevsky informed the Fifth Guards Army commander that the Germans might seek to break through at Prokhorovka and he must move quickly. During the night, two of the army's divisions began forming a second defense line in the Psel-Prokhorovka sector: 95th Guards Rifle on the left, and 9th Guards Airborne directly across Leibstandarte's projected line of attack. Like their Luftwaffe counterparts, Russian airborne troops were by this stage of the war configured more for ground fighting than for jumping out of planes. But they saw themselves as an elite—doubly so since acquiring Guard status. If any division in the Red Army's order of battle was likely to give the SS all the fighting they wanted, 9th Guards Airborne was top of the list.

Marshal Vasilevsky visited the headquarters of 2nd Tank Corps shortly after 4:00 A.M on July 11, asked for a situation report, then interrupted to deliver his real message. Hold on at all costs for twenty-four hours. Tomorrow things would improve. Fifth Guards Tank Army would attack in this sector. Hold on!

Leibstandarte's main thrust was down its sector's middle. The 2nd Panzer Grenadiers, backed by assault guns and the four Tigers that had done such good work on July 10, would follow the railroad to and over Hill 252.2. Simultaneously, the reconnaissance battalion was to clear the villages along the Psel and link up with Totenkopf's vanguards. Once the panzer grenadiers had opened the way, the panzer group—fifty-two tanks and the half-track battalion—would go forward to Prokhorovka. This thin offensive gruel reflected and replicated Citadel's fundamental dilemma. Neither the division north of the corps nor the Fourth Panzer Army had any reserves left. Hausser's intention was to allow Das Reich to have as much of a down day for rest and refitting as the Russians might allow, in order to exploit Leibstandarte's expected breakthrough. That meant Leibstandarte had to provide its own flank security. Instead of lending weight to the main attack, a full panzer grenadier regiment was responsible for clearing threatening Russian positions—likely to be a full day's work in itself. To make matters worse, Leibstandarte had nowhere near enough artillery to neutralize the Soviet batteries. The Luftwaffe again reported the weather too bad to fly. But riflemen were still able to walk. Almost immediately, they were driven to ground by overwhelming fire from the front and both flanks. Adrenaline-fueled Soviet combatants described over two dozen German AFVs disabled or destroyed—including Tigers. Then the sun shone, the ground mist cleared, and the Stukas that had been ready for takeoff since before dawn intervened.

From Citadel's beginning to its end, successful German attacks depended heavily on the pinpoint-accurate close support delivered in particular by the obsolescent Ju-87s. Absent German air cover gave the ubiquitous Soviet antitank guns increased opportunities for close-range kill shots. Now, as dive-bombers struck and silenced artillery positions, panzer grenadiers pushed toward Hill 252.2, the few Tigers leading as their turret and frontal armor defied nearly continuous shell hits. By 10:00 A.M., the preliminaries were finished: the SS and the Guards Airborne met and grappled.

Vasilevsky's speech at 2nd Tank Corps headquarters reached the rifle companies in blunter form: "Remember Order 227! Not a step back!" By 10:30, the minefields had been sufficiently cleared for Leibstandarte to commit its panzer group. This was as much a response to desperate Soviet resistance as an attempt to develop a breakthrough. The Luftwaffe cooperated with an eighty-plane strike, but the key defensive positions remained functional, if not entirely intact. It required the commitment of Leibstandarte's half-track battalion to secure the crest of 252.2 around 1:30 P.M. About the same time, the reconnaissance battalion broke through in the 95th Guards Rifle sector. As the hasty initial deployment of the two Russian divisions began to show strain, the Germans pressed toward the October State Farm. The defenders, a mixed bag of riflemen low on ammunition and gunners firing over open sights, held out for more than two hours as the Germans probed for weak spots. Russian accounts speak of an absence of centralized command, handicapping the direction of supporting artillery fire and the allocation of reinforcements. The Sixty-ninth Army, nominally in charge of the sector, was fighting an even more desperate battle against Breith and spared no time for Prokhorovka. Three things, however, can be discerned. Russian units did erode under pressure; officers were stopping fleeing men at pistol point. Russian casualties nonetheless indicated they fought with grim determination; 2nd Tank Corps's motorized brigade alone reported six hundred dead, wounded, and missing. And the SS overwhelmingly spoke respectfully of their opponents as soldiers and tankers.

Apart from a few occasional fighters, thus far the Red Air Force had been conspicuous by its absence—particularly in the ground troops' judgment. Most of Voronezh Front's available air assets had been sent south against III Panzer Corps, and much of the rest were deployed covering, to good effect, the vulnerable rear zones against German medium bombers. Those dispositions, however, had subtexts. Increasing losses to German fighters combined with the high number of sorties were generating stress-based caution. Voronezh Front's Second Air Army had replaced some of its hardest-hit formations, including an entire fighter division, and the newcomers needed adjustment time. Voronezh Front also ordered the temporary grounding of its Shturmoviks as a preliminary to Vatutin's intended offensive. In late afternoon, an emergency Shturmovik strike temporarily held back the Germans around the October State Farm. Around 5:00 P.M., the panzers came again, only to be caught in a series of counterattacks mounted by what remained of the 95th Rifle Division and 2nd Tank Corps. Frontline units spoke of heavy casualties, die-hard resistance from cutoff Russians, and daylong stifling humidity. Prokhorovka remained just out of German reach—about five hundred yards from its outskirts was the best the panzers could manage before securing for the night.

In its daily report, Leibstandarte blamed what it called limited success primarily on Totenkopf and Das Reich. Their failure to keep pace had created a salient badly exposed on both flanks and a strongly defended tactical objective, Prokhorovka, unlikely to be carried by an armored rush. The division command recommended suspending operations in their sector and concentrating all corps assets on bringing Totenkopf forward next morning. That task completed, Leibstandarte and Das Reich could finish off the Russians around Prokhorovka. Hausser phoned Leibstandarte, consulted his own staff, then agreed.

Leibstandarte still hedged its bet slightly, proclaiming its intention of continuing the attack next day—but only "with the strongest Stuka preparation" and only once Totenkopf secured Hill 226.6, thereby establishing solid contact. In mitigation, Totenkopf could have pleaded a long, hard day in the mud. One of its panzer grenadier battalions was holding defensive positions east of the crossing site on the Psel's south bank. Its initial mission was to secure Totenkopf's right flank and the bridges, and Totenkopf considered a good offense the best defense—especially since this was the closest unit to Leibstandarte's open left flank, about two miles distant. Around noon, a battalion of the Totenkopf Theodor Eicke Regiment, whose "honor title" commemorated a former commandant of Dachau, started toward the village of Vasilyevka. By 2:00 P.M., it had most of the burning houses in hand but was driven back by a tank brigade counterattack, in its turn checked at short range by German rocket launchers. Totenkopf committed a tank battalion. Panzers and panzer grenadiers cleared the village of Soviet armor by 2:40 P.M., but Soviet riflemen held on in Vasilyevka's eastern half: a desolation of mud, smoke, flames, and rubble.

Not until almost 3:00 P.M. did the engineers report the bridges over the Psel ready for use, forcing Totenkopf's commander to apply his math skills. His tank losses had been light and his mechanics busy; Totenkopf could now muster almost a hundred tanks, ten of them Tigers, and twenty assault guns. Had the last two days gone as planned, they might be deploying on Leibstandarte's left as muscle to carry the SS into Prokhorovka. As matters stood, the Russians were massing for another attack on Vasilyevka despite the best efforts of Totenkopf's division artillery. Tanks and trucks were having more problems than ever getting through the mud; fuel and ammunition reserves were limited. Losses for July 11 totaled 450 dead and wounded—most of them in the battalion that had done most of the fighting and that would carry the burden of covering the tanks. True nightfall was about four hours away, and most of that time would be required to move into position for an attack in Leibstandarte's direction. This meant going forward into the kind of broken terrain that, unless patrolled and cleared, was natural cover for antitank guns. Totenkopf resolved this particular round of scissors-paper-stone by informing Hausser that it would not be able to attack until next morning.

Das Reich spent most of July 11 handing over the southern part of its sector to the 167th Infantry Division, shifting its panzer grenadier regiments to the left to concentrate on the attack on Prokhorovka. One regiment did not begin arriving in its new sector until after noon. By that time, the other regiment had been caught up in a Soviet attack aimed at the Leibstandarte flank it was tasked with screening. The division and corps reports refer to "strong resistance" and heavy counterattacks, with woods and the high ground in front of the advance strongly occupied. All in all, July 11 was not one of Das Reich's more spectacular days.

If the Germans had fallen short of expectations, the Russians were explaining defeat. The Fifth Guards Army's commander admitted his people had been surprised. Vatutin, at 7:45 P.M., informed the commanders of the Sixty-ninth Army and 2nd Tank Corps that the German advance was the result of their carelessness and poor preparation, and ordered the lost ground to be retaken immediately. Fifteen minutes earlier Sixty-ninth Army had issued similar orders. At 11:00 P.M., it reported the situation stabilized despite continuous attacks by German air and armor. The unstated subtext was that more could not be expected at that late hour. Certainly the attacks made during the rest of the night by the frontline rifle divisions never came within small-arms range of October State Farm.

From Vatutin's perspective, a variety of threats remained as the day turned. The Germans were reaching the limits of the front zone's prepared defensive belts. If they got through Prokhorovka, the next field fortifications were twelve to fifteen miles away, deep in Voronezh Front's rear. To be sure, the Fifth Guards Tank Army barred that way. But the Germans also had the option—which had concerned Vatutin for three days—of swinging left, across the Psel and toward Oboyan. Rotmistrov's counterattack was intended to prevent that alternative. But a good share of Rotmistrov's projected start lines were now in German hands—a fact calling for more improvisation on top of earlier improvisations almost German in their scale, and not calculated to improve the front commander's peace of mind.

Nor did Stalin remain dormant. Around 7:00 P.M., Vasilevsky turned up at Rotmistrov's headquarters, unannounced and unexpected. The army commander reported his plans and dispositions. Vasilevsky approved and informed Rotmistrov that the Vozhd had ordered him to coordinate and render all assistance to the Fifth Guards and Fifth Guards Tank Armies. As a start, Vasilevsky proposed taking advantage of the waning daylight to visit the positions that 29th and 18th Tank Corps would occupy for the morning's attack. As the generals drove along, Rotmistrov indicated the positions into which his tanks would move during the night. Suddenly Vasilevsky ordered the driver to stop and turn off the road. The now clearly audible noise of tank engines gave way to the vehicles themselves. Vasilevsky turned to Rotmistrov and asked why exactly tanks intended to attack by surprise were moving about so close to the front in daylight, under German eyes. Rotmistrov looked through his binoculars and replied that they were German!

Vasilevsky responded that the enemy must have broken through somewhere and was aiming for Prokhorovka. Rotmistrov ordered two of his own tank brigades forward as a gesture, and the two generals returned to Fifth Guards Tank's HQ. Rotmistrov and his staff promptly revised the details of their tactical plan: artillery support, formation sectors, routes of attack, and everything else. The unexpected, unperceived German gains required recalibration—most of it at the level of brigades and regiments, whose commands and staffs were likely to find improvisation difficult and who were by now fully absorbed in their own detailed preparations. The situation worsened as it became plain that 2nd Tank Corps was too enmeshed on the front line and had suffered too heavy casualties to be a major factor in the next day's offensive.

With his strike force reduced by a fifth, and constrained to find new start lines by midnight, Rotmistrov was in no position to begin from scratch. The plan was to deploy 2nd Guards, 29th, and 18th Tank Corps in the first line, with 5th Guards Mechanized Corps following to exploit success and react to emergencies. The

2nd Tank Corps would contribute what it could. The attack would go in at 3:00 A.M.: 2nd Guards against Das Reich, the other two corps against Leibstandarte and any of Totenkopf's units that came in range.

Rotmistrov put his expectations on the initial shock. Five hundred AFVs were going in. Vatutin had combed his rear echelons for a brigade of artillery, five independent rocket and mortar regiments, and a full division of antiaircraft guns. The leading brigades of 29th and 18th Tank Corps were front-loaded with an extra battalion of T-34s. Their light T-70s might be little more than moving targets, but they could at least draw fire and provide distraction. Against the Tigers and their excellent gun sights, against the Stukas and the rocket launchers, across the twelve miles of open ground west and southwest of Prokhorovka, the armor's best chance was to get as close as possible as quickly as possible—five hundred yards was the generally accepted range for a T-34 facing a Tiger. Given the stress and fatigue levels in the tank companies, an advance straight ahead at full speed was probably the most promising in human terms as well. Sophisticated situational awareness would not be at a premium when the alternatives were stark: Kill or die.

Chapter VI

HARD POUNDING

HAUSSER WAS READY TO OBLIGE. His orders for July 12 were straightforward. No more fooling around. This time apply the panzers' mantra: *Klotzen, nicht kleckern* ("Stomp, don't tickle" is an approximate rendering of the German colloquialism). That, however, did not mean a massed frontal attack, three divisions abreast, into the teeth of Russian guns. Hausser intended a sequential operation. Totenkopf's armored battle group would cross the Psel and push north, then turn east on reaching the Karteschevka–Prokhorovka road, which on the map offered a clear route into the rear of the main Russian position.

Leibstandarte's 1st SS Panzer Grenadier Regiment with a panzer battalion attached would move out at 4:50 A.M. and establish a left-flank guard. The rest of the division was to capture Hill 252.4, the Stalinsk State Farm, then Prokhorovka—but only once Totenkopf's attack had destabilized the Russians: no need to risk getting an extended finger broken. Das Reich would in turn drive straight east, take the high ground south of Prokhorovka, and establish positions for extending the attack on July 13. Das Reich's orders also made it clear that the division was expected to accelerate its pace and keep in touch with its partners regardless of threats to its southern flank.

Corps maintenance crews worked through the night to put more than three hundred tanks and assault guns on line. But in both corps and army higher headquarters, the question loomed ever larger: Where was III Panzer Corps? On the Eastern Front, willingness to shovel manure was a necessary mind-set. But when work just kept piling up and there were no more shovels . . . ?

I

Three panzer divisions' worth of shovels had been held almost in place since Citadel's inception. Even in best-case circumstances, any success the SS gained at Prokhorovka was going to be limited, when not ephemeral, if III Panzer Corps failed to appear in force from the south. On the morning of July 9, its circumstances had not appeared especially promising.

Against the freshly reinforced 35th Guards Rifle Corps, the Germans ran into another day of hard fighting for limited results. Just before noon, four Tigers, the last operational ones in III Panzer Corps, led a panzer grenadier company onto Hill 211.1 in 19th Panzer's sector. But Russian tank counterattacks grew so heavy that 19th Panzer's attached infantry regiment gave ground, then reported it could no longer hold. The division commander managed to restore the line, but by day's end, 19th Panzer had only a dozen of its own tanks operational. Kempf reported that III Panzer Corps could make no further headway. Manstein responded by paying Kempf a presumably inspiring visit and ordering the attack to continue.

The 7th Panzer's experience was similar. Not until around 4:00 P.M. did its tanks manage to push forward—thanks in good part to a Luftwaffe handicapped all day by low-hanging clouds that took advantage of a break in the weather to mount an incendiary strike on the forest facing the 7th's front line. But that attack too produced no more than an almost indefensible salient. All this sound and fury was a long way from a breakthrough and drive north to support the SS that was III Panzer Corps's new primary mission.

A junior staff officer of 6th Panzer Division, sent to Hoth's headquarters as liaison on the evening of July 10, described a mixture of energy and resignation against an overall background of fatigue. The atmosphere at Kempf's HQ was about the same. Manstein, a believer in the restorative qualities of a night's sleep, waited to take action until the next day, when he met with Hoth and Kempf to discuss the situation. Citadel, he said, was fragmenting. Given that the Ninth Army was stuck fast, given the rapid increase of Soviet forces in the southern sector, was it time to suspend Army Group South's attack as well?

Hoth initially recommended continuing the attack, but he picked up Manstein's subtext that Kursk was now out of reach. He responded by suggesting the more limited objective of destroying the Soviet forces south of the Psel. Kempf was less sanguine. Hoth's plan depended heavily on the rapid intervention of III Panzer Corps. And although aerial reconnaissance reported that only one prepared defensive line remained, behind that line waited at least a tank corps and a dozen rifle divisions—enough to make the few map miles between III Panzer Corps and Prokhorovka a very long distance indeed on the ground.

Erhard Raus, the clearest military thinker in Kempf's command, summarized the dilemma in postwar retrospect. Given a successful breakthrough, a drive north needed the full armored strength of III Panzer Corps. That in turn would be possible only if the Russian forces remaining in the Donets Basin could be destroyed or thrown back. Both operations must be executed simultaneously. Since Citadel's beginning, however, Kempf had been shifting inadequate resources from place to place for at best limited successes. The Fourth Panzer Army had no help to offer. Even if the chimeric reinforcement of XXIV Panzer Corps arrived, Kempf argued it would be too little and too late.

Hoth called Kempf a pessimist. Manstein decided to see for himself and went to Breith's headquarters. The discussion's exact balance between arm-twisting and consensus is unclear. Its outcome had Manstein ordering Breith to concentrate two of his panzer divisions, break through the Russian defenses at all costs, and give the SS Panzer Corps maneuvering room by driving the Sixty-ninth Army eastward. And Breith reciprocated with something like good news. The day before, Kempf and Breith had returned 7th Panzer Division's battle group to its parent division. The 7th Panzer then took over part of 6th Panzer's sector, enabling the latter division to concentrate its resources for a breakthrough effort. The 6th Panzer's commander, Brigadier General Walther von Hünersdorff, was openly anti-Nazi, but he was skilled and promising enough to have been promoted in spite of that. His division had forty tanks left on the morning of July 11. The 503rd Panzer Battalion, attached to his division, was operating as a unit for the first time in Citadel. Its indefatigable mechanics added nineteen Tigers—a number affirming the design's fundamental survivability.

The potential effect of what might seem a small force was enhanced because the Sixty-ninth Army had no armor at all and limited reserves. Its mission was unchanged: Keep the Germans from crossing the Donets and breaking out to the north. Breith's orders were for the 6th Panzer Division, in the center of his line, to attack north toward Miasoedovo. The 19th Panzer, on the left, and the 7th, on its right, would support the 6th—with the 19th having the secondary mission of forcing its own bridgeheads across the Donets.

Covering the panzers' flanks in turn were two of Citadel's forgotten divisions: 168th Infantry on the far left, 198th on the far right. Both had been indispensable since July 5. Their horse-drawn artillery pieces and locally acquired supply wagons looked Napoleonic among Breith's tanks and half-tracks. But in blocking counterattacks, supporting the panzers, and frequently taking the main role in the local attacks that had brought Army Detachment

Kempf as far as it had come, the *Landser* had fought themselves to near exhaustion: *immer bereit, still zu verbluten im feldgrauen Kleid*, "always ready to bleed out quietly in field gray."

The strophe is evocative and accurate despite its right-wing provenance. It applies no less to the Russian riflemen across the battle line—specifically to the men of the 35th Guards Rifle Corps on the morning of July 11. The panzer corps artillery began its barrage around 2:00 A.M., followed by massed attacks from VIII Air Corps's Heinkel 111s. Three hours later, the ground attack began. The 19th Panzer, operating with all of its combat battalions for the first time in days, ran onto a hill so well fortified that the trenches were invisible at five yards. The German report also took pains to note that most of the defenders were "Asians," whose primitive level of development was said to have made them psychologically immune to the shock of Stukas and panzers. Attempts to bypass this strongpoint were frustrated by marshy terrain and minefields. Not until around 3:30 P.M. did elements of the 19th break through. Their tanks and panzer grenadiers, with Stuka support, reached the villages of Kisilevo and Kholokovo and beyond.

The 19th Panzer Division's daylong grapple attracted enough Soviet attention for the 6th Panzer's armored battle group to shoulder its way forward and through the defenses in its sector. Again the Tigers made the difference. They led the way and they got the jump, breaking through the remaining antitank positions, gaining ground steadily. The Tigers continued north, toward the first objective of Olkhovatka, supported by whatever the neighboring 7th Panzer Division could provide on the fly.

Both halves of the maneuver succeed. The 35th Guards Rifle Corps cracked, then gave ground. The 6th Panzer's tanks were able to spot and bypass a minefield, then keep going. The 7th Panzer could muster only eleven tanks, but they covered a mile and a half before encountering serious resistance. The Tigers of the 503rd rolled into Olkhovatka virtually unopposed, and the advance continued for another mile and a half before encountering another series of strongpoints. With Russian antitank guns on the flanks and Russian infantrymen flinging Molotov cocktails to the front, a Tiger commander saw only one solution: "Stand on it!" This particular tank made it through at top speed. The battle group, however, was checked by nightfall, and by resistance that defied the fighting power of the panzer grenadiers who managed to remain with or catch up to the armor. But the 6th Panzer had reached the village of Kazache, the center of the Sixty-ninth Army's second defensive line and a total gain of seven and a half miles. A Soviet division commander decided to "relocate" his headquarters to the rear, leaving subordinates to their own devices on a (literally) dark and stormy night.

It was a good day's work: the best for III Panzer Corps since Citadel's inception. It was not a breakthrough in the style of 1940 and 1941. But it was a break-in, and even a short July night to rearm, repair, and rest boded well tactically for July 12. The commanding general of Army Group South concurred. As noted earlier, Erich von Manstein preferred scientific games as recreation. Neither blackjack nor roulette was likely to have been high on his list of ways to lose money. But as he evaluated the day's reports, Manstein saw not exactly a gamble, but an opportunity that hinged on Breith.

For July 12, III Panzer Corps was to continue its main axis of advance north. As the range closed, Breith was to swing his left wing west and cooperate with the southern, or right, wing of II SS Panzer Corps in finishing off the Sixty-ninth Army. With Hoth's unequivocal approval, Manstein also ordered XLVIII and II SS Panzer Corps to, respectively, establish bridgeheads across the Psel and capture Prokhorovka. The next step would be to reverse fronts and deal with the enemy remaining between Kempf and Hausser, like a large boil in the right armpit. According to Hoth's chief of staff, Manstein originally proposed detaching a panzer division and an infantry division for the purpose. Hoth argued that this was insufficient—if Citadel had proven anything, it was that no serious operation could succeed if mounted on a shoestring. He made a powerful case for using the entire SS Panzer Corps.

With or without Hoth's proposed addenda, Manstein's plan invited careful consideration as being unacceptably risky. German air and ground intelligence had provided a reasonable sense of what Stavka was concentrating around the salient the Fourth Panzer Army had created. Mounting a major offensive into the teeth of an even more massive Soviet attack was something approaching a dice roll. But the panzers' strengths were mobility and flexibility. The best chance of defeating the Red Army was to confuse it, to turn it back on itself. An encounter battle promised far more in that context than holding in place.

That again brought the focus back to III Panzer Corps. If Breith broke through to the north in force on July 12, even if Prokhorovka remained out of reach, it might begin the process of throwing the Reds off balance for the first time in this misbegotten operation. Across the front, the Sixty-ninth Army had managed to put together a defense line that still held the panzer spearheads fifteen to twenty miles away from Prokhorovka. But its reserves were nearly exhausted. For practical purposes, it had no AFVs at all. The Sixty-ninth's commanding general was sufficiently dubious about his prospects that late on July 11 he appealed to Vatutin for help.

Stalin was looking over the shoulders of both generals, demanding action. The III Panzer Corps proposed to give Lieutenant General Vasily Kriuchenkin even more to worry about on July 12. The action began when Breith ordered 6th Panzer Division, on the corps's left and the closest to Prokhorovka, to reach the Donets at Rshavets and establish a bridgehead, enabling 19th and 7th Panzer to cross and mount a full-strength drive toward the Waffen SS. The initial plan was for a full-scale daylight attack. The commander of the 11th Panzer Regiment and the CO of its panzer battalion developed an alternate: a high-risk, high-gain nighttime operation that might have an even more decisive morale effect than another direct attack.

Shortly before midnight, the battle group moved out: two weak tank companies, a panzer grenadier battalion, truck-mounted so as—hopefully—to be less conspicuous, and the Tigers, bringing up the rear in a situation where speed and surprise were essential. On point were two captured T-34s, manned by German crews and clearly marked with the German *Balkenkreuz*, the Greek cross, replacing the Red star. In passing, given the Wehrmacht's nearly systematic abuse of deception tactics, this one was an accepted ruse de guerre, legitimated since eighteenth-century navies incorporated one another's captured ships and captains had to pay attention to colors flown rather than hull and rigging designs.

Assisted by a moonless night, the German column advanced for three hours, encountering only a Russian truck convoy, which it allowed to proceed on its way. Then the T-34 leading the main body broke down in the middle of the road! Still no Soviet reaction, even from bystanders. One can almost hear tired men muttering, "Let the damn *tankisty* do their own work!" as German crewmen climbed out and reboarded the remaining vehicles. Around 4:00 A.M., the vanguard, a platoon's worth of Panzer IVs led by the remaining T-34, entered Rshavets and passed through the town unchallenged. Whispering, the commander reported around two dozen T-34s in his immediate vicinity. The officer in charge of the strike force, the tank battalion's commander, was a reservist: Major Dr. Franz Bäke. Most Wehrmacht officers with doctorates held them in some branch of the humanities. Bäke was a practicing dentist in peacetime. In war, he had built a reputation as aggressive, successful, and lucky. He took a tank company forward, setting a fast enough pace that no Soviet straggler sought to hitch a ride. Then the Germans met a column of T-34s going in the opposite direction. The Russians were tired and felt safe in their own rear zone. When a voice from the lead German tank said in Russian, "Keep right," the Soviet column obligingly made place, until someone noticed that they were making way for tanks with German markings. The resulting melee featured grenades, submachine guns, and hand-delivered explosive charges as well as point-blank gunfire. When the fighting died down, about a dozen Russian tanks had been knocked out, several of them by Bäke and one of his crewmen running from tank to tank and placing hollow-charge bombs by hand.

The French colonial army had a word, *baraka*. Its original meaning was religious and referred to spiritual force. Its militarized version meant "fighting man's luck," and surely the *baraka* had been with 6th Panzer's pencil thrust into the Soviet rear. But Bellona, the goddess of war, is no one's trull. Bäke's lead tanks were within three hundred yards of the bridge when a series of explosions announced its destruction. The Germans had driven past the turn leading to it. Check—but not yet mate. At around 6:00 A.M., 6th Panzer Division's battle group was twelve miles from Prokhorovka, with a good road ahead. The column's panzer grenadiers threw a footbridge across the Donets, then expanded it to a bridgehead. Taken by surprise, Russian tanks and infantry fell back in small groups instead of counterattacking. A division staff reported being encircled by three hundred tanks. A division commander declared himself so chivied about by other German tanks that he had lost control of his formation for fourteen hours. And Sixty-ninth Army HQ repeated its call to Voronezh Front for help.

Still, the situation was not all that promising for the Germans. But more had been made from less since Barbarossa's first days. Leading from the front, Hünersdorff and his command group set up shop on the Donets's north bank to expedite and coordinate the bridgehead's expansion. About the same time, the Luftwaffe began softening-up raids on the Soviet positions ahead. A group of Heinkel 111s coming in at low altitude spotted a number of tanks and vehicles in the open: the kind of target increasingly difficult to find as Citadel progressed. They mistook the Germans for Russians and took out 6th Panzer's forward headquarters. Fifty men were killed or wounded, including Hünersdorff himself and two regimental commanders. The Heinkels had guided in on a clearly visible T-34 in the midst of the massed vehicles! Friendly fire and combat karma with a vengeance. The subsequent investigation declared that all precautions had been taken and no one should be held responsible.

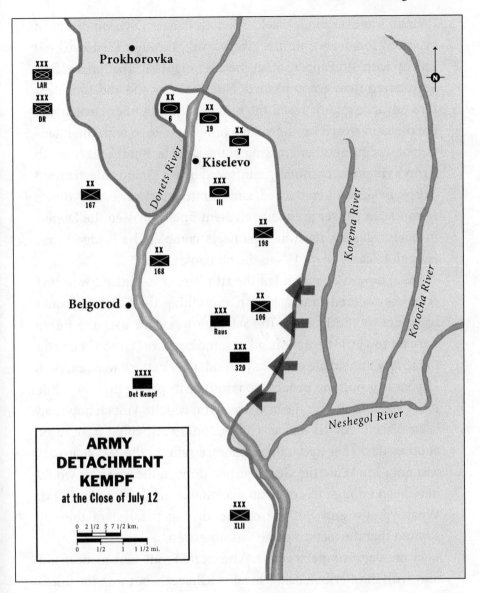

Though local counterattacks rendered control of Rshavezh uncertain until around 9:30 A.M., by 10:00 A.M. the village was in German hands and they were reinforcing the bridgehead. The Tigers' weight still kept them on the river's far side, but by 11:15 the Germans were making clear progress. Had those hundred tanks seen by Vatutin's airmen actually been available, the Russian situation would have been grim. The crucial question now became,

"Where was everybody else?" The 19th Panzer Division had been expected to advance up the river's bank, through Kiritsevo, and link up with 6th Panzer sometime after nightfall. That proved easier ordered than accomplished. Not until 2:15 P.M. did 19th Panzer's advance guards reach the 6th's positions. Other elements of the division closed on the village of Shchplokovo with the intention of forcing another crossing of the Donets. But the Sixty-ninth Army's riflemen, eventually reinforced by 5th Guards Mechanized Corps, held, counterattacked, and counterattacked again. Around 11:00 P.M., a panzer grenadier element finally crossed the Donets in boats. Shortly afterward, pioneers completed a bridge heavy enough to carry Mark IVs to the far bank.

Bäke, now in command of the 11th Panzer Regiment, was nevertheless ordered to attack with everything the Germans could bring across the Donets. The set time was 6:00 P.M.: the forces were far too little to make headway; the hour was far too late to do the SS any immediate good. In the end, Bäke's attack was canceled. His battle group was ordered to reinforce its parent division while 19th Panzer took over the bridgehead on which so much hope had been placed. For III Panzer Corps, tomorrow would have to be another day. That declarative sentence reflects the fact that 1943 was not 1941. What the Germans had done in the morning would have been enough to create an exploitable breakthrough in 1941. What Vatutin and Rotmistrov did during the rest of the day showed that the tactical game was now even.

From Vatutin's perspective, Voronezh Front had to deal not only with the German bridgehead at Rshavezh, but with the unexpectedly successful advance of the 168th Infantry Division. Disregarded by the Russians as Kempf's left-flank security force, it fought its way to the Donets, took more than two hundred prisoners, and was working to force a river crossing with its own resources. Germans across rivers, in whatever strength, was a bad omen. Specifically, Breith's panzer battle groups had shown a high standard of mobility, repeatedly turning up unexpectedly where they had no business being. And as the Sixty-ninth Army began shuffling its forces one more time to cope with the morning's developments, the continuous line of defense in their sector facing Army Detachment Kempf grew even more ragged.

At 1:15 A.M. on July 12, Stalin, increasingly concerned about what seemed an unstoppable German advance, issued orders to Steppe Front to concentrate a rifle army and two mechanized corps for dispatch to the threatened southeast sector of the Kursk salient. The deadline, however, was the end of July 13. That left Vatutin to restore the immediate situation with his own resources. The Sixty-ninth Army had taken a predictable initiative by ordering its counterintelligence department—a uniformed branch of SMERSH (the Russian acronym for "Death to Spies")—to prevent further abandonment of the battlefield. By 4:00 P.M. on July 13, the responsible senior officer reported 2,842 officers and men "detained" and the mass retreat stopped. Otherwise, the front commander was playing with an empty pocket. Every available formation of any useful size was committed to the defense or the counterattack. Russian air intelligence tended to count armored half-tracks in with the panzers—a logical action given the absence of such vehicles in the Red Army at the time. As a result, reports indicated about two hundred tanks in the break-in zone. Rotmistrov calculated twice as many.

Perhaps that was why he cooperated so thoroughly with Vatutin's completely unexpected order at 5:00 A.M. on July 12 to dispatch a strong force to the Rshavezh area. Rotmistrov instructed his deputy, Major General K. G. Trufanov, to assemble the 2nd Guards Tank Corps, two mechanized brigades from 5th Guards Mechanized Corps, and supporting units, turn south, and destroy the enemy in the area of Rshavezh. Trufanov was also to report his progress every two hours. It was a substantial downsizing of the Fifth Guards Tank Army's main assault force. But having three panzer divisions emerge on an open flank while frontally engaged with the Waffen SS was an even bleaker prospect.

Trufanov's fire brigade arrived in increments, reaching its concentration areas by 2:15 P.M.: 160 tanks, each of them a welcome sight to the men of Sixty-ninth Army and their commander. Trufanov did not have a headquarters; the two subordinate formations, 5th Guards Mechanized and 2nd Guards Tank, took charge of whatever units they found in their geographic zones—a quasi–battle group system that diffused effort and transformed an intended large-scale counterattack into hole-plugging and sector-level ripostes.

That is the hindsight version, formed by consulting orders, reports, and maps, with as many hours to evaluate decisions as commanders had minutes to make them. The 11th Mechanized Brigade went in around noon against 19th Panzer. Its chief political officer later reported the brigade was thrown in without intelligence information, without artillery preparation, and on an untenable defense line. The results included failure of air-ground cooperation, poor liaison with neighboring units, and haphazard exercise of command.

Fighting in this sector was fierce from the beginning, and the defenders were left largely to their own devices. Companies and battalions—what remained of them—abandoned positions without orders even in the absence of German pressure. One battalion commander led his unit away from the front until the rout was stopped by the division chief of staff, around Alexandrovka. Russian tanks opened fire on one another while Shturmoviks shot up the positions of the rifle division the tanks were supposed to be supporting. In the same sector, a tank regiment's ordered withdrawal (ordered at least according to the official report) drew groups of infantry with it. Antitank guns mistook the result for a German breakthrough and were barely prevented from opening fire on the whole mass. The commander of the 81st Guards Rifle Division ordered his regimental commanders to "introduce the strictest discipline" and "implement Order No. 227."

Order No. 227, mentioned earlier in the text, was Stalin's "not a step back" directive of July 28, 1942, forbidding any commander to retreat without orders and allowing the summary execution of "panic-mongers and cowards" by specially organized "blocking detachments." That aspect of the order had been unofficially dropped a few months later. But on July 12, the Sixty-ninth Army's SMERSH detachment improvised seven of them. But if the Soviet defenses were shaken, the front never cracked. The 19th Panzer Division was still fighting its way through its immediate opponents at day's end.

Voronezh Front was staging no celebrations. On the night of July 12, Vasilevsky informed Stalin that the threat of a breakthrough from the south was real and that he was doing everything possible to reinforce the sector with the rest of 5th Guards Mechanized Corps and four additional antitank regiments. Nevertheless, the Soviets had stabilized their positions without resorting to large-scale summary courts and ad hoc executions. The Germans were unable to convert their advance into a breakthrough.

One might call this an and/or/both proposition. The fighting in this sector on July 12 has been relatively neglected, even in detailed accounts of the battle. Usually the Germans are given credit for their gains, with a deduction of varying size for falling short of the objective. In fact, the experience of Breith's corps reflects the intersection of two performance curves. The Russians, both the original defenders and Rotmistrov's reinforcements, were learning how to respond to emergencies on the spot and not resort to the large-scale retreats and advances that had highlighted their tactics as late as the aftermath of Stalingrad. For their part, the Germans were showing the effects of wear, tear, and grit in the machinery. Here, as elsewhere in Manstein's sector, it was not just a matter of too few tanks at the sharp end. Too many veteran crewmen, too many experienced company officers, were gone. Too many of the replacements were learning the nuances of their crafts on the job, against an enemy whose tuition rates were increasing. And although records, memoirs, and memories combine to deny it, the strain of combat seems to have begun eroding not so much courage as judgment: the fingertip feel, the situational awareness, central to the German approach to war. Opportunities, discovered or created, were not being developed with the speed and flair of earlier months, to say nothing of years. That required an obliging enemy—and the Red Army was not all that obliging.

II

Turning to the opposite flank, Voronezh Front had spent most of July 11 providing the muscle for the straight right-hand punch of its intended counterattack. The orders were delivered at various times during the afternoon and evening of July 11. According to First Tank Army commander Mikhail Katukov, Vatutin on July 10 said he was not expecting much: a kilometer or two of ground, and keeping the Germans in the sector from reinforcing Prokhorovka. But Katukov's orders were more optimistic—or so it seemed. He told his corps commanders that the objective was a deeper penetration. After all, men with limited objectives could not be expected to fight with the determination of those set to break through the full depth of the enemy defenses. Motivational psychology Red Army–style, circa 1943.

The revised plan assigned 3rd Mechanized and 31st Tank Corps, reinforced by two rifle divisions, to hold their positions east of the Oboyan road, taking the offensive only when the Germans gave way to the main attack of 5th Guards Tank and 10th Tank Corps against Grossdeutschland and 3rd Panzer at 8:30 A.M. Katukov was not acting entirely on his own initiative. Intelligence reports had revealed both XLVIII Panzer Corps's tactical reshuffling and the movement of two infantry divisions from LII Corps to cover the flank positions now occupied by 3rd Panzer Division. From a Russian perspective, the developing German deployment looked like a smaller version of the SS salient at Prokhorovka. A break-in there was worth a try, especially given the expectations placed on Rotmistrov's attack. And the best opportunity was while the Germans were regrouping, settling into new positions, and reconnoitering potential routes of advance.

Grossdeutschland's sideways shuffle went as according to plan as anything ever did on the Russian front: artillery and antitank units moving out first, with the reconnaissance battalion and a panzer grenadier regiment waiting for 3rd Panzer to shift into place. But the German tankers had taken heavy casualties the day before, and the route of advance was thick with mines, German and Russian, many of them randomly sown. By 5:00 P.M., the Russians had advanced nearly ten miles in 3rd Panzer's sector and come close to throwing 332nd Infantry Division into the Psel River. A panzer grenadier battalion and the division's antitank gunners did blunt the Soviet drive, and 3rd Panzer was even able to mount a counterattack as the day ended; but when losses were tallied, 3rd Panzer's operating tank strength had been reduced by the evening of July 12 to around twenty. Not only could the division offer Grossdeutschland no help, it would require support against what seemed a Soviet attack with the potential power to split XLVIII Panzer Corps in half.

That the German front held owed a fair amount to the delay of 19th Tank Corps, on 5th Guards's left, in going forward. With more than 120 AFVs, it had the muscle to give First Tank Army the initiative. But by Katukov's account, the corps commander failed both to deploy his units appropriately and to clarify orders that had been previously explained in detail. On the other hand, those orders amounted to little more than "drive on and keep going"— toward objectives ten or twelve miles away. Perhaps the corps commander considered his assignment a mission impossible and intentionally fudged the preparations. Perhaps his performance was affected by the wounds he had suffered a few days earlier. Perhaps Katukov was looking for a scapegoat. Nevertheless, once the Russian attack did go in, Grossdeutschland, with no help in any form arriving from the west, had more than it could handle in its sector despite the command confusion that initially slowed the Russian attack. Rocket-firing Shturmoviks of the 291st Ground Attack Division joined in. Without air cover of their own, first the reconnaissance battalion and then the panzer grenadiers were "temporarily compelled . . . to withdraw."

198 · ARMOR AND BLOOD

Anodyne officialese obscures the hand-to-hand fighting that resulted in the annihilation of an entire Grossdeutschland company and impelled a battalion commander to ignore two wounds and lead the counterattack that retook his lost forward positions. By some German accounts, the Russians were on the verge of breaking into Grossdeutschland's rear areas—until once again German armor saved the situation. This time it was Grossdeutschland's organic tanks that did the job in a counterattack as well timed as it was well executed. The Tigers made a particular impression on already tired Soviet gunners and riflemen. All but the latest design of 76 mm armor-piercing rounds bounced off side and frontal armor alike. Lighter antitank guns did no more than dent the thick steel even at close range. However, Grossdeutschland's hard-hammered infantry were unable to do more than retake some of their original positions—and that as much through local Soviet withdrawals as by counterattacks on any scale.

At around 4:00 P.M., First Tank Army essentially shifted to a holding action across its sector—a decision encouraged by 11th Panzer's successful attack on its left-flank rifle division. The 11th Panzer remained a bone in the throat of the Russian offensive. The panzer grenadier companies were down to two or three dozen exhausted men, and the attacks and counterattacks had taken a disproportionate toll of junior leaders and their potential successors. But what the 11th had left proved enough—just enough. When the 5th Guards Tank Corps's commanding officer reported that he could no longer advance, Katukov ordered him to halt in place and hold his present lines.

Analysis and recriminations indicate that the Rusians were significantly disappointed with the results of July 12 in the Oboyan sector. Vatutin and his staff perhaps had overestimated Voronezh Front's capacity to shift from to-the-last-man defense to flexible offense in a matter of hours. If, however, personal responsibility is to be assessed, it is reasonable to describe Katukov as more cobbler than blacksmith. He could stitch and mend; his gifts did not extend to swinging the nine-pound hammer of a mass armored assault. It should also be noted that the First Tank Army had borne the brunt of the German northern drive for a week. Staff and line, officers and men, including the commanding general, had fallen into a tactical routine without time to shift mentalities to another approach. Tank and mechanized brigades had been shuffled and borrowed so often to meet emergencies that not merely chains of command but command relationships had been disrupted. And in the Red Army, obeying orders from the wrong general could be as professionally and personally fatal as obeying orders from the right general. A reasonable conclusion is that the front command and the army commander expected their subordinates to demonstrate German-style flexibility and initiative. That time would approach—but it was months and miles, and many dead bodies and burned-out tanks, ahead.

Across the fighting line, at the end of the day prospects for an immediate advance on Oboyan were as close to zero as XLVIII Panzer Corps's staff could determine. Grossdeutschland, with the drive's key role, was already shifting to a defensive posture, concentrating its by now extended panzer grenadiers and grouping its tanks behind the grenadiers' as a sector counterattack force. Around 4:00 P.M., Manstein appeared at corps headquarters. In contrast with Model, Manstein rarely made impromptu visits to the front; they were not a usual part of his command style. His presence indicated a corresponding concern. He did not, however, challenge Knobelsdorff's eventual orders for July 13–14. The 11th Panzer would hold in place and try to restore contact with Totenkopf. Grossdeutschland was to send its armor group—what remained of it—to reinforce 3rd Panzer, with the combined force then attacking not north toward Oboyan, but west.

Hoth concurred but remarked that he had seen the need himself that morning. Knobelsdorff's proposed strike was at right angles to the corps's original axis. Its objective, the Rakovo–Kruglik road, lay in the middle of nowhere in particular. If it was reached, the most likely result would be to cut the Russians' local supply lines and relieve local Russian pressure. Yet that relief had become vital to Knobelsdorff's corps and to the Fourth Panzer Army. The corps's left flank was hanging by a thread, making an advance farther northward out of the tactical question. The Oboyan sector had become a high-risk salient whose best hopes lay elsewhere in the southern sector. As on the Fourth Panzer Army's right flank, the situation on the left can best be described as balanced—but on a knife's edge.

III

The creation of that balance set the stage for Kursk's defining event: the tank battle at Prokhorovka. All the elements of myth were at hand. Prokhorovka offered a head-on, stand-up grapple between the elite troops of the world's best armies, on a three-mile front under conditions that left no room for fancy maneuvers or for air and artillery to make much difference. The drama is heightened by a familiar image of both sides attacking simultaneously—an encounter battle in the literal sense, suggesting predators in rut. Like Pickett's Charge at Gettysburg, Prokhorovka offered an emotional turning point: afterward, nothing was ever the same. Afterward, the tide of war rolled only one way—toward Berlin. Marshal Konev called Kursk the swan song of the panzers. He was in a position to know. Prokhorovka had its Homer as well: Pavel Rotmistrov, whose dramatic narrative of a heroic attack that left dozens of Tigers ablaze was for years one of the centerpieces of Soviet commemoration and one of the few accounts from the Red Army's front lines generally available in the West.

As for the Germans, they could and did content themselves with countermyths of fighting to the last man and the last tank. That was no trifling detail in the context of a Western culture of heroic defeat that celebrates last stands from Thermopylae to the Alamo, Dien Bien Phu, and beyond, no matter their provenance or matrix.

Throughout the night of July 11–12, the frontline elements of

Leibstandarte and Das Reich were kept awake by the ubiquitous single-engine "sewing machines" of the night witches and by the sound of Russian tank engines—a lot of tank engines. The question was, Were the Soviets concentrating for an offensive or redeploying elsewhere? Shortly after midnight, a panzer grenadier battalion, pushed forward as a reconnaissance force, provided the hint of an answer when it fell back before strong and alert resistance. The next step to confirmation came at dawn, when Shturmoviks materialized out of the fog. Coming in at treetop height, they shot up everything that crossed their gun sights, no matter its direction. Around the same time, Russian artillery opened fire—initially not a massive barrage, but ranging fire. That meant the real barrage might begin at any time, and as mortars joined, Leibstandarte began adjusting its frontline dispositions to meet what was becoming the certainty of a full-scale attack at daylight.

The attack Hoth and Hausser had ordered was contingent on Totenkopf's advance on the SS left. Leibstandarte's intention was to hold in place until the Death's-Head tanks began applying pressure to the Russian flank. Now that mission appeared more complicated. Totenkopf's forward artillery observers reported large tank formations approaching Leibstandarte's left flank. Patrols and observers confirmed increasing ground activity to the division's front, including exhaust fumes heavy enough to smell even at long range. Among the panzer grenadiers, the focus by then was not on attacking in any direction, but on preparing to hold out against what appeared to be the most powerful Soviet attack since Citadel began.

By the book, Leibstandarte had the ground in its favor. The terrain to its front was relatively open; the ravines crossing it randomly from end to end were shallow; the extensive fields of grain and sunflowers were not high enough to shelter any force larger than an infantry patrol. Antitank guns began moving cautiously forward into ambush positions. The Germans had the further advantage of being able to reverse some of the Russian defenses they had captured on July 11. In two world wars, a significant and overlooked difference between Germans and their British and American opponents was that the *Landser* did not object so strenuously to digging. And if reversed entrenchments were not as effective as the original version, the trenches and bunkers occupied by the SS, especially on Hill 252.2 in the center of their line, were nevertheless a significant improvement over a grave-sized foxhole scratched out with entrenching tools. Even the replacements were not so young and so green as to think, "Let 'em come!" But as extra grenades were brought to hand, as the MG 42s and their ammunition belts were rechecked, there was no sense that the cigarette lit during the intervals was the last one. Best not to think about it. Best to do one more equipment check and trust to "soldier's luck."

Rotmistrov's tankers were no less nervous. They fiddled with engines and breechblocks. They loaded extra ammunition and additional gasoline, accepting the corresponding increase in the risk of being torched by even a glancing hit. A T-34 halted was a T-34 destroyed; fuel was even more vital to survival than were shells. Crewmen waited "with dry mouths and wrenching stomachs." A political officer described conducting discussions "on the subjects of the military oath, their knowledge of the Stavka directives, hidden sabotage, the approach of the hour of revenge. . . . Applications for Party membership were written up. . . . The political awareness and morale were high."

Morale was probably better served by the hot meal provided to most of the forward units—at least for those able to eat it. Even more welcome was the vodka that accompanied the food—or replaced it. Everyone knew that the attack would have to cross open ground. It did not help to know that the T-34, designed to save internal space, was not easy to get out of in an emergency and that its poorly fitted turret hatches frequently jammed of their own accord. Nor was it useful to remember that tankers' uniforms had no fire resistance. Germans regularly commented on the burning tanks that spawned human torches, when a pulled trigger meant a mercy shot and not a war crime.

Not all the Russian tankers at Kursk were men. How many died there remains unknown. But women had been folded into the Red Army's tank units since before Stalingrad, being particularly valued as drivers. Their generally smaller size made it easier for them to fit into the T-34's cramped forward compartment—and to get out as well. Others were commander/gunners. Aleksandra Samusenko was decorated for destroying three Tigers and eventually became Russia's only woman tank battalion commander, killed in action during the Battle of Berlin.

Like so many other details of Kursk, exactly when and how what one survivor called "the devil's waltz" began remains obscure. Rotmistrov arrived at the command post of 29th Tank Corps just before dawn and was told all was ready. At 5:15 A.M., he informed Vatutin that everything was in order. The full artillery preparation would start at 8:00 A.M. and the tanks would go in thirty minutes later. Leibstandarte's records, on the other hand, describe a number of probing attacks around that time, but no serious Soviet movement. Probably the best evidence against either a preemptive or a simultaneous German attack was that the men of a Leibstandarte tank company in the target sector, exhausted by the previous day's fighting, were literally caught in their blankets as the Russians completed their final deployment. The company commander banged his head and nearly stunned himself when he came crawling out from under his tank in response to a summons from his battalion commander. The order he received was vague: Make contact with the infantry and prepare to intervene if they needed support.

Since the company had only seven tanks that morning, "intervene" was all that it could do. Captain Rudolf von Ribbentrop had returned to his unit and was drinking coffee when he looked eastward and saw "a wall of purple smoke." Purple was the color of the flares and shells that announced a tank attack. A motorcyclist from the panzer grenadiers appeared in a cloud of dust, pumping his fist in the signal to advance. When the panzers reached the crest of the high ground to their front, "what I saw left me speechless. . . . In front of me appeared fifteen, then thirty, then forty tanks. Finally there were too many of them to count, rollling toward us at high speed."

Ribbentrop responded by taking his tanks downslope toward the Russians—not on a suicide run, but to keep from being silhouetted on the crest. An advance made sense as well, because the Soviet barrage was falling short of expectations and requirements—at least in hindsight. There was an ample number of gun tubes and rocket launchers somewhere in the combat zone. But regiments and batteries had moved into position in a helter-skelter fashion that led to a neglect of communications. Ammunition supplies were similarly distributed at random. The assault brigade commanders were too concerned about their own missions to coordinate systematically with the gunners supporting them. Target acquisition was also random: available sound and flash equipment failed to range the guns with anything like precision.

The result was a Russian artillery preparation closer in method and effect to 1915 than to 1943, let alone the barrages that would open the Red Army offensives of 1944–45. In German reports, the overall impression is that the SS infantry found the shelling disturbing, but not devastating—not the kind that drove men to the ground and silenced any reaction beyond a near mindless wanting it to stop. Nor was Hausser's corps artillery quiescent. Its counter-battery fire grew increasingly effective, especially against Prokhorovka itself and the roads leading from it toward the Russian positions.

Rotmistrov was able to do no more than report to Vatutin that the artillery preparation was insufficient. Rotmistrov was well aware of something that later accounts and analyses tend to overlook: this was the Fifth Guards Tank Army's first battle. It was newly organized—indeed, one might say thrown together—from units with limited experience working together. Ordinarily, the quality of individual senior officers would have been less a central issue. All they would have to do was get their tanks forward, never mind how, and pin the Germans down until succeeding waves could complete the breakthrough and exploitation. But Vatutin's early-morning order to reinforce the front's left flank against Breith had cost Rotmistrov three brigades from his already weak second echelon. Moreover, Rotmistrov had independently created his own flank guard from independent assault gun regiments— more striking power unavailable for the main attack.

When all the chopping and changing was done, Fifth Guards Tank Army's deployable reserve was down to two brigades with fewer than a hundred tanks between them. Front intelligence credited the Germans in Rotmistrov's sector with 250 to 300 tanks— but provided no detailed information of the possible number facing Rotmistrov's attack. Although his plan was hardly unraveling, enough grit was finding its way into the machinery that Fifth Guards Tank Army's first wave would have to do more than just bull its way forward until it was expended. One of its corps commanders, moreover, was new to that level. Rotmistrov considered the other of sufficiently dubious quality that he sent the army chief of staff to keep an eye on him. Communications between corps and brigades, and brigades and battalions, were so haphazard that the kind of control prescribed by Red Army doctrine and encouraged by experience would prove difficult to maintain.

The time for tinkering ended at 8:30 A.M., when the last Katyusha salvo was fired. The guns and launchers fell silent—the signal to attack. The code word for the attack went out over the army's radio network: "Steel! Steel! Steel!" Repeated over and over, it released a spring by now tautened almost to the snapping point. Some of Rotmistrov's *tankisty* might well have anticipated the order. Now the rest gunned their engines and raced at full throttle for the heights to their front. At 9:20 A.M., Vatutin notified Stalin that Voronezh Front had gone over to the offensive according to plan. But "no plan survives contact with the enemy," and Voronezh Front's was no exception. Rotmistrov declared that as Fifth Guards Tank went in, the Luftwaffe mounted a massive air attack. Hausser had requested air support against the armored threat suddenly looming in his sector. Brigadier General Paul Deichmann, commander of the 1st Air Division, had put everything he had into preparing to support Hausser's originally projected attack. Ground crews had worked around the clock to restore planes to the order of battle. As a result, VIII Air Corps could reply immediately that two ground-attack groups were on their way.

That was just the beginning. Messerschmitts cleared the sky above and ahead of the attack planes. Wave after wave of medium bombers sought out artillery positions. Guided by a still-efficient ground control system, the Henschels of Schlachtgeschwader (Attack Wing) 1 and JG 51's tank destroyer squadron would combine for almost 250 sorties on July 12. The twin-engined Henschels had repeatedly proven their worth against armor. Working with them were not only the conventional dive-bombers, but a new variant. The Ju-87G was a pure tank buster, with additional armor and two 37 mm cannon in underwing pods. Even with their heavy earlier losses, the Stuka wings were manned largely by experts, and none was better than Hans-Ulrich Rudel. A veteran of more than a thousand combat sorties in the Ju-87, he was an early advocate of the specialized tank killer and now flew one of the first delivered.

Like many another pilot, Rudel could tell a war story to advantage: "The first flight flies behind me in the only cannon-carrying airplane.... In the first attack four tanks exploded under the hammer of my cannons; by the evening the total rises to twelve. We are all seized with a kind of passion for the chase...." The number and timing of Rudel's kills remain controversial. But on that day and in that place, his claims are reasonable. The effect of the hits the Germans scored was enhanced by the extra fuel carried by the cautious Russian tank commanders. The best place to carry extra cans was on the rear deck, and machine-gun fire from above was usually enough to turn the vehicle into a torch as blazing gasoline came through the ventilators and reached engines already running hot.

The attacking planes had the further advantage of relatively limited aerial opposition. The Russians had neither the Germans' sophisticated air-ground liaison system nor the Luftwaffe's smoothly working maintenance capacities. Russian sortie times were appreciably longer, especially in high-stress situations. The Russian fighters made a showing poor enough that ground-force reports uniformly described air support so limited that the Germans were able to pick their targets without interference.

To the men beneath the wings, it seemed as if the entire Luftwaffe were overhead and seeking to kill them specifically. One rifleman spoke for many: "I did not see an aircraft diving toward us, but moments after a warning was yelled the ground in front of us levitated. It was like a giant had grabbed the battlefield and shaken it. I was knocked to the ground but was dragged to my feet and the platoon was told to look to its front and stand firm. . . ." Even when they did not find a target, the bombs aided the German defenders by contributing to the clouds of dust thrown up by the charging tanks. At many points, the Russians were advancing almost blindly. The T-34 may have been the best battle tank of World War II, but its four-man crew required the commander also to act as the gunner. That made it nearly impossible for him to ride with the hatch open like his German counterpart, looking for obstacles, threats, and opportunities.

With losses about to mount, this is a good time to address the still-vexing question of numbers. History may not tolerate the subjunctive but is frequently forced to accept it. Just how many tanks ultimately confronted one another in the fields around Prokhorovka? The answer depends in part on how the battle zone is defined and in part on whose reports from what time periods are given most credence. The numbers also incorporate a mythic element. For Germans and Russians alike, the longer the odds, the greater becomes the heroism. But the Russians encounter a certain paradox. The Soviet Union's success in World War II was and remains in good part defined in contexts of mass: the ability of the USSR and its people to submerge the Fascist monster in matériel and drown it in blood. The more tanks available, the more convincing is the meme.

Cutting to the chase against that background, the most recent and detailed analysis of the Russian forces puts 234 tanks in the first attack wave. The 181st Tank Brigade was on the right, next to the Psel River. The 170th was next, opposite the German positions around the October State Farm. The 31st and 32nd Tank Brigades of 29th Tank Corps aimed at Hill 252 from the right. The corps's 25th Tank Brigade went forward on the army's far right flank, south of the railroad. A senior officer riding with the 32nd described the scene:

> Instantly the field, which had seemed barren of life, sprang to life. Crushing shrubs in their way and churning up the crops with their tracks, the tanks rushed forward, firing on the move.... The commanders understood the Tigers would take advantage of every halt, slightest hesitation in motion, or amount of indecision.

Initially, they faced only Ribbentrop's company of Leibstandarte's tank battalion. Tankers, like pilots, can tell stories to advantage. Ribbentrop's might be titled "Alone at Prokhorovka." For the first few minutes, at least, his seven Panzer IVs suffered an embarrassment of targets. Going for flank shots against relatively thin armor, each tank covering another, they were flaming Russians at under a hundred yards' range. The only question was whether their ammunition or their luck would run out first. Ribbentrop's own tank was bypassed in the Soviet charge. He found himself taking Russian tanks and infantry by surprise from the rear as he struggled to return to his starting point, ultimately winning a death duel with a T-34 at gun-barrel range.

Then, unexpectedly, the Russian momentum was broken—not from ground resistance or air strikes, but by an antitank ditch dug as part of the original Soviet defensive system. It was fifteen feet deep, and the speeding tanks drove right into it. There appears to have been no knowledge of its presence at any level of 29th Tank Corps. As a rule, such obstacles were clearly marked on relevant maps. But for the sake of security, map distribution was severely restricted, and Rotmistrov's tankers were new to the sector.

Erich von Manstein on his way to a field command post
Bundesarchiv, Bild 146-1991-015-31A / Heinz Mittelstaedt

Hermann Hoth (left) and Manstein at a conference
Bundesarchiv, Bild 101I-022-2927-26 / Heinz Mittelstaedt

Hoth observing from a trench
Bundesarchiv, Bild 101I-218-0530-10 / Geller

Tiger in the field
Bundesarchiv, Bild 146-1978-020-01A / Friedrich Zschäckel

German Marder II self-propelled antitank gun
Bundesarchiv, Bild 101I-197-1238-16 / Henisch

German half-track with 37 mm antiaircraft gun
Bundesarchiv, Bild 101I-022-2926A / Wolff/Altvater

JU-87G Stuka, showing 37 mm cannon
Bundesarchiv, Bild 101I-646-5184-26 / Niermann

Infantry of Das Reich advance with Tiger support
Bundesarchiv, Bild 146-1973-080-50 / Friedrich Zschäckel

Infantry of Grossdeutschland move forward
Bundesarchiv, Bild 101I-732-0135-22 / Gottert

Column of Panzer IIIs in open country
Bundesarchiv, Bild 101I-219-0595-03

Tiger on target!
Bundesarchiv, Bild 146-1973-098-48 / Gronert

It was a horse-powered war for both armies on the Eastern Front.
Bundesarchiv, Bild 101I-578-1950-05 / Bayer

Cigarette break at Prokhorovka
Bundesarchiv, Bild 101I-219-0553A-10 / Koch

Panzer III crew rests during a halt
Bundesarchiv, Bild 146-1981-143-14A / Friedrich Zschäckel

Ground reconnaissance might have changed that, but fighting was still going on during the night.

The result of this nighttime fog and friction was that next morning, drivers blinded by smoke, dust, and adrenaline raced headlong into a ditch designed to stop Tigers. Other tanks, swerving to avoid the ditch, collided with their neighbors. Gasoline flared and metal flew. Like World War I infantrymen facing barbed wire, tanks sought the few available crossing points as others piled into the melee. Ribbentrop described "an inferno of fire, smoke, burning T-34s, dead, and wounded Russians." It speaks much for the ruggedness of the Russian tanks that so many were able to keep going after shocks and crashes that would have disabled any of their German counterparts. Command and control eroded, however, as senior officers, going forward to restore order and momentum, lost contact with front and rear alike. In Guards tank units, platoon commanders had radios, but they were fragile. Concussion from glancing hits often knocked them out of action. To the other two radioless tanks in a platoon, the rule was still to follow the leader. Limited visibility, large numbers, and German fire reduced practical maneuver options to two: forward or back.

By this time, Leibstandarte's artillery regiment had come into action, laying a curtain of fire between the antitank ditch and the division's frontline infantry. What started as a rush turned to a grind as the Soviet armor fought its way forward almost on an individual basis. The 31st Brigade lost around half its tanks in the mad rush to contact. But enough tanks reached their objectives to give the Germans some of Citadel's fiercest fighting.

Most of the T-34s were carrying infantry—both the brigades' organic "tank marines" and passengers shifted from the supporting rifle divisions. Other infantry on foot followed the tanks despite imminent risk of being run over by their own tanks or shot by their own men. But the Soviet riflemen, especially the 9th Guards Airborne, pressed forward, working their way past the junkpile at the antitank ditch. As the T-34s led the way to Hill 252.2, the panzer grenadiers used everything that came to hand:

grenades, satchel charges, machine guns—the latter to hose off the tank-riding infantry before they could dismount and come to close quarters. On Hill 252.2, the Russians overran the headquarters of a Leibstandarte panzer grenadier battalion. Its commanding officer, the later notorious Jochen Peiper, personally took out a T-34 with a bundle of hand grenades—not the usual mission of a senior officer, even in the Waffen SS.

Ribbentrop's tank and two others made it back to their own lines. German statistics credited Ribbentrop alone with fourteen kills in the brief melee. Another crew accounted for seven—five after the tank was disabled and firing in place. The exact numbers are debatable, but the Russians may well have done as much damage to themselves as did the half-dozen Mark IVs. But whether directly or indirectly, Ribbentrop's tanks added significantly to the debacle at the antitank ditch.

Ribbentrop's crews also bought time for the other two companies of Leibstandarte's tank battalion to deploy in support of their hard-pressed infantry. Arguably of more significance, Ribbentrop's stand enabled the division's Tiger company to take hull-down positions left of Hill 252.2, covering October State Farm. The 18th Tank Corps's leading brigades had been tasked to break through Leibstandarte's left flank, still wide open in the absence of Totenkopf's panzers. Initially, four Tigers blocked their advance. One of them was commanded by an even more iconic SS hero than Ribbentrop. The legends enveloping Michael Wittmann obscure the facts that even at this early stage of his career, his comrades considered him unique for situational awareness and a cool head. That made him the right man in the right spot as a hundred Soviet tanks surged toward October State Farm. Beginning at ranges of eighteen hundred yards, the Tigers methodically picked off one T-34 after another. And there were too few Tigers to give the supporting Russian artillery a target.

The Soviet tanks nevertheless kept coming. As the ranges closed, their alternatives grew fewer. A Tiger's real killing range began at around a thousand yards. But for a T-34, even damaging a Tiger at ranges much over eighty or a hundred yards required a steady aim and a lot of luck. And Bellona tends to bestow fortune on those who do not need it. Experienced Tiger drivers—the only kind left by July 12—had learned to halt at an angle, so even direct hits on the frontal armor were likely to glance off. When T-34s flamed, Tigers threw sparks.

Desperate Russian tankers set nearly suicidal examples to reduce the odds. The most familiar, arguably Citadel's defining incident, occurred when a T-34 was hit at near point-blank range and set on fire. The crewmen pulled the badly wounded commander to safety. Then the driver saw a Tiger approaching. He reentered the burning tank and set out to ram the German. Rotmistrov's version of the story has the effort succeed, with the resulting fire and explosion destroying both vehicles. The German account is more detailed. The German crew was startled when the flaming T-34 started for them. The commander ordered an advance, to get clear of the smoke. The gunner fired—and the shell bounced off. The Russian kept coming and rammed the Tiger. As flames covered both tanks, the German suddenly backed up. At five yards' distance, the T-34 exploded. The Tiger resumed its original position with little more than scratched paint and—presumably—five sets of shaken nerves.

If the point of the story needs establishing, it is that even after a week of close-quarters, high-tech combat, courage was not a scarce commodity on either side. And though courage was no proof against 88 mm armor-piercing rounds, surviving tankers of the 170th had enough fighting spirit to enter the still-desperate melee on Hill 252.2. Their commander died there—according to Peiper, in hand-to-hand combat with an SS officer who killed the Russian with his own knife. It was not enough. Even when the battered Soviet remnants were finally ordered back, for the rest of a long afternoon, episodic Russian attacks continued. The overall result was to keep the exhausted Germans in the sector pinned firmly in place.

The 25th Tank Brigade escaped the debacle at the antitank ditch, but ran full tilt into the 1st SS Panzer Grenadier Regiment and, more important, Leibstandarte's antitank battalion. Its lightly armored, open-topped, self-propelled vehicles were no direct match for a T-34. But their high-velocity three-inch guns were deadly firing from concealed positions. SS riflemen tackled the tanks directly, boarding them to grapple with the survivors of the "tank marines," pry open hatches, and drop grenades inside fighting compartments. The regiment's commander described seeing half-track drivers repeatedly attempting to ram T-34s with their lighter vehicles. "Everywhere," recalled a German antitank gunner, "were the shells of burning tanks. . . . One hundred twenty tanks or more were supposed to have been in the attack. . . . Who counted?"

It is easy enough to write repeatedly from the comfort of a book-lined study, facing no risk greater than a paper cut, about burning and exploding tanks. After the war, a veteran of the 10th Tank Corps in the Oboyan sector wrote:

> The T-34 has 3 100-liter fuel tanks on the right side, and an additional 100-gallon drum with motor oil on the left side. When an armor-piercing shell penetrates the side, fuel oil or motor oil spills into the tank and a cascade of sparks falls on the uniform and everything blazes up. God forbid a living being from ever having to witness a wounded, writhing person who is burning alive, or ever have to experience the same. That is why there exists among tankers a unique, unofficial measure of courage . . . the number of times you've been on fire inside a tank. . . ."

Twenty-six of the thirty-four T-34s that led this attack were destroyed. All of their supporting assault guns were lost, at least one of them in ramming a German AFV. The level of heroism was such that the number of decorations awarded was unusual in the context of a failure. And failure it was. The German line held. The attacks subsided and the fighting broke off, partly from mutual

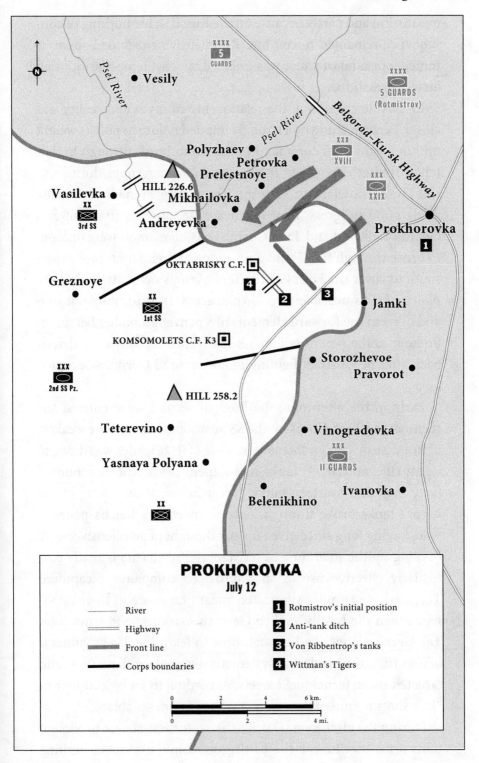

PROKHOROVKA
July 12

River	**1** Rotmistrov's initial position
Highway	**2** Anti-tank ditch
Front line	**3** Von Ribbentrop's tanks
Corps boundaries	**4** Wittman's Tigers

exhaustion and partly because on the Russian side nothing of consequence remained to commit. Rotmistrov's attack had spent its force; Leibstandarte, too, was finished, at least temporarily, as an attack formation.

In Das Reich's sector, the relationship of myth and reality was closer. Perhaps stung by a strongly implied failure to pull its weight on July 11, division command proposed to break through in battalion strength on its left, then move its *Panzergruppe* through to roll up the Russians to its front. The panzer grenadiers initially made good progress, then ran headfirst into the attack of 2nd Guards Tank and 2nd Tank Corps. The Guardsmen were ordered to break through the German positions to their front, then swing south to cover the Fifth Guards Tank Army's main attack and exploit as far as possible their own success. Instead, they ran into and overran the forward elements of a panzer grenadier battalion, broke into the parent regiment's rear echelons, and were driven back after fierce street fighting in and around German-occupied villages.

Early in the afternoon, the Russian second wave entered the scene as 2nd Tank Corps hit the SS positions. This was the weakest of Rotmistrov's major formations. One of its brigades was down to eighty rifles and twenty tanks, half of them T-70s. Another counted forty men and fourteen tanks. Nevertheless, about thirty of the corps's tanks broke through, only to meet Das Reich's panzers, who, having long since given up any thought of an offensive, were backing up the main line of resistance. The Germans made particularly effective use of an improvised company of captured T-34s, whose familiar silhouettes meant far more to their opponents than the hastily applied German markings and paint jobs. The German crews had enough time to learn the T-34's vulnerabilities from the inside and systematically went for flank shots and targeted the external fuel barrels. According to an official report, "In a short period of time all 50 tanks . . . were set ablaze."

During the afternoon, Das Reich's sector was struck by violent rainstorms that turned the battleground into a morass, limiting the mobility of even the T-34s. The 2nd Guards Tank skidded and slipped back to its start lines, leaving dozens of wrecks behind and reporting that the Germans were hot on the corps's heels. Das Reich's headquarters in fact understood that the division was unable to do anything more than secure its own positions and see what its opposite numbers were able to do the next day. But as the Russians fell back in disorder, Das Reich's panzer grenadier regiments pushed forward. Their local counterattacks were nothing like a serious attempt at a breakthrough or a flanking movement, but served to keep the Soviets well off balance as the day waned. Around 5:00 P.M., Rotmistrov arrived at 2nd Tank Corps headquarters and issued orders to renew the attack at 6:30. But a few hours later, Vatutin was informing Stalin that major reinforcements were urgently necessary to complete the destruction of the enemy. Das Reich was not the only headquarters playing for time as July 12 came to a water-soaked end.

Events on Das Reich's and Leibstandarte's fronts were heavily contingent on Totenkopf's performance. At dawn, Totenkopf's advancing panzer group discovered that the Russian infantry to its front had been relieved by the Fifth Guards Army's fresh 3rd Guards Rifle Corps: three divisions reinforced by extra guns, rocket launchers, and antitank guns. Its orders were to destroy the German bridgehead across the Psel. Each side's plans were disrupted when the attacks got in each other's way. Totenkopf's panzer grenadiers were sufficiently hard pressed that tanks repeatedly had to be brought forward in support. Heavy Soviet artillery fire forced SS riflemen to seek protection under their own tanks—a last resort for an experienced infantryman. Then the Shturmoviks joined in—unopposed. The initial objectives of Totenkopf's armor, however, remained: two hills high enough to command the surrounding terrain.

Occupying that ground were two Guards rifle divisions. The 52nd, moving into its own assault positions, was taken by surprise when the SS appeared to the front. But the Guardsmen were a match and more for Totenkopf's panzer grenadiers in both courage and tactical skill. According to a political commissar, their political spirit was also high. Positions changed hands so often that the exact course of events remains vague. The SS, with Stuka support as welcome as it was belated, made enough initial progress to generate hope for the long-delayed linkup with Leibstandarte. Then the armored battle group's leading elements encountered more and more tanks from Rotmistrov's 181st Brigade. German accounts describe spectacular explosions, huge fireballs—and enough losses of their own to instill caution by the time Hill 226.6 was firmly in German hands. The tanks and panzer grenadiers encountered a series of defensive positions, some prepared and others improvised, all bristling with antitank guns. Totenkopf's tankers made a point of crushing trenches and foxholes, burying defenders alive under their treads. But not until 3:00 P.M. did the Germans begin breaking Soviet defenses beyond immediate restoration.

Not all the comrades were valiant. Some of the 52nd's regiment and battalion commanders reported sick, straggled to the rear, or just ran away. When the panzers reached Hill 236.7, elements of the 95th Guards Rifle Division also broke and scattered. But around 4:00 P.M., 33rd Corps ordered maximum protective fire: every gun and rocket launcher that could come to bear was to target Totenkopf's tanks, even if they were in Russian positions. The barrage removed the impetus from an SS attack already eroded by a defense stubborn enough in some positions to be suicidal.

Small-scale advances nonetheless continued. As of 10:45 P.M., Totenkopf was comfortable reporting that its panzer group had reached the Karteschevka–Prokhorovka road—a day late and a large number of men and tanks short. On the map, only a few miles separated Totenkopf from the road leading into Voronezh Front's rear zone. On the ground, Leibstandarte's reconnaissance battalion had established fingertip contact but was itself too stretched out to be more than a trip wire with nothing behind it. In absolute terms, the day's casualties had not been high—a few more than three hundred. But the losses were cumulative. By now,

Totenkopf's panzer grenadier companies were down to fifty men or fewer, so tired after days of close combat that the standard stimulants were having an opposite effect. The panzer regiment had lost almost half its tanks fighting its way out of the Psel bridgehead. Forty-five had been destroyed or damaged, including all the Tigers. The crews of the fifty-six remaining Mark IIIs and IVs were exhausted. Fuel and ammunition were low. Although only a few of the disabled tanks were permanently lost, the maintenance crews were on the far side of the Psel. Either bringing their men and vehicles forward or moving the tanks backward meant challenging higher priorities of food, gasoline, and ammunition in one direction, or evacuation of the wounded in the other. The bridges remained vulnerable to air attack and to the still-existing possibility of a surprise enemy breakthrough.

Totenkopf's original cadre came from the concentration camps. Its first commander had spent time in a mental hospital—not a usual step to high command even in the Third Reich. Not surprisingly, the division's ethos was to get the job done at whatever cost; imagination was not a valued virtue. So when on the evening of July 12 Totenkopf expressed concern about the Soviet forces and the number of reinforcements that seemed to be arriving by the hour, when it began buttoning up in preparation for an even stronger attack on its still-small bridgehead, it was a clear signal that the SS Corps had been fought to a standstill—at least in the minds of those bearing the brunt of the day on the Soviet side and reading the decoded radio interceptions.

IV

Much—perhaps too much—has been made of the myths of Prokhorovka, which in good part still define the Battle of Kursk. The original, Soviet version has more than fifteen hundred tanks, half German and half Russian, grappling tread to tread in a three-mile-wide arena that at day's end was strewn with over four hundred disabled or burning panzers, seventy of them Tigers. It was a fair price for what even Rotmistrov admitted were roughly equivalent Red Army losses.

Back-of-the-envelope arithmetic based on long-available statistics tells another story. The SS divisions involved, Leibstandarte and Das Reich, had a combined total of around two hundred AFVs available on July 12. The reports for July 10–13 for Leibstandarte and Das Reich list three tanks as total losses. The commander of a Leibstandarte tank company noted only one for July 12, despite odds of ten to one. The best calculation of material losses has over three hundred Soviet armored vehicles destroyed. Most of their crews were blown up or incinerated. Rotmistrov's tank corps listed more than seven thousand casualties. More—thirty-six hundred—were dead or missing than wounded: an unusual statistic even on the Russian front. Replacing such losses was only half the generals' problem. Stalin made a point of requiring immediate phone reports on major operations. Neither Vasilevsky nor Rotmistrov would have dared to dissemble regarding the Fifth Guards Tank's losses. Like God, the Vozhd was not mocked. Stalin, famous for describing a million deaths as a statistic, called Rotmistrov to account, demanding to know what had happened to his "magnificent tank army." Loss of command, perhaps a court-martial, may have been threatened and was certainly implied. A one-on-one session with Stalin in November 1942 had left Rotmistrov shaking from the stress and with no desire for a repeat experience. His response, supported by Vasilevsky and Khrushchev, presented a highly embellished account that mollified the Vozhd and was memory-holed by a subsequent field performance solid enough to bring Rotmistrov assignment as deputy commander of Red Army armored and mechanized forces in November 1944. With face saved all around, Rotmistrov's 1972 memoirs repeated the embellished story, giving it canonical public status while the Soviet Union endured.

Stalin remained sufficiently disturbed to transfer Vasilevsky to the Southwestern Front and personally order Zhukov down from the Bryansk Front as a troubleshooter despite the imminent launch of a major offensive in that sector. Zhukov's presence was not required. For the revisionist accounts describing Fifth Guards Tank Army's Prokhorovka attack as a mistake, a defeat, a fiasco have obscured the situation on the other side of the line.

On the evening of July 12, Manstein "thanked and praised" the SS divisions for their "outstanding success and exemplary conduct." Reports of Soviet tank losses, and the firsthand accounts of what had happened to them, further reinforced Manstein's belief that chances were good the Reds had been bled white. Breith's corps was on the move. Manstein was so confident of further armored reinforcements, in the form of XXIV Panzer Corps, that at 9:10 P.M. on July 12, Hoth's headquarters ordered II SS Panzer Corps to make room in its rear areas for the newcomers.

The actual situation merited a more subdued mood. Hoth was edgy. Both of his leading corps had been hit hard across their fronts by Soviet tanks whose numbers far exceeded the original concern that had led Hoth to plan for the SS turn toward Prokhorovka in the first place. Nor had subsequent intelligence and reconnaissance reports prepared the Fourth Panzer Army's command for tank corps and tank armies that seemed to materialize from the very forests and steppes. For XLVIII Panzer Corps to continue its offensive, the threat to its left, or western, flank must be removed. Neither the panzer army nor the army group had any reserves to send. Knobelsdorff would have to cope. And his coping mechanisms were limited. Among them, the corps's three panzer divisions counted about a hundred tanks when the day's fighting ended. It was reasonable to expect that number to increase by morning once the repair shops set to work. At best, however, the increase would be in the low double figures.

The day's personnel losses were not in themselves crippling. The SS counted around 200 dead, and missing presumed dead. But the numbers of wounded were far higher. Leibstandarte alone reported 321 wounded, most from the tank and rifle companies. And—to repeat Citadel's universal threnody—nothing could replace the veterans, the platoon and company commanders, the tank commanders, and the noncommissioned officers who were increasingly sacrificing themselves by taking suicidal risks to compensate for declines in skill, energy, and morale in overtired, undermanned units.

Mentally, emotionally, and physically, the SS tankers and the panzer grenadiers, the riflemen and the gunners, had been tried to the limit by the nature and intensity of the fighting since July 5. A fair number of men still in the ranks were lightly wounded or mildly concussed, preferring to stay with their outfits than chance an overworked medical evacuation system. The combination of humid heat and torrential rain took its toll as well. Thirst to the point of dehydration was a special problem for the tankers. Food was if and when, with anything hot, even coffee, a welcome anomaly. The universal constant, however, was lack of sleep. When darkness ended the fighting, the digging and carrying began. When these tasks were concluded, finding a dry spot for anyone not a vehicle crewman was pure serendipity. Harassment from the air was a constant. Daylight began around 4:00 A.M. So did the next cycle of stress. A Tiger crewman described diarrhea so severe that he relieved himself outside the tank regardless of the situation—"nothing mattered to me any more." By Citadel's end, his weight had dropped below 110 pounds.

It belabors the obvious to note that things were no better on the Russian side of the line. But what in 1941 was an already toxic combination of ideological racism and cultural arrogance in the German military was two years later becoming a survival mechanism. Given the overwhelming Russian material advantage, soldierly superiority and warrior spirit were mutating into survival mechanisms. Anything—anything at all—that challenged those defense mechanisms was a harbinger of collective disaster and individual death sentences. For the Germans at Kursk's sharp end, denial was not the proverbial river in Egypt.

On the whole and on balance, by the evening of July 12 Prokhorovka nevertheless seemed a vindication for the Fourth Panzer Army's commander. He had foreseen since Citadel's beginning the threat provided by Rotmistrov's powerful tank army. He had planned for the contingency of its deployment almost exactly where it emerged. The two tank corps that were its offensive core had been crippled by the SS at a very acceptable price. Hoth considered breaking off the attack northwest and returning the SS Panzer Corps to its original axis of advance. Two panzer corps might be able to succeed in destroying the Russians in the Oboyan sector where one had not. But as closely and successfully as the SS appeared to be engaged, fighting it out in two sectors, even though they faced in two directions, was the better option. Fourth Panzer Army's initial orders to Hausser for July 13 were delivered by phone at 6:35 P.M.: Continue the flanking operation from the Psel bridgehead. When Manstein called later in the evening, Hoth stated that he considered Totenkopf's opposition to have been sufficiently weakened during the day's fighting that solid prospects existed for a breakthrough against weakened Soviet forces.

Around 8:45, Hoth's final orders arrived. They described Fourth Panzer Army's intention to hold ground in the center and expand its flanks—in other words, gain maneuvering room. The SS Panzer Corps was to begin concentrating on the Psel's northern bank, the bridgehead zone, and begin enveloping the armored formations around Prokhorovka with the aim of encircling them. Any offensives farther east and north would depend on the success of that encirclement.

Hausser's early situation reports reflected neither triumph nor ambition. Neither did the corps intelligence summary submitted at 9:00 P.M. It described major atttacks across the sector, their repulsion with heavy loss—and at least three hundred operational enemy tanks remaining. The SS Panzer Corps was facing three tank corps plus three or four rifle divisions. Additional reserves seemed on their way from neighboring fronts. Radio intercepts indicated Soviet intentions of resuming the offensive on July 12. In short, the intelligence chief declared, the enemy intended to stop the German offensive across the Psel at all necessary cost.

222 · ARMOR AND BLOOD

Hausser responded to Hoth by ordering Das Reich to consolidate its positions, organize a reserve, and hold its assault gun battalion ready to support the 176th Infantry Division on its right. Leibstandarte would develop a main line of defense on its right but hold its left-flank elements, ready to cooperate with Totenkopf when that division's armor appeared from the Psel bridgehead. Totenkopf was ordered to resume its attack early on July 13. The division's reconnaissance battalion would screen the left and reestablish contact with 11th Panzer Division. One of its panzer grenadier battalions supported by assault guns would clear the Psel area. The panzer group would drive down the Karteschevka road into the rear of 18th and 29th Tank Corps, with as much air support as the Luftwaffe could provide given the weather and the general situation. An accompanying warning to the SS antiaircraft units that the Hs 129 should not be mistaken for a Soviet twin-engine bomber suggests that Hausser was not optimistic in his expectations.

Compared with the missions assigned Leibstandarte and Das Reich, Totenkopf was somewhere back in the halcyon days of 1941 in terms of doing much with little. Hausser's orders split the division's fighting force, and the attention of its headquarters, in three different directions. The Germans had begun Citadel as a battle of armies and corps. Now the offensive's focal point in a critical sector was an attenuated tank regiment and a couple of worn-down battalions of panzer grenadiers.

Chapter VII

―――

CROSSOVERS

LIKE CITADEL ITSELF, the perspective of this account has shrunk steadily and inexorably: from a two-front, army-level nut-cracker, to the maneuvers of corps and divisions, to the level of regiments and battalions. It is now time to shift from battlefield microhistory to the influence of strategy and grand strategy on a gridlocked operation.

I

The direct aspect of that development began on July 11. It involved a still-overlooked operation that is arguably better evidence of the Red Army's progress than the so frequently cited battle to the south. When all is said and done, Kursk, seen from a Russian perspective, was a traditional Russian battle. Echoing Zorndorf and Kunersdorf, Friedland and Borodino, it was a test of endurance intended to enable the Red Army to begin setting the pace. Operation Kutuzov, the assault on the German-held salient that began on July 12, was something fundamentally different.

The German and the Russian ways of war approached operational art from opposite directions. The Prussian/German army had developed its version of operational art as a response to the constraining of campaign-level tactics in an age of mass armies. The Russians came to it through a developing understanding of how Russia's vast spaces could complement the metastasizing armies made possible by industrialization and bureaucratization. Large forces executing major attacks on a broad front, cavalry masses breaking deep into an enemy's rear, field armies coordinating offensives over hundreds of miles—all were integrated into theory and practice between the Crimean War and the Revolution of 1917. The Red Army had added the concepts of deep battle, and had evaluated the use of mechanized forces to exploit initial breakthroughs and the value of consecutive operations: coordinated attacks all across a front that might cover the Soviet Union from Murmansk to the Caucasus, mounted in such quick succession that the enemy had time neither to recover nor to shift reserves from place to place.

Predictably, each of these concepts had their turns in the barrel and their time in the sun. The political infighting of the 1920s and the purges of the 1930s further complicated internal, professional disputes on force configuration and strategic planning. Operation Barbarossa caught the Red Army in the midst of a complex reconfiguration with many contradictory aspects. What David Glantz aptly calls its rebirth was a two-year process. But one thing that remained consistent was Stavka's—and Stalin's—commitment to consecutive operations. From the winter 1941 counteroffensive to the Stalingrad campaign, the USSR's ultimate goal was on a grand strategic level: a series of timed, coordinated offensives that would turn Russia into the Wehrmacht's graveyard.

The problem lay in implementation on the operational level: communications, logistics, coordination. To date, the Soviets' greatest offensive successes had been achieved with assistance from the weather. Snow and cold, mud and rain, had been as important as the new generations of generals and weapons. At Kursk, the Red Army had demonstrated it could match the Germans in high summer when standing on the defensive. Now for the first time it would show that it could implement consecutive offensive operations when the days were long and the sun quickly dried storm-saturated ground.

Preparations for Kutuzov were overseen and coordinated by Zhukov, and by another Stavka representative: Marshal Nikolai Voronov, chief of artillery—the latter assignment an indication of the tactics to be employed. As at Kursk, the operation involved two fronts. On the left, General Vasily Sokolovsky deployed the Eleventh Guards and Fiftieth Armies in the front line, with 1st and 5th Tank Corps in support: more than 200,000 men and 750 AFVs. On the right-hand sector, General Markian Popov's Bryansk Front had, from left to right, the Sixty-first, Third, and Sixty-third Armies, supported by two tank and a rifle corps—170,000 men and 350 AFVs.

The plan was for Popov's Third and Sixty-third Armies to hit the front of the salient, with the Sixty-first Army conducting a supporting diversion on the right. Sokolovsky would go in where the northern bulge began, break through, and extend east toward Orel, coordinating as the situation developed first with the Bryansk Front and then with Rokossovsky's Southwestern Front, which on July 15—at least in theory—would attack north out of its positions around Kursk. Behind the Western Front, as a second-wave exploitation force, Stavka concentrated the Eleventh Army and Fourth Tank Army, the latter with another 650 armored vehicles.

The senior command teams were solid. The tables of organization were complete. The men were relatively rested. The sector had been quiet for months, and the front commanders applied *maskirovka* comprehensively to keep Army Group Center unaware of what was concentrating against it. At the operational and tactical levels, arguably the major German advantage was flexibility: the ability to respond to Soviet initiative by organizing ad hoc blocking forces that on paper and on the ground seemed fragile but that time and again had proven all too capable of delaying or derailing the Red Army's best-planned initiatives.

Timing was even more critical than surprise. Rokossovsky had to bleed and fix Model's Ninth Army at Kursk to a point where it could not redeploy in time to do any good. But if Kutuzov jumped off too late, even by a day or two, the Germans might be willing to write off Citadel, cut their losses, and be in a position to counter each Soviet attack in turn. The possibility that the planned Allied invasion of Sicily might draw German troops westward does not seem to have been factored into Stavka planning. Even if the British and Americans finally chose to act, the prospect of a few divisions probing the remote fringes of "Fortress Europe" hardly impressed a Red Army that saw itself as fighting a war of army groups on its own.

In developing Kutuzov, the Red Army confronted an obliging enemy. In terms of force structure, the Germans obliged by treating Army Group Center as an inactive sector. This was more a matter of practice than policy. It had begun gradually, and months earlier: it involved replacing full-strength divisions with those worn down elsewhere, then increasing their fronts and lowering their priorities for replacements. It also involved transferring air assets and heavy artillery and reducing mobile reserves. Secondary defensive lines and fallback positions were constrained because neither the men nor the material to develop them were available.

The situation was exacerbated by the distractions occasioned because Army Group Center's headquarters, itself physically isolated, was in late 1942 and early 1943 the locus of a serious plot to arrest and execute or kill Hitler when he visited in March 1943. Field Marshal Günther von Kluge was disgusted by Germany's behavior in Russia and believed declaring war on the United States had been a disastrous mistake. Although ultimately refusing to support the conspiracy, he was sufficiently aware of it and involved on its fringes that making the best of his army group's tactical situation took second place. Pressing the Führer for reinforcements scarcely appeared on the field marshal's horizon.

Two years earlier, under Heinz Guderian, the Second Panzer Army had led the drive on Moscow. On July 11, that army confronted Operation Kutuzov with fourteen ragged infantry divisions, most composed of inexperienced replacements and recovered wounded, a panzer grenadier division, and, ironically, a single panzer division. All told, a hundred thousand men and around three hundred AFVs, with only local reserves available. The order of battle showed pitilessly how the balance of forces had changed on the Eastern Front. Divisional sectors averaging twenty miles and more made a "continuous front" that was no more than a line on a map; reality was a series of strongpoints more or less connected by patrols. As an additional force multiplier, the Soviets achieved almost complete surprise. In evaluating the Red Army's *maskirovka*, it is appropriate to ask whether it was that good or German intelligence was that bad. By this time under Reinhard Gehlen, Foreign Armies East, as the German intelligence operation on the Eastern Front was called, was better at gathering information than at processing it, and not particularly good at either. Certainly Gehlen's service failed to discover the Soviet concentrations on Army Group Center's left and against the salient's nose. As late as mid-May, Army Group Center and the Second Panzer Army increased alertness in the front lines and carried out extensive mine and wire laying, but only as a commonsense effort to improve its readiness. Aerial reconnaissance was limited by a lack of planes. The attenuated front lines inhibited aggressive patrolling in favor of something like a "live and let live" approach. Russian partisans and reconnaissance units were less cooperative and more informative. By mid-July, both Western and Bryansk Fronts' assault formations had up-to-date information on what they faced where in the projected attack sector.

Kutuzov's exact launch time was determined by the successful German advance on Oboyan and Prokhorovka. Early on July 11,

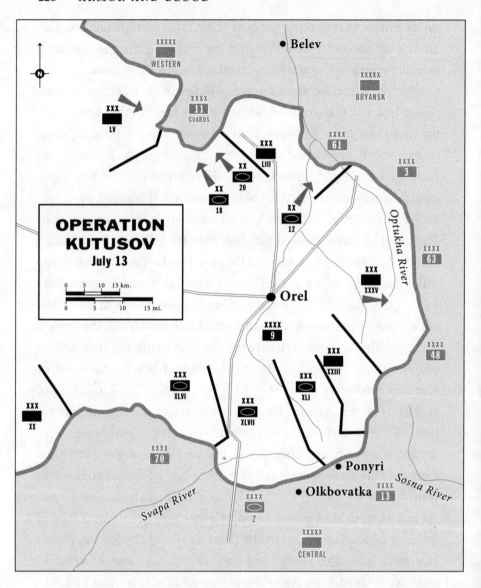

OPERATION
KUTUSOV
July 13

0 5 10 15 km.

0   5   10   15 mi.

patrols were replaced throughout the attack zone by battalion-strength strikes on German outposts. That night, Russian bombers attacked bases throughout the salient. Fresh rifle units took over the line at 3:00 A.M. At 3:30, the artillery barrage began: the heaviest and best coordinated in the history of the Eastern Front. Two and a half hours later, the first assault waves and their supporting armor took position and the initial bomber and Shturmovik strikes went in. At 6:05 A.M., the main attack began. On Second Panzer Army's left, six Guards rifle divisions hit the previously reconnoitered junction between two German divisions, breaking through easily enough that by the afternoon, the Eleventh Guards Army committed its second line to expand the breach and the two reserve tank corps were readying to exploit southward.

Airpower played a major role in the shifting tide of battle. Believing the Western Front's attack was only a diversion, the Luftwaffe kept most of its aircraft in Citadel's sector, to the east. Initially, the Red Air Force owned the sky on Eleventh Guards Army's front, and Shturmoviks hammered the *Landser* unmercifully. By the afternoon, when 1st Air Division began diverting sorties north, the Eleventh Guards' leading elements were safely under the cover of heavy forests. But Stuka *Gruppen* hit follow-up elements to such effect that small-scale counterattacks mounted by 5th Panzer Division were enough to delay 1st Tank Corps. The Eleventh Guards Army doubled down and committed 5th Tank Corps. Its T-34s were more than six miles into the German rear by nightfall, when 5th Panzer managed to slow their pace as well.

With the Stukas concentrating on the few roads passable by tanks, the army commander decided against a further blitz and ordered a set-piece attack for the next morning. Ivan Bagramyan had had his ups and downs since June 1941. His vigorous advocacy of the abortive Kharkov offensive of 1942 had led to his temporary eclipse. Restored to favor and combat command, he led the Sixteenth Army so successfully that it was renamed the Eleventh Guards Army and given a key role in Kutuzov. Bagramyan had learned from experience that against the Germans, a closed fist was preferable to a broken arm. But his decision to trade time for shock reflected as well the processing of German radio reports, specifically from 5th Panzer Division, that stated that immediate reinforcements were required to avert disaster in the northern sector. The only source of those reinforcements was Model's Ninth

Army. Give Fritz a few hours to sweat, decide, and begin moving tanks. Then, Bagramyan calculated, strike before they reached the field.

In the salient's nose, Bryansk Front found the going tougher. The Germans there belonged to XXXV Corps, under Major General Lothar Rendulic. Rendulic paid attention to intelligence reports and aerial reconnaissance that confirmed a concentration against the junction of his two frontline divisions. He redeployed his infantry, concentrated his artillery and antitank resources, and on July 12 made Bryansk Front pay yard by yard for its gains.

Fourteen Soviet rifle divisions on an eight-mile front seemed ample for the task of breaking through—especially when supported by heavy tanks. These were KV-2s: a prewar design, obsolescent by 1943 standards, underpowered and undergunned for their weight. But their fifty-plus tons included enough armor to make them invulnerable to any gun smaller than three inches. Instead, the KV-2s ran onto an unreconnoitered minefield. By day's end, sixty Soviet tanks were destroyed or disabled. The Germans had been forced out of their forward positions but were still holding the main line of resistance. They owed a good part of their success to the Luftwaffe. German fighter pilots were consistently successful in separating the Shturmoviks from their escorts, then scattering the escorts. Stukas and medium bombers struck repeatedly and almost unopposed, with VIII Air Corps diverting more and more aircraft from Oboyan and Prokhorovka to the Orel salient. The price was familiar: further overextension of already scarce ground-attack aircraft and already tired crews. One dive-bomber pilot flew six attacks in twelve hours. That kind of surge performance could not be continued indefinitely.

It was correspondingly obvious from Rendulic's headquarters to Kluge's that the sector could not hold without immediate reinforcements on the ground. That meant panzers. And the nearest concentration of panzers was in Ninth Army. In two sectors in a single day, Kutuzov confronted the Germans with a game-changing situation and very little reaction time. Model responded to the new crisis with a rapidity his principal English-language biographer, Steven Newton, calls suspicious. Newton argues that Model and Kluge were both expecting a major Soviet attack in the Orel salient, especially after the failure of Ninth Army's attacks in Citadel's northern sector. Rather than challenge Hitler and the OKH directly, they agreed, with a wink and a nudge, to commit to Citadel armor that would be more badly needed elsewhere in a matter of days. Certainly the divisions Kluge offered deployed slowly. Certainly, too, Model did not push the attack of XLVI Panzer Corps in the Ponyri sector on July 11. Late in the afternoon of July 12, Model flew to the headquarters of the Second Panzer Army and assumed its still-vacant command without relinquishing command of the Ninth. He and Kluge had previously agreed on this arrangement, which made Model directly responsible for the Orel salient and half the Kursk reentrant. It also gave him as free a hand to transfer forces over as wide an area as any senior officer of the Third Reich could expect.

Thus, on the morning of July 13, 4th Panzer Division's commander was ordered to cancel his planned attack, shift to defensive mode, and take over the positions of his neighbor, 20th Panzer Division, which was redeploying north. Recent communication between Model and Kluge had been carried out by unlogged telephone calls and confidential face-to-face meetings. Kluge, Newton asserts, could thus tell Hitler he had not ordered the abandonment of the offensive against Kursk. Model was just doing what he was recognized for doing: responding decisively to an unexpected development, living up to the reputation as a "defensive lion" he had earned in the crisis winter of 1941.

It all makes for another fascinating and unprovable story among the many spawned in the Third Reich. What the records show is that by the night of July 13–14, Ninth Army's 2nd Panzer Division and 8th Panzer from the high command's reserve were moving into Rendulic's sector. The 12th, 18th, and 20th Panzer were backing the sorely tried 5th Panzer against Bagramyan. That simple statement had a backstory. Emergency German redeployments on the Eastern Front might have become routine, but the process was anything but. The 12th Panzer had spent a week vainly seeking a breakthrough in the direction of Kursk. At 12:45 A.M. on July 12, it was ordered to the Orel sector. The order was a surprise, and its timing could not have been worse for all those trying to catch some sleep in the four hours before sunrise. But by 1:00 A.M., the 5th Panzer Grenadier Regiment and the reconnaissance battalion were on their way—eighty miles on dirt roads pounded to dust by weeks of military traffic. An hour later, the leading elements were taking position around Bolkhov, the previously anonymous spot on the map where army headquarters deemed their presence most necessary.

The tanks took longer. So did the rest of the division. The 12th Panzer moved ad hoc, by small improvised groups each going all out, each eroding as fuel tanks emptied, transmissions failed, and engines quit. To drive with windows and hatches open was to choke on the fine dust. To shut them was to broil in the heat. Vehicles were loaded and dispatched almost at random. Rest stops were equally random. A company commander took an unauthorized twenty-minute halt in Orel to check on the well-being of his aunt, a nurse in the local soldiers' home. Roads were blocked by collisions and breakdowns. Tanks, each hulled in its own dust cloud, lost contact with one another. Less than half of 12th Panzer's original starters made the finish line.

Model, predictably, lost his temper with the regiment's commanding officer—and just as predictably gave him command of one of the battle groups the field marshal and his staff officers were throwing in as fast as they could be organized. By this time, everyone in Second Panzer Army's rear areas was seeing Russians everywhere, and 12th Panzer was risking dismemberment as rear-echelon officers demanded tanks and men to restore their situations and calm their nerves.

The 5th Panzer Grenadier Regiment had been on the front line from the war's first days. Poland, France, Barbarossa, Leningrad: its men had seen as much combat as any in the Wehrmacht. So when its veterans spoke of Bolkhov as "the threshold to battle hell," it was more than retrospective melodrama. The regiment reached its assigned sector around midnight on July 12, and began advancing at 9:00 A.M. on July 13. At first all seemed routine: a steady advance against light opposition. Then suddenly "all hell broke loose." Bryansk Front had sent in the Sixty-first Army and its supporting 20th Tank Corps. The strength, intensity, and duration of the supporting fire exceeded anything the regiment's veterans had experienced: a "fire ball" that enveloped the entire front. Under the shelling, the panzer grenadiers' advance slowed, then stopped, then inched forward again. First the Stukas, then twenty or so of the division's tanks, sustained the momentum for a time, until dug-in tanks and camouflaged antitank guns drove the infantry first to ground, then to retreat.

As in the other sectors of the offensive, there was no breakthrough, but limiting the Soviet advance nevertheless took its toll on the defenders. Thus far, they had held—but for how long could another large-scale tactical stalemate be sustained? The reports and the recollections of the divisions that fought first in Ninth Army's attack on Kursk and then in the Orel salient convey an unwilling, almost unconscious sense that this time there was something different about the Russians. It was not only the intensity of their artillery fire. It was the relative sophistication. It was not only the depth of the defensive positions or the determination of their defenders. It was a more general sense that the Red Army's mass and will were being informed by improving tactical and operational sophistication—the levels of war making most likely to influence and frustrate German frontline formations directly, and in ways impossible to overlook.

II

If, to paraphrase Napoleon after Wagram, the animals were learning something, the consequences became clear in Kursk-Orel's wider context. For the first time in World War II, Nazi Germany found itself in a strategic, as well as a grand strategic, cleft stick. On July 10, the British and Americans invaded Sicily. Even before that, the Reich's position was shaky. The Mediterranean theater was geographically extensive and operationally complex. Success required combined arms: a synergy of land, sea, and air the Wehrmacht had been able to achieve only in the limited context of the Norwegian campaign. The destruction of the Axis forces in North Africa had confirmed Allied air and sea superiority in numbers and effectiveness. Even on land, growing partisan activity in the Balkans combined with the endless demands of the Russian theater had left German forces stretched to the limit.

Militarily and diplomatically, Italy was a broken reed. The government was requesting war material on an unprecedented scale, and it was obvious that the German war industry could not possibly fill the inventory. There was not much less question, in Berlin, at least, that Italy knew it. The all too logical conclusion was that Italy was looking for an excuse to withdraw from the war and from the alliance. Politically, Mussolini's Fascist regime was straining at its seams. By 1943, casualty lists were growing longer, Allied bombing raids heavier, German contempt more obvious. Political and economic elites who had collaborated with Mussolini for advantage were developing projects for throwing the Duce under the wheels of the war he had bestowed on Italy. And the Germans were making their own plans to disarm and occupy Italy at the first sign of disaffection—perhaps earlier if expedient or convenient.

It is difficult to imagine a less promising situation for a Wehrmacht whose way of war was based on flexibility and maneuver. An Allied invasion was a foregone conclusion. But where? Hitler favored the Balkans as a likely site. Sardinia and Corsica were natural bases for a future invasion of southern France. Sicily was in the same position relative to Italy. The eventual outcome was a more or less even distribution of available forces in the three most obviously threatening sectors. It absorbed the bulk of Germany's available mobile divisions, most of them formations destroyed in Tunisia and reconstituted with inexperienced men. The Italian troops deployed in forward sectors were seen as little more than filler. An already badly stretched German army would have to take over the Mediterranean theater's entire tactical/operational spectrum.

Objectively, Hitler's concept of "Fortress Europe" called for recalibration. Objectively, the Reich's policy and strategy in Russia merited reconsideration. But the short-term crisis demanded immediate attention. On July 12, Field Marshal Albert Kesselring, Germany's Oberbefehlshaber Süd (Commander in Chief South), weighed in. His reputation for optimism had earned him the nickname "Smiling Albert," and it was a corresponding shock when he reported the situation as hopeless. Almost as disconcerting was Kesselring's request for another mechanized division to help hold the ring in Sicily until an evacuation could be prepared and implemented. Hitler authorized sending the 29th Panzer Grenadiers—and that left the Reich's panzer cupboard close to empty.

What all this meant for the Eastern Front was that for the first time since Barbarossa, it would be at best competing for resources and probably expected as well to provide men and machines for the emerging southern European front. At all levels, the Reich's strategic can had been kicked down the road since December 1941. On July 10, 1943, it bounced into a rut.

Hitler's decision on Citadel may well have been made by the time he summoned Kluge and Manstein to his East Prussian headquarters for a conference on July 13. These were the senior officers most immediately involved in relevant major operations. Manstein later grumbled that Hitler should have come forward to the army group headquarters rather than remove their commanders at such a crucial time. One might say that his complaint was a trope for the way the Reich and the Wehrmacht fought and lost World War II: by microfocusing. Manstein was not encouraged when he arrived in the early morning and discovered that the conference would be held that evening. A swim in a nearby lake did little to cool him off. Nor did a chance meeting with Erwin Rommel, just recalled from Italy and being touted by the army's rumor mill as the new commander in chief of the Eastern Front. Rommel described himself as taking a sunlamp cure: soaking up sun and faith. Manstein had taken his swim in the nude and was at a corresponding disadvantage conversing with someone fully dressed. When he asked Rommel if they would meet later under more formal circumstances, the reply was, "Of course, under the sun-ray lamp."

The reference to Hitler, impossible to miss, was no substitute for clear thinking. Hitler's presentation was on the apocalyptic side. Sicily, he declared, was finished. The next step would be larger-scale Allied landings in Italy or the Balkans. Meeting such a threat would require entire fresh armies, and the only possible source of such forces was the Kursk salient. Citadel must be canceled. Kluge agreed. Already there were three deep penetrations on the Second Panzer Army's front. The Ninth Army had been stalemated even before the latest Russian attack, its losses already amounting to twenty thousand men. Its remaining resources were vitally necessary to keep not merely the Orel sector but Army Group Center's entire front from collapsing. Citadel was finished. It could be neither continued nor resumed even should the Orel crisis be successfully resolved.

Manstein was either more sanguine, more cautious, or more contrary, depending upon one's perspective. In Army Group South's sector, he asserted, the battle was at its decisive point. To break it off would be to throw victory away. The field marshal cited the victories of July 12, gained against not only the forward Russian elements, but their operational reserve as well. He described the destruction of eighteen hundred Soviet tanks in a week. If the Ninth Army could hold in place the Russians on its front, Manstein was confident that he could break them in his sector once he was authorized to send his reserve, XXIV Panzer Corps, to reinforce Army Detachment Kempf. The SS and XLVIII Panzer Corps would then face north, cross the Psel, and take Oboyan on a two-corps front, then hit the Russians from behind.

What began as pincers was therefore to become a hammer and anvil. What happened afterward would depend on developments in the Orel salient. If the Ninth Army had no chance of resuming its original attack against Kursk, Manstein asserted, his proposed operation would at least give his army group time and space to disengage: "an easy respite." But halfway measures, inflicting only partial damage, would mean a crisis in Army Group South's operational area even greater than anything befalling Army Group Center.

Hitler agreed that the Fourth Panzer Army should continue its efforts to destroy the Russians facing it south of the Psel, but undertake only limited offensives north of the river. Army Detachment Kempf would cover these attacks, operating to the east. Hitler also finally released XXIV Panzer Corps to Manstein—but not for use at the field marshal's discretion. Any successes against Soviet forces in Manstein's sector were to be utilized only for breaking contact and withdrawing forces for use elsewhere. Operation Citadel was to be concluded forthwith. Manstein's new mission was to prepare his army group to meet a major Russian offensive farther south, in the Donets Basin region, whose resources Hitler considered vital to the Reich's war effort.

That prospect was far down Manstein's list of concerns. The conference had reflected a significant shift in the opinions of the two field marshals involved. Kluge had been a leading advocate of Citadel in its planning stages. Now he made obvious his conviction that it was time to fold the hand. The Ninth Army had failed to break through, and the chances of its ever succeeding were receding almost by the hour. The Russian attack on the Orel salient, on the contrary, was succeeding all too well. Manstein, who had expressed consistent doubt when Kursk was on the drawing board, now spoke as though confident of victory, with XXIV Panzer Corps to be its instrument. Manstein had sought since the begin-

ning to convince Hitler that Citadel must be an all-or-nothing
proposition—no bets hedged, even if it meant putting the Donets
Basin at risk. Kluge finished the job by reiterating that there was
no way the Ninth Army could hope to resume the offensive at
Kursk. Rather than even holding its present positions, the Ninth
was going to have to retreat in the coming days.

This was a game Hitler had played like a champion since his
political career began: bring opposing viewpoints together, let the
proponents exhaust themselves, and hold back his decision until it
was a welcome end to gridlock—and until the unhappiness of one
party was balanced by the other party's sense of having won the
Führer to its point of view. The conference ended with Hitler repeating his decision to shut down Citadel, adding that he was acting as well in response to the escalating requirements of the
Mediterranean theater.

By then it was too late in the day for either commander to return to his army group. They joined Rommel in the headquarters
guesthouse for what Manstein's aide described as a convivial evening, with enough good wine to loosen tongues and invite confidences. Kluge was the first to retire. His evening benediction was
to declare that the end would be bad and to announce his willingness to serve under Manstein in an implied consequence of that
catastrophe. Rommel lingered, and as the wine continued to cir-
culate he also predicted "the whole house of cards" would collapse.
Manstein replied that Hitler would resign the supreme command
before that happened. Rommel said Hitler would never give up
command. When Manstein stood up, preparing to exit, Rommel
too declared himself "prepared to serve" under him.

Turning to the wider issues raised in the marshals' discussion,
the relationships of the participants to the German resistance are
outside the scope of this work. It is nevertheless appropriate to
contextualize this exchange with an increasing number of similar
ones taking place in 1943. In the seventeenth century a Scottish
general declared, "He either fears his fate too much / Or his des-
erts are small / That dares not put it to the touch / To win or lose it

all." The point is clear, though the Earl of Montrose was referring to love, not war. Suggestive as well is the fable of the mouse who fell into a barrel of whiskey and emerged licking his whiskers and slurring, "Bring on that [expletive deleted] cat!"

If Manstein was conscious of having been nominated to bell the beast, he gave no sign of it upon returning to his headquarters on July 13. Erich von Manstein is arguably the first great captain since Julius Caesar to define his own place in history through his writing. *Lost Victories* depicts the field marshal as the embodiment of the German way of war: master alike of strategic planning, operational command, and tactical innovation, a consummate professional who earned and kept the respect of his peers, the confidence of his subordinates, and the trust of his troops. Always thinking ahead, remarkably successful in most of his engagements, above all this Manstein is cool, rational. Not for him the emotions and enthusiasm of a Model or a Rommel. Not for him a visceral commitment to last stands and lost causes.

The real Manstein was proud to the point of hubris. He knew his worth to the last reichsmark. In the Crimea, at Stalingrad, and during the following months, he had developed in his own mind into the Reich's master of lost causes: creating triumph when others saw only disaster. He attended and departed Hitler's latest conference believing he could once again restore a desperate situation on his terms. His approach to evaluating the results of July 13 in the sector of Army Group South was a logical extension of that premise.

III

Across the battle line, Vatutin's headquarters had been doing the same thing, albeit with less righteous certainty. Vatutin was all too aware that the SS had held their ground, and even gained ground, against the best and the most Voronezh Front could throw at them. He was equally aware that the Germans were digging in along their front, but that did not preclude further offensive operations. Late in the afternoon of July 12 he and Vasilevsky, still at Rotmistrov's headquarters, compared notes. They agreed the best response was to maintain pressure. Vatutin's orders for July 13 tasked Voronezh Front with forestalling what he considered the most likely German initiatives. Specifically, the front's armies were to prevent reinforcements from reaching Prokhorovka, to destroy the Psel bridgehead and the forward units of III Panzer Corps, and to continue attacking in the Oboyan sector. How all this was to be done given the losses of July 11–12 was not specified. Typical was Vatutin's injunction to the commander of the Fifth Guards Army not to shift to the defensive prematurely. Measures were being taken to destroy the enemy; until they should be implemented, Fifth Guards's pressure in its sector would yield a great deal. Therefore, act with more energy—and by implication, trust the system!

Vatutin also informed Stalin that no fewer than eleven German tank divisions had been concentrated in his sector. Despite that massive opposition, Voronezh Front had held its ground and inflicted heavy casualties. Encircling and destroying what remained would constitute a major defeat for the Hitlerites. That, however, would require a greater superiority of force than the front possessed. Vatutin requested reinforcements: a tank and a mechanized corps, plus a full corps of Shturmoviks. The request was countersigned by Nikita Khrushchev.

By all accounts, Stalin was not pleased. Stavka had been pouring resources into Voronezh Front since Citadel began. Rokossovsky had successfully made do with bits and pieces. The Vozhd responded by sending Zhukov by air and Vasilevsky by car to Vatutin's headquarters. Konev, whose Steppe Front would be first in line to provide the requested support, was also present at the resulting council of war in the early morning of July 13. That was an unusual concentration of alpha personalities and high-profile talent out of Stalin's direct reach, even at this stage of the war. The stated purpose of the meeting was to coordinate Voronezh and Steppe Fronts' roles in future offensive operations. Unstated but implied was a parallel task: evaluating, and if necessary sorting out, the immediate situation. The result was a stated intention to mount a counteroffensive on the heels of the retreating enemy. The necessity was first to compel that retreat. Zhukov ordered energetic counterattacks to keep the Germans off balance. Neither he nor Vatutin, however, specified how the army and corps commanders were to implement the process. Unstated but clear enough was the general recognition that Voronezh Front, and the Fifth Guards Tank Army in particular, would need some time, at least a day or so, to regroup and refit.

That last was the highest priority for Rotmistrov's tankers. Removing disabled tanks was handicapped by the lack of specialized recovery vehicles. Generally, tanks were used for this work, to the detriment of their own engines and transmissions. Across the front, the Germans were able to recover or demolish most of the tanks that lay between the lines. As for maintenance, welding equipment and machine tools were in short supply, making it difficult to repair even simple parts. There were no breakdown teams in forward units, so mechanics had to be taken from repair jobs to supervise stripping parts from disabled vehicles. Major repairs, to engines, guns, turrets, were carried out at tank corps level. These depots were manned by trained mechanics, many of them uniformed civilians from tank factories. However, they were inexperienced in working under field conditions. Overnight, for example, the 29th Tank Corps was able to repair only four of its fifty-five knocked-out tanks and assault guns by the next morning. Nor could replacements be brought forward quickly from depots that lay as far as two hundred miles to the rear.

Militarily, the night of July 12–13 was quiet in the SS sector. Violent thunderstorms provided most of the flash and noise; small and cautious patrols did most of the shooting. Cooks and first sergeants did what they could to provide hot food and coffee to men falling asleep on their feet. Officially and unofficially, alcohol was becoming standard issue to combat what today would be diagnosed as ongoing traumatic stress.

That point has been made so often, in this account and in most other discussions of the Eastern Front, that it risks validating the Wehrmacht meme that German soldiers were at a more refined stage of mental and emotional development than the brutish Slavs they confronted. To a significant degree, Russian mythology contributes to the trope by stressing the Soviet soldier's toughness: his unique ability to endure and overcome any conditions he faced.

Alleged racial/cultural differences were far less relevant than the fact that the consequences of combat exhaustion were more salient for the Germans than the Russians. Russian doctrine was based on control from above. At the sharp end, what was ultimately important was the will to obey. The Germans, on the other hand, were forced to compensate for numerical and material inferiority by intangibles: flexibility, initiative, situational awareness. Blunted by stress and fatigue, they could not readily compensate. A company commander in Leibstandarte's reconnaissance battalion presented his mental state in a diary entry written several days later: "I couldn't deal with it. It was too much for me. The mental pressure threatened to tear me apart. . . . I don't want to list all the dead here. . . . How old our men have become."

Wehrmacht mythology has Hitler living in a world of shadows and abstractions. How many corps, army, and army group commanders as well were by the time of Citadel acting on their own illusions about the men they kept ordering forward? How many plans were based on the half-conscious subtext that "the boys up front" could make anything work? These are by no means rhetorical questions. The Soviets facing Manstein had been badly shaken by the fighting on July 11–12. But any chance of exploiting their condition depended on the kind of smoothly working German response that would not only regain the initiative, but shorten reaction times and exacerbate stress points across the battle line. Was that still possible?

The answer began emerging on Totenkopf's front. During the night, Rotmistrov had reinforced the Psel sector with two brigades of his 5th Guards Mechanized Corps and the 6th Guards Airborne Division, fresh from reserve. There was no time for the usual camouflage, and German reconnaissance aircraft duly noted and reported the newcomers' presence and positions. Then at 9:30 A.M., Totenkopf informed Hausser that the panzer group still could not be resupplied because of the road conditions. This neat example of delaying bad news and hoping for a miracle was especially significant because Totenkopf's tanks had been under increasingly heavy attack since dawn. Should the Russians break through, the Psel bridgehead was a matter of yards rather than miles away. Division ordered a retreat—back to Hill 226.6, still a charnel house from the previous day's fighting. Its garrison of panzer grenadiers was promptly hit by Rotmistrov's two fresh tank brigades.

The SS fought as hard to hold the hill as they had to capture it, but the Russians kept coming. By 11:15 A.M., the tough Guardsmen had forced the defenders down the reverse slope. With heavy rainstorms blinding artillery observers and grounding Stukas, the way to the Psel bridges seemed open. But minutes later—three minutes by Russian reports—the armor appeared. One of Totenkopf's tank battalions had managed to take on enough ammunition to reenter the fight. Its guns did just enough damage to halt a Soviet thrust that itself had been bled white on Hill 226.6. A counterattack caught the Soviets before they could consolidate, splitting the infantry from their supporting tanks. By 12:30 P.M., Hill 226.6 was back in German hands. By 3:00 P.M., the Russians had been pushed back almost to their original start lines. Some idea of the day's shock and frustration is indicated by a Soviet tank corps report describing an attack by no fewer than thirty-three Tigers—more than the whole army group could field—and listing as trophies of the day one machine gun and a lone machine pistol.

Events on Totenkopf's left took a similar, no less dramatic course. In that sector, a Russian battle group overran a panzer grenadier battalion and made for the bridges. Totenkopf threw in its half-track panzer grenadier battalion as a tank substitute. Its desperate charge scattered the Soviet infantry and confused the tanks, relieved the overrun battalion, then itself foundered against hastily emplaced antitank guns. A second Russian wave, supported by Shturmoviks and another of the sophisticated barrages the Red Army artillery was now capable of unleashing on small scales, ran into a battery of hull-down assault guns that held long enough for Totenkopf's tank battalion and an antitank battery to add their high-velocity guns to the defense. The antitank gunners, manning a dozen open-topped, lightly armored, highly vulnerable vehicles, were credited with thirty-eight T-34s by the end of the day.

At 6:45 P.M., Totenkopf informed SS Panzer Corps headquarters that the Russian breakthroughs had been halted, the division was reoccupying its former positions, and the Luftwaffe was still nowhere to be seen. The rain and overcast skies had not kept the Shturmoviks from incessant attacks on the bridges and the supply columns struggling to cross them, but their successes were harassing rather than decisive. As the skies cleared in the early evening, German fighters reemerged. Tactically, it had been a good day for Totenkopf. The bridgehead was intact. Over sixty Russian tanks littered the killing grounds. Hill 226.6 was in SS hands. The Russians had been sufficiently hurt that a tank brigade and an assault gun regiment were entirely withdrawn.

Operationally, however, July 13 in the Psel sector was somewhere between a disaster and a catastrophe. SS Panzer Corps's movements had been predicated on Totenkopf's breakout from the bridgehead. Instead, the division had been fought to a near standstill just to stay where it was. The last of its Tigers had been bogged down or disabled. And lest the day's events be considered an aberration, an intercepted Soviet dispatch declared that the bridgehead must be taken at all costs. Based on recent experience, that order was best interpreted literally. During the night, Russian ground patrols and their harassing aircraft seemed everywhere.

Mortar, artillery, and rocket fire deluged forward positions and rear echelons. Just before midnight, corps headquarters confirmed the obvious and ordered Totenkopf to hold its positions against all attacks. Any renewed German offensive would have to be sparked by someone else, somewhere else.

That someone else would not be Leibstandarte. Its positions came under air and artillery attack at daylight. An attempt by the reconnaissance battalion to make contact with Totenkopf was stopped almost immediately. Then the Soviet attacks began. Rotmistrov had ordered a start time of 8:00 A.M. His forward units, still stunned from the day before, were slow off the mark and poorly coordinated; they made no headway. At 11:40 A.M., Rotmistrov informed Vatutin that the SS seemed to be preparing a major attack for the next day and strongly hinted that he wished to suspend operations and prepare an appropriate reception. Vatutin called the Fifth Guards Tank Army's offensive essential and ordered it continued, promising air support.

Rotmistrov saluted electronically, then spent the rest of the day shadowboxing. So did Hausser. His initial attack orders for Das Reich were frustrated internally by "administrative delays": a euphemism for everybody still shaking off the previous forty-eight hours. After token gains of ground, Das Reich halted for the day. Das Reich's commander declared himself unwilling to order a full-scale attack without appropriate preparation and air support—a fairly emphatic gesture of defiance, especially in the Waffen SS. Fourth Panzer Army's daily report described II SS Panzer Corps as repelling heavy, tank-supported infantry attacks. It mentioned Totenkopf's withdrawals. It also, however, described ground reconnaissance reports of a Soviet retreat from what seemed an exploitable pocket developing between Breith's advancing corps and Das Reich. Though unverified by the Luftwaffe, this at least suggested an opportunity. *If* Das Reich made one more effort, and *if* Nehring's panzer corps came up behind them, and *if* Breith did his part closing the gap with Army Detachment

Kempf . . . well, who knew? One last throw of the dice had decided many a battle for Prussia and Germany, ever since Fehrbellin in 1675.

Manstein too was looking to Army Group South's flanks. The XLVIII Panzer Corps, variously and legitimately described as dazed and mechanical, had spent July 13 regrouping, patrolling north, and shoring up its trailing left flank. On the right, the forward elements of III Panzer Corps were less than nine miles from Prokhorovka on the night of July 12. The 7th Panzer Division was stalemated and pinned. The 6th Panzer was down to fourteen tanks at day's end. But the corps as a whole mustered sixty-two, including half a dozen Tigers. With 7th Panzer covering the flank, 6th and 19th Panzer Divisions went forward on the morning of July 13, gaining ground slowly in the teeth of a well-coordinated "shield and sword" defense: frontline infantry fighting—almost literally—to the last man, supported by armored counterstrikes that repeatedly set the Germans back on their heels. The defenders' tactics differed from the Red Army's norm for Citadel in that there had not been time to prepare more than rudimentary defensive positions. Instead the intention was to stop the Germans by inflicting unsupportable losses in the open. The tankers and riflemen of Trufanov's task force did not fall short by much. When the fighting died down, III Panzer Corps was nowhere near in any of its divisional sectors to a junction with the SS around Prokhorovka.

From Manstein's perspective on his return from Rastenburg, none of these developments stopped him from translating the general intention he had developed over the few previous days into a revised plan. Although July 13 might seem a lost day, if Army Group South had been able to catch its breath, time remained—and time was vital. The XLVIII Panzer Corps and the SS would still carry the main burden, but in a new direction: driving north to Oboyan, then shifting west, and crushing the Russians along the Psel. But for that attack to succeed, a continuous, solid front to the east/northeast was necessary. In other words, III Panzer Corps must not merely link up with the SS, but take over its southern positions, allowing Das Reich in particular to add muscle to the drive on Oboyan. And that would require finishing the Russians south of Prokhorovka, specifically the Sixty-ninth Army and the tank units that had just reinforced it.

The plan was christened Operation Roland: perhaps a semi-conscious reference to the Carolingian paladin mythologized for a forlorn-hope operation in the Pass of Roncevaux. The XLVIII Panzer Corps pulled itself together on the night of July 13 for one more effort. Totenkopf's reconnaissance battalion had established tenuous contact with 11th Panzer Division but had been strained to its limits on July 13 holding its own positions. The chances of meaningful support from the SS were correspondingly nil. As was increasingly the case, a disproportionate hope and a dispropor-tionate burden were placed on an elite formation. Once again it was Grossdeutschland's turn to carry the flag—and the can.

The division's orders for July 14 were to shift its axis left and cooperate with 3rd Panzer Division in enveloping Oboyan from the west. This turned out to be an old story on a different page. Grossdeutschland, which had reassembled most of its elements during July 13, attacked at 4:00 A.M. into a wasteland of shattered trees, burning underbrush, and random minefields—and into the teeth of Fifth Guards Tank Corps and 10th Tank Corps. Gross-deutschland's intention was for its armored battle group to skirt the western edge of the devastated forest and continue north. A second battle group, built around the division's assault gun bat-talion, would flank the forest from the opposite direction. As soon as Grossdeutschland's leading elements crossed their start lines, however, they came under heavy fire from Soviet tanks, then faced an assault across ground supposed to be controlled by 3rd Panzer. That division, ordered and expected to go forward on Gross-deutschland's left, began its attack at 7:00 A.M., encountered a minefield, and lost two tanks. Unsupported, the panzer grenadiers were unable to crack the Russian defenses. "Requested" by Gross-deutschland to shape up and close up, 3rd Panzer's headquarters called for air support. The response was that the Stukas were otherwise engaged.

A Soviet counterattack drove the 3rd's riflemen back as the tanks evaded the minefield, only to be immobilized in a mudflat. The 3rd Panzer shouldered forward against increasingly heavy opposition. The Luftwaffe now went all out to help. Heinkel 111s of VIII Air Corps were diverted from their normal targets in the rear echelons to support the panzers directly and did especially accurate work bombing just ahead of 3rd Panzer's attack. Half a dozen of the increasingly scarce Stukas were shot down by Soviet fighters and light flak. Not until late afternoon, however, did the division's 3rd Panzer Grenadier Regiment close in on the Russian positions around Hill 258.5. And not until 6:30 P.M. did it capture the objective and finally clear the way for Grossdeutschland.

That division's advance had been thrown on its heels around 11:00 A.M. by a surprise tank-infantry attack with devastating rocket and artillery support. A battalion of the 332nd Infantry Division, ordered forward to take over ground presumably occupied by Grossdeutschland's panzers, found empty space. Corps headquarters had lost contact with Grossdeutschland's headquarters. It was 5:30 P.M. before the advance resumed, helped as much by 3rd Panzer's initiative as from any fresh internal momentum. The forward elements immediately came under fire from local Russian reserves hastily redeployed. Gains averaged a little over a mile—a long way from the morning's expectations. The XLVIII Panzer Corps had failed. The 3rd Panzer was a spent force. Grossdeutschland was almost as badly worn. Only a handful of Panthers remained operational or repairable. Aircrew losses included two *Gruppe* commanders, one with seventy-eight fighter victories and the other with seventy Stuka sorties.

The First Tank Army was staggering but had done its job. On July 13, Vatutin visited Katukov's headquarters and extended congratulations all around. The army, he declared, deserved Guards status for its work since July 5. In fact, he had already submitted the recommendation. That was the good news. The bad news was that while First Tank might hope for reinforcements, Stavka had decided: Not one man, not one vehicle. That meant repairing damaged tanks and returning lightly wounded to their units, both as quickly as possible. Then Vatutin concluded with the other good news: First Tank Army was to be withdrawn into reserve and begin preparing for its future role in the great summer offensive.

At 10:00 A.M. on July 16, Vatutin ordered Voronezh Front to "go over to the stubborn defense of its current lines." That sentence reflects the difference ten days had made in the tactical, operational, and strategic situations on the Eastern Front. The Russians were able to replace their battle-worn formations and able to hold ground as opposed to attacking across it. And one of Manstein's projected windows of opportunity was closed.

IV

Vatutin and Rotmistrov were no less anxious about the situation on their left flank than Manstein and Kempf were hopeful. The advance of III Panzer Corps had been on a northeast axis that left the Sixty-ninth Army and its reinforcements caught in a narrow salient between Breith's panzers and Das Reich, with limited maneuver room and a chance of being cut off at the salient's base. Vatutin's initial orders for July 14 were for the Sixty-ninth and Fifth Guards Tank Armies to destroy the Germans. Stavka-pleasing rhetoric out of the way, the real mission was to above all prevent a breakthrough on either flank of the newly created salient. Voronezh Front backed its words by reinforcing the Sixty-ninth Army with a number of artillery, antitank, and Katyusha units. But its rhetoric of attack was challenged by reports from the front line. The 81st Guards Rifle Division was typical. It described its men as physically exhausted, without food and water for as long as three days, a fifth of them unarmed. Another rifle division reported such a shortage of horses that it had been forced to abandon eight guns and a quarter of its artillery ammunition.

Such statements read like excuses to political officers. Efforts to restore discipline included, again, creating blocking detachments of "thoroughly checked" officers and men, with the assignment of "detaining" everyone moving to the rear without authorization and sending them back. By July 17, almost seven thousand shirkers had been accounted for. Enough men remained in the ranks, however, to hold ground tenaciously and give ground stubbornly on Breith's sector throughout July 14.

Army Detachment Kempf had been informed that it could expect help from SS Wiking Division—eventually. Until then, Breith was on his own. The III Panzer Corps attacked north-northwest in the early morning of July 14 with 6th and 7th Panzer Divisions, and 19th Panzer to secure the left, or western, flank. Linking up with the SS was part of the corps's objective, but the wider intention, as outlined in Operation Roland, was to create and seal a pocket, disrupting or trapping the Soviet forces south of Prokhorovka, then to relieve the SS so they could cooperate with XLVIII Panzer Corps in attacking toward Oboyan. The 6th Panzer Division, on the corps's right, would block any Soviet advance around Alexandrovka, capture the town, then continue attacking northwest with an armor-heavy battle group. Depending on the circumstances, 7th Panzer, in the center, was to either support the 6th or drive for Prokhorovka independently while 6th Panzer covered its right. The 19th Panzer, badly worn from the previous days' fighting, would hold the bridgehead and follow up any Russian retreat northward.

A clear indication of Breith's intended *Schwerpunkt* was his order that all of the corps's effective Tigers would be assigned to 6th Panzer. That amounted to a single company from 503rd Panzer Battalion: eight Tigers, repeatedly battered, repeatedly repaired, shedding parts, but able to lead out one more time. The ubiquitous pioneers cleared minefields. The panzer grenadiers discovered paths the Russians had overlooked. And what remained of the division's organic tanks, a composite battalion of twenty or so Mark IIIs and IVs, waited for a chance to break out.

That opportunity was long in coming. Alexandrovka's forward positions fell to the tanks' cannon and machine guns as the Tigers crushed riflemen under their treads and T-34s exploded. But then the tank-to-tank fighting grew closer and the work grew harder. One Russian report described a German tank somehow opening radio contact across the battle line to lure the T-34 that responded into an ambush. As pioneers and riflemen improvised paths across the second defensive line's antitank ditch, the panzers engaged the guns covering it. A Russian gunner described the consequences of a missed shot: "We . . . saw the turret traverse toward us. The next thing I remember was lying on my back—I went back to find . . . just scraps of uniform and a gory mess."

It was evening before Breith's headquarters received definitive word of Alexandrovka's capture. By then, losses in men and tanks had been so heavy that the best that could be done was to set up a defensive perimeter and regroup. Across its sector, 6th Panzer had gained ground and taken a locally impressive toll of tanks, antitank guns, and artillery pieces. But 6th Panzer was still a long way from Prokhorovka—or indeed any other operationally useful objective. The 19th Panzer, reinforced by a panzer grenadier battalion from the 6th and a battalion of 88s, had also had a good day checking Russian infantry assaults. But these successes as well were on the wrong side of Operation Roland's ambitions and intentions.

In its men's perspective, III Panzer Corps might be advancing slowly, almost yard by yard and certainly a far cry from a blitz. The corps and division commanders facing it, however, had been fighting Germans long enough to be well aware of the tactical risks of one of their rapierlike breakthroughs. Vasilevsky's report to Stalin that the Fifth Guards Tank Army's units in the sector were "behaving splendidly" was less complimentary about the riflemen. Early on July 15, Vatutin responded to what seemed a destabilizing situation by making Rotmistrov and the Sixty-ninth Army's commander personally responsible (Red Army code for execution as a possible price of failure) for counterattacking immediately. The order came a day too late. Sixty-ninth Army had already authorized withdrawal to a new defensive line. Trufanov, screening the operation by well-timed, small-scale counterattacks, managed one of the Red Army's smoother retrograde movements. By dawn of July 15, most of the threatened troops had reached their own lines.

Whether the Russians were ever actually surrounded remains debatable. But Zhukov too had given orders: In the context of the major offensive under way in the Orel sector and the one planned for the Donets and Mius Rivers in the south, local withdrawal in the face of encirclement was acceptable. Arguably of more consequence, and certainly suggestive in any case, was the failure of III Panzer Corps to comprehend that the Russians in front of them were retreating rather than shifting to new entrenchments and new ambush sites, as had been the case since Citadel began.

Das Reich's panzer grenadiers had attacked at 4:00 A.M. on July 14, aiming first for the Pravorot road and then toward Prokhorovka and a junction with III Panzer Corps. Instead, they ran into elements of Trufanov's battle group from Fifth Guards Tank Army. For the rest of the day, Germans and Russians slugged it out at gun-barrel range and from house to house. Stukas of VIII Air Corps again were crucial in preparing the grenadiers' way to, through, and beyond the strongly defended village of Belenikhino. During the night, Das Reich's workshops had restored the panzer regiment to about a hundred tanks. But even this relatively impressive armored force was stopped by massed antitank guns when it attempted a breakout. Only with the close support of their own artillery and rocket launchers, and at a much more measured pace, did the tanks reach the next village, Ivanovka. By then it was 5:15 P.M. Heavy clouds to the east had prefigured rain most of the afternoon, and the skies opened around 7:00 P.M. It was already growing dark. The torrential rain eroded visibility to the vanishing point. Roads and fields—it was increasingly difficult to perceive much difference—turned to thick mud that bogged tanks, half-tracks, and wheeled vehicles alike. The advance skidded to a halt well short of the Pravorot road and even farther from Breith's divisions.

The closest III Panzer Corps came to a linkup with the SS on July 14 was when elements of the 7th Panzer Division, in a reprise of the glory days of the French campaign in 1940, reached a dot on the map called Malo Jablonovo before they too bogged down for the night. Around 6:00 A.M. on July 15, they established radio contact with Das Reich. Das Reich's efforts to strengthen the connection were frustrated by mud so formidable that around noon the division's artillery reported that moving its guns forward was impossible. Fuel and ammunition supplies were mired even farther back. Luftwaffe assets had been shifted north to the Orel sector and diverted to strike Soviet forces building up a hundred miles eastward, across the Donets. During the day, Das Reich and 7th Panzer reinforced their contact. But the pocket that junction might once have sealed was now empty of anything but abandoned entrenchments, tanks, and guns, plus a few stragglers.

The fragile, now pointless linkup bothered Manstein less than it might—and probably should—have. In the course of the day, the commander of Army Group South had further refined and reconceptualized his proposed battle. Totenkopf's stand in the Psel bridgehead, plus the successful, albeit limited, advances of III Panzer Corps and Das Reich, combined to support Manstein's growing belief that the massive counterattack that occasioned the initial eastward turn of the SS panzers had been defeated. That provided an opportunity, he later explained to Hoth, to strike and destroy the Soviet forces south and west of the Psel. Totenkopf would hold the bridgehead, no longer as a springboard for an advance farther eastward, but as a flank guard and pivot point. The combined strength of the Fourth Panzer Army and Detachment Kempf would roll the Soviets up from east to west across the front of XLVIII Panzer Corps and drive them into the rear areas of the Russians facing LII Corps on the army group's far left. The XXIV Panzer Corps, which had begun assembling in the region of Kharkov on July 12, could be committed with two days' notice. At the

254 · ARMOR AND BLOOD

moment, its constantly fluctuating order of battle included only two divisions. But Wiking and 23rd Panzer had more than a hundred AFVs between them and ought to be able to provide any additional muscle needed to exploit the resulting confusion.

On the evening of July 15, Manstein met with Hoth and Kempf at Kempf's headquarters. He informed them of the orders he had received from Hitler and of his plans for implementing their intention, if not their letter. Translated into movement orders, essentially Das Reich was to take over 11th Panzer's northern-facing sector, while Leibstandarte redeployed behind XLVIII Panzer Corps's line as a tactical reserve. The 7th Panzer would move from III Panzer Corps to Knobelsdorff's corps as further reinforcement of the projected attack. Totenkopf would hold its position; Army Detachment Kempf, temporarily under Hoth's command, would guide north on Totenkopf. And 11th Panzer Division would replace Leibstandarte on the eastern flank, essentially as a reserve for that sector.

Two plausibilities lay behind Manstein's immediate plan. The "optimistic" one is the judgment that the Russian reserves were sufficiently exhausted that one more hard blow might be just enough to start the Russians down defeat's slippery slope. The "pessimistic" interpretation suggests Manstein was sufficiently worried about the situation on Model's front, and sufficiently aware of the powerful Soviet forces massing to the east and southeast, that he perceived the necessity of creating space and force for the mobile, flexible defense that was his great talent as a commander. That in turn was best achieved by giving the Russians as bloody a nose as possible in the shortest possible time, then breaking contact and withdrawing southwest.

The credibility of both, however, is called into question by the orders for redeployment presented above. The terrain across which Manstein's divisions were expected to move, difficult to begin with, had been turned to an obstacle course by shell fire, tank treads, aerial bombs, and rain. The near exhaustion of the combat formations repeatedly highlighted above was replicated in the service echelons—and not least in the higher headquarters. Nothing in the behavior of Rotmistrov and Vatutin suggests either would have been indifferent to such large-scale troop shuffling. Finally, the Russian reserves in the Kursk sector, the tactical skill displayed by the Russian commanders, and the fighting power demonstrated by the Russian troops meant XXIV Panzer Corps was unlikely to revitalize Manstein's offensive—even had Hitler allowed its commitment.

As much to the point, Voronezh Front's command was already leaning forward, thinking ahead to its role in Stavka's planned offensive on the Belgorod–Kharkov axis. Operation Rumyantsev, named for a heroic commander in the eighteenth-century Russo-Turkish wars, was aimed at destroying not only the Fourth Panzer Army but the other main components of Manstein's army group, the Sixth Army and First Panzer Army. Its final geographic objective was the Black Sea, more than 120 miles away. Even in the initial stages, an operation of that scope was unlikely to encourage a narrow focus.

A final indication of the limited prospects for Manstein's projected revision of Citadel came in the sector of XLVIII Panzer Corps. At 5:30 A.M. on July 15, 3rd Panzer Division went forward once more into the Tolstoye Forest. Rain, mud, and caution held it back as the Russians in its path slowly withdrew. Grossdeutschland in the center had a similar initial experience, then encountered resistance sufficient to hold it in place for most of the afternoon. The 11th Panzer was barely able to maintain its positions in the face of repeated Russian attacks. By day's end, the Russians had been forced back to more or less their original start lines of July 12. But all three of Knobelsdorff's divisions were worn dangerously thin by ten days of constant head-down combat. Russian fighting power, on the other hand, seemed undiminished. The mood at Knobelsdorff's headquarters was somber, with overt recriminations showing up even in official documents. Far from further attack in any direction, the corps would be doing well to stay where it was.

Manstein's variant shifted definitively to Citadel's file of might-have-beens on July 16. That day, Leibstandarte and Das Reich were ordered to establish "main battle lines" where they stood—in other words, shift to the defensive. This was in the context of Manstein's plans for Operation Roland, and the corps staff was implementing detailed preparations for the next set of troop movements when word came through by teletype from Army Group South: "The Führer has ordered the immediate withdrawal of the SS Panzer Corps and its earliest possible concentration west of Belgorod." At 7:30 P.M., the Fourth Panzer Army ordered the destruction of all war material remaining on the battlefield.

Citadel's last avatar was off the table. But Hitler's decision to revoke his earlier authorization to Manstein to continue attacking was anything but spontaneous. Stalin and Stavka were anxious to begin the projected southern offensive as soon as possible. Zhukov did not exactly counsel caution, but he did insist both Voronezh and Steppe Fronts would require a few days of recovery and regrouping before they could play their assigned parts. That meant taking extra pains to attract German attention elsewhere. On July 17, the Southwestern Front struck the First Panzer Army and the Southern Front attacked the Sixth Army along the Mius River. Neither were feint attacks or diversions, in the sense the Germans understood the term. These were full-scale operations, spearheaded by Guards rifle armies and tank and mechanized corps, backed by air, armor, and artillery assets their overextended opponents could not come near countering.

Hitler and the Army High Command, without fully comprehending the grand Soviet plan of a series of sequential offensives across the entire Eastern Front—another spectacular failure of German intelligence—finally recognized the obvious. The Orel offensive was not a local, one-off enterprise to disrupt Citadel. No structure and no plan could survive a continuous series of the kinds of emergencies the Red Army was now capable of creating. Citadel had been an attempt to regain the initiative. Now not only was Citadel *im Eimer* ("in the bucket"), but the whole southern

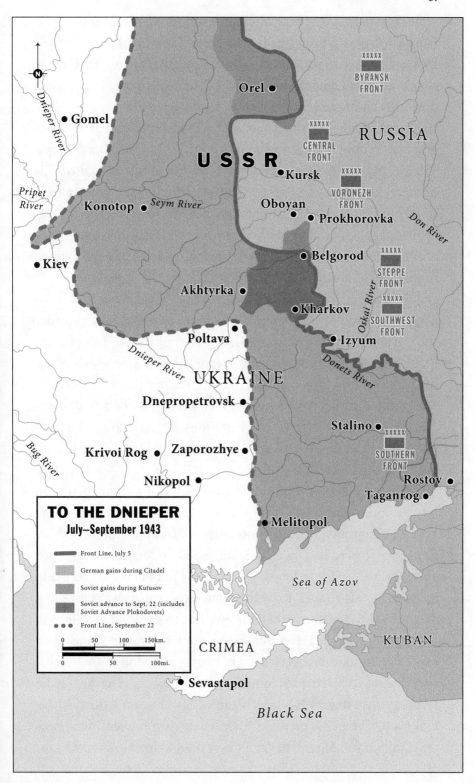

N

Dnieper River

• Gomel

Pripet River

XXXXX
BYRANSK
FRONT

Orel •

RUSSIA

XXXXX
CENTRAL
FRONT

U S S R

Konotop •   *Seym River*

• Kursk

Oboyan
•

XXXXX
VORONEZH
FRONT

• Prokhorovka

Don River

• Kiev

• Belgorod

XXXXX
STEPPE
FRONT

Akhtyrka •

Oskai River

XXXXX
SOUTHWEST
FRONT

• Kharkov

Poltava
•

Dnieper River

UKRAINE

• Izyum

Donets River

Dnepropetrovsk •

Stalino •

XXXXX
SOUTHERN
FRONT

Bug River

Krivoi Rog •   Zaporozhye •

Rostov •

Nikopol •

Taganrog •

• Melitopol

TO THE DNIEPER
July–September 1943

━━━ Front Line, July 5

   German gains during Citadel

   Soviet gains during Kutusov

   Soviet advance to Sept. 22 (includes
   Soviet Advance Plokodovets)

••• Front Line, September 22

0   50   100   150km.

0   50   100mi.

Sea of Azov

KUBAN

CRIMEA

• Sevastapol

Black Sea

sector was at risk. The first, obvious response was to commit XXIV Panzer Corps as a fire brigade. The second was to take a long, hard look at the Orel sector. Hitler had accompanied the original July 13 cancellation of Citadel with orders to Model to restore the original line. This command proved out of touch with reality as the Central Front began applying pressure on Model's right flank and Bagramyan reinforced his attack on the left with a fresh tank corps. The already worn-down divisions Model committed against this drive melted away to a point where Model relieved a panzer division commander for refusing to make a counterattack he considered suicidal. All that remained in some sectors were elements of rear-echelon security divisions, better suited to executing Russian civilians than destroying Russian T-34s.

That the German front in the Orel salient held more or less together reflected in good part Model's disregard of Hitler's order that no secondary defensive positions be established. Even before Kursk, Model had initiated the preparation of a series of phase lines that by the time of Kutuzov were more than map tracings. Model handled his sparse reserves with cold-blooded skill, committing them by batteries and battalions in just enough force to blunt and delay Soviet attacks. The decisive tool in his hand, however, was the Luftwaffe.

The 1st Air Division mounted over eleven hundred sorties on July 18 alone, almost half by Stukas and ground-attack planes. The next day, Bagramyan's lead tanks emerged from the forest and the Germans struck at dawn. The Stukas, Henschels, and Fw 190s bored in at altitudes so low that one Hs 129 pilot flew his plane into the tank he was attacking. By this time, experience and rumor had taught the Russian tankers all they wished to know about German attack planes. Some crews undertook random evasive maneuvers, scattering in all directions. Others simply abandoned their vehicles. The 1st Air Division claimed 135 kills on July 19 alone. Soviet records admit that by July 20, 1st Tank Corps had only thirty-three tanks left. The pilots credited themselves with preventing a "second Stalingrad." Model, never an easy man to impress, wired congratulations for the first successful halting of a tank offensive from the air alone.

On July 19, Bryansk Front threw the Third Guards Tank Army into the attack. Over seven hundred AFVs, supported by the full strength of the Fifteenth Air Army, advanced almost eight miles by nightfall and kept hammering. Despite Stalin's direct "encouragement," what was projected as a breakthrough became a battle of attrition. Model used his aircraft to compensate for steadily eroding ground strength. Luftwaffe medium bombers were flying as many as five sorties a day, and 88 mm flak guns pressed into antitank service claimed more than two hundred tank kills. Russian and German fighters grappled for control of the air, with one Soviet report describing a pilot landing near a downed Me-109 and capturing the pilot himself. What counted was that as 1st Air Division's planes were ruthlessly shifted and ruthlessly committed, pilot judgment diminished and aircrew losses increased. A disproportionate number of them were among the veteran flight and squadron leaders, correspondingly irreplaceable at short notice.

V

As early as July 16, again strictly against orders, Model had begun work on a fallback position along the Desna River at the salient's base. On July 20, Hitler forbade any further retreat by Army Group Center. Model requested Kluge to change the Führer's mind. The current position was untenable. The storm emerging in Manstein's sector meant the redeployment of the indispensable air assets sooner rather than later. Germany's strategic and political position in the Mediterranean was steadily eroding. As the Allies advanced through Sicily, Mussolini's hold on reality and power grew increasingly tenuous, and Hitler met with him on July 19 for a final, very one-sided discussion. On July 23, Mussolini was deposed and arrested. By then, there were sixteen German divisions in Italy.

Were they there to defend the country, to occupy it, or both? What was certain was that in neither case would they be available for the Eastern Front. It is easy, moreover, for British and American scholars, with their deep roots in cultures of sea power, to over-look the influence on the Germans of Allied naval supremacy—no longer even superiority—and what seemed an accompanying, nearly mystical power to strike when and where they would at a time of their choosing. Operationally as well as strategically, the Reich seemed suddenly caught between enemies able to behave similarly: one on sea, the other on land.

On July 22, Hitler had agreed to an elastic defense on Model's immediate front. On July 26, he summoned Kluge and informed him that the SS Panzer Corps was to be transferred to Italy imme-diately. Other unspecified divisions would be taking the same route. This meant, the Führer asserted, that the Orel salient must be evacuated, also immediately. When a shocked Kluge men-tioned that the fallback positions for that contingency were barely under construction, Hitler stood firm. On July 28, the OKH issued the specific orders.

Army High Command and the Führer had responded to the Red Army's southern offensive by dispersing not only Manstein's long-sought reinforcements, but the core of the Fourth Panzer Army. SS Wiking was assigned to the First Panzer Army. The 23rd Panzer was sent to the Mius. It was followed by the SS Panzer Corps—minus Leibstandarte, which was eventually dispatched to Italy. Grossdeutschland, pulled out of the line at short notice, ini-tially went north to reinforce the hard-pressed Army Group Cen-ter. On a tactical level, Citadel's dismantling went unpredictably smoothly. From corps to companies, a sense of relief at getting out of Citadel's killing ground is palpable alike in official reports and private communications. From the Russian perspective, events were progressing sufficiently according to plan that no pressure was applied for close pursuit. In particular, Voronezh Front and its component armies had taken the kind of mauling that made even dedicated Communist warriors require some breathing space—like the Union army after Gettysburg.

The same might be said for Manstein. Hitler's orders brought him back to his kind of war—both against the Russians and against his superiors. He recorded his perceptions in his memoirs. The Russians facing his army group enjoyed a seven-to-one superiority in men and material, providing the capacity to strike at will. They had a related capacity to replace losses that the Reich could not match. The Germans still possessed a qualitative edge, though it was wearing thin in the crucial categories of experienced frontline soldiers, company officers, and (not least) field officers. From Citadel's beginning to the end of August, Army Group South alone lost 38 regimental commanders and no fewer than 252 battalion COs.

Such assets must be expended with care, for maximum advantage—not wasted in last stands for lost outposts. And that was the responsibility of the senior commanders. Bean counting and number crunching had never characterized the German way of war. What mattered at high command levels was willingness to forget odds and trust one's *virtu.* If that meant clashes with superiors and subordinates, so be it. Germany's ultimate assets, at least in their own opinions, were generals like Erich von Manstein. "If," he informed Zeitzler, "the Führer has a commander or an army group headquarters that has better nerves . . . that shows more initiative . . . that improvises better . . . I am ready to give up my post." He concluded the message by declaring, "As long as I am at this post, I must have the possibility of using my own head."

For a few days, Army Group South seemed to be fighting Manstein's war. The SS restored the Mius sector. The First Panzer Army mounted a locally successful counteroffensive. But Manstein and his staff were incorrect in their estimate of the time required for the full-scale Soviet attack to materialize. Fog and friction were in fact omnipresent on the Russian side. Citadel's losses in men and equipment had been made up haphazardly, if at all. Written orders did not appear until two days after the attack began—and the Red Army was not precisely geared to verbal transmission. Operation Rumyantsev nevertheless commenced in earnest on August 3, with nine armies, two tank armies, and two air armies. The initial sector was well chosen. Its defenders, still worn from Citadel, had spent two weeks retreating—not to prepared positions, but to whatever the *Landser* could scratch out of the earth and the tankers could improvise. Their logistics and their maintenance were not much better than those of the Russians. Their replacement situation was worse, especially in the infantry divisions. In a day, Voronezh Front opened an eight-mile gap between the Fourth Panzer Army and Army Detachment Kempf. It was a fitting coda to Citadel, a valedictory for the rejuvenated Red Army. It was also only a beginning.

For the next two months, Manstein shored up sector after sector as the Soviet offensive steadily expanded. Citadel's stalwarts, Totenkopf, Das Reich, and a once more hastily redeployed Grossdeutschland, played central roles in a one-way process. They bought days—but not time. In Robert Citino's trenchant words, "The situation maps were a blizzard of red arrows heading west." On August 8, Zeitzler paid an unannounced visit to Manstein's headquarters, to be confronted with two stark alternatives. Either transfer no fewer than twenty divisions to Army Groups South and Center or conduct a fighting retreat to the Dnieper River. When Hitler authorized a reinforcement of half a dozen divisions, Manstein dismissed this as temporizing. Instead of committing every available division to sustaining the southern Russian front, Hitler was fretting where the next Allied blow in the Mediterranean would fall—a contingency Manstein dismissed as "just as improbable as it was unimportant."

With the Orel salient's evacuation successfully in progress, Hitler flew to Vinnitsa on August 27 and met with Manstein. After some preliminary fencing, the field marshal repeated his alternatives: Either immediately reinforce Army Group South with at least twelve divisions or abandon the Donets area. According to

Manstein, Hitler agreed to provide whatever could be spared from other sectors in Russia. In the context of other developing Soviet offensives, that turned out to be nothing. Manstein compared experiences with Kluge, who had received essentially the same response. On September 2, he warned Zeitzler again that delaying reinforcements until the Allies committed to a second front risked immediate disaster in the East. And on September 3, Kluge and Manstein met with Hitler at Rastenburg. They made a common point: Either send substantial reinforcements to their army groups or authorize "mobile operations"—anodyne language for organized withdrawals screened by local counterstrikes. This time Hitler was entirely uncooperative, denying his subordinates both reinforcements and initiative. He was even less responsive to their suggestion of addressing the emerging problems of a strategically expanded war in the East and a two-front war emerging in the West by creating a unified high command.

Hitler's renewed intransigence reflected events on the other side of the continent. On September 3, the British Eighth Army landed in Calabria, at the tip of the Italian boot. The same day, Italy signed an armistice with the Allies. And on September 7, Manstein informed the OKH that unless something was done immediately, Army Group South might not remain "in control of the situation." The next day, Hitler visited Manstein's headquarters— behavior at least susceptible of interpretation in context as the mountain coming to Muhammad. Manstein responded with a detailed briefing that focused on the situation facing his army group. Hitler reacted by allowing the Sixth and First Panzer Armies to withdraw and by once more promising reinforcements to the Fourth Panzer Army and Army Detachment Kempf, now retitled the Eighth Army. He repeated that promise as he boarded his plane.

Manstein nevertheless followed the meeting with a message reiterating the need for prompt and major reallocation of forces on the Eastern Front and between the East and the war's other theaters. That same day, September 9, British airborne troops seized

264 · ARMOR AND BLOOD

Taranto, and elements of the U.S. Fifth Army landed at Salerno. And on September 14, Manstein informed the OKH that either it authorize a withdrawal or the entire army group would fall back across the Dnieper on his authorization. He received the reply not to act until the matter was discussed with Hitler. Manstein in turn demanded a private meeting with the Führer, with only Zeitzler attending. The next day he flew to Rastenburg, where he made his points with a slight but significant spin. He described retreat to the Dnieper as a consequence of previous promises of reinforcements not being kept and of orders to send them not being obeyed. Manstein declared himself confident, however, that the orders *he* intended to issue next day *would* be obeyed. No doubt remained what those orders would entail.

This was a glove not thrown at Hitler's feet, but flicked across his face. Manstein's foremost military biographer correctly comments that no dictator can accept such a challenge. Nor can a leader of a democracy accept this kind of defiance with equanimity: the Korean War's Truman-MacArthur controversy comes to mind. Faced with the alternative of dismissing Manstein on the spot, Hitler authorized retreat to the Dnieper. He also spoke again of reinforcements. But even had the Führer suddenly become willing to denude occupied regions of their garrisons, there was no time left to shift them to Russia. Nor were there many quiet sectors left in "Fortress Europe." As a particularly ironic counterpoint, the 16th Panzer Division, sent to Italy only in June, came close to throwing the Salerno landing into the sea on August 14.

Since mid-July, at least, Kluge and Manstein had acted from a common matrix. They agreed the Reich's strategic and grand strategic circumstances were sufficiently desperate to require a major change in the Wehrmacht's high command structure, with the immediate aim of restoring the military situation in Russia and the long-term one of concluding the war in an acceptable fashion—a Teutonism for some kind of compromise peace. It was an open secret that both headquarters contained men more or less aware of the resistance. Colonel Rudolf von Gersdorff, of Army Group

Center's intelligence staff, had gone so far as to attempt to assassinate Hitler by immolating himself as a suicide bomber. He described Kluge as sending him to Manstein with a proposition. After a successful putsch, Kluge would offer his colleague the post of chief of the Wehrmacht general staff—in other words, supreme command of the armed forces.

Gersdorff was sufficiently cautious to couch his message initially in terms of the need for a united command and the curbing of Hitler's propensity to control everything himself. Manstein agreed but said he lacked Hitler's trust, especially since "foreign propaganda" described him as seeking high command for himself. Only Kluge or Marshal Gerd von Rundstedt had the seniority, the gravitas, and the influence to approach the Führer with this kind of proposal. According to Gersdorff's memoirs, the discussion sharpened when he suggested to Manstein that the field marshals should confront Hitler and "hold a gun to his chest"— presumably metaphorically. Manstein's alleged answer, that Prussian field marshals do not mutiny, has become a trope for the mentality of the entire senior officer corps. His emendation that Hitler's removal would lead only to chaos was accompanied by his assurance to Kluge that he, Manstein, would always stand loyally at the service of legitimate state authority.

For Manstein, the stated subtext of this encounter was his expressed belief that the war was not yet lost—not quite. He repeatedly insisted in his memoirs that he was fighting for a draw—a *Remis-Frieden*. *Remis* is a word usually associated with chess and sports. The Russo-German War, and, indeed, all of Germany's World War II, fit neither category. How was such a draw to be achieved politically? What would be its terms? On those points, the "simple soldier" is simply silent.

An alternate subtext may well have been a common one among the Wehrmacht's senior officers after 1942: self-imposed tunnel vision, focusing on immediate problems that were daunting enough in themselves, legitimated procrastination. In terms of character, this reflected a doubled-down commitment to what Isabel Hull calls "one-sided actionism": combining intellect, will, and reck-lessness to make the best of a desperate situation. This lofty echo-ing of the *Nibelungenlied*'s heroes was likely to be accompanied by the consideration that should the war be lost, colonels and gener-als would become shoeshine boys and bellhops—the lucky ones, that is. And the two combined to obscure a moral question. Is an oath one-sided? Can—indeed, must—an oath be defined in con-text: to whom it is given and how it is used?

It was easier not to think about it—easier to fight a war. As Army Group South and Army Group Center fell back, they scorched the earth. Neither Manstein, Model, nor Kluge consid-ered it necessary to consult higher authority. Apologists declared they were only following precedents set by the Russians them-selves in the first months of Barbarossa. A clearer precedent had been established by a Führer order in Stalingrad's aftermath: Should withdrawals be necessary, destroy anything materially useful; evacuate all men between fifteen and sixty-five. This was no mere torching of villages and looting of houses, but the system-atic destruction of anything, in Manstein's words, that might af-ford concealment or shelter to enemies; anything that might remotely assist Soviet war production. In total war, that meant ev-erything. The swath of devastation covered hundreds of square miles. What was not burned was blown up. As an occupying power, Germany was required to protect civilians under its con-trol. Instead, thousands were driven west with what they could carry, with the alternative of risking execution as suspected parti-sans or simple shooting at random. The Russians, in the words of one of Manstein's infantrymen, "should find nothing but a field of rubble."

Files labled "Protests" and "Refusals" are conspicuously absent from otherwise well-kept German records. What was important was that the despoliation be carried out in an orderly fashion and under command. German soldiers were not mere brigands. Be-lieving that required Orwellian levels of doublethink. And it is reasonable to suggest that, like any example of doublethink, believing it required shutting off elements of mind and spirit that are crucial to generalship at its highest levels.

Manstein conducted his retreat with consummate professionalism. The Red Army stayed on Army Group South's heels. Vatutin aphorized its motive: "They are burning our bread." Few Soviet soldiers had not experienced hunger. By the time Army Group South reached the Dnieper, it was down to fewer than three hundred operable tanks. The average infantry division's frontline strength was around a thousand men; its average sector was around twelve miles. The men were so tired and apathetic that a report from the elite Grossdeutschland Division said its men no longer cared whether they were shot by the Russians or their own officers.

Army Group Center was in no better condition. By September 1944, one of its army commanders said his total rifle strength had been reduced to no more than seven thousand. An auto accident on October 12 took Kluge out of action; he never returned to the Eastern Front. Only Russian regression to tactics making Passchendaele and the Somme appear sophisticated eventually enabled the Germans to stabilize—more or less—that sector for part of the winter. But wherever the Red Army drove forward, it was with renewed determination to carry the fight to a finish, as long as it took and whatever its cost.

Conclusion

WATERSHEDS

IN EVALUATING AND CONTEXTUALIZING KURSK, a spectrum of issues meriting consideration remains. First come statistics. In terms of material, the Soviet claims were of almost 2,800 tanks and assault guns destroyed. German archives provide a figure of around 250. Only 10 of those were Tigers. Similar exploration of Soviet records gives 536 total AFV losses for Central Front, between 1,200 and 1,400 for Voronezh Front and the reinforcements from Steppe Front. Put together, the totals vary between 1,600 and over 2,000—about eight to one. More than 54,000 Germans were killed, wounded, or missing. Total Russian casualties exceeded 320,000.

These figures help address some of Kursk's prevailing myths. The German army on the Eastern Front was neither bled white nor demodernized by Citadel's human and material losses. Its Tigers were masters of the field wherever they appeared. Even the often denigrated Ferdinands did yeoman service in Model's sector when used appropriately, in their intended antitank role. Intangibles may well be another story. Whether in a context of irreplaceable combat experience lost to death and wounds or irreplaceable confidence lost in a battering confrontation that left the Russians standing and the Germans on one knee, after Kursk it was the Germans reacting to Russian initiatives.

For the Red Army, Kursk was one of its bloodiest and least sophisticated battles, one that drew in corps and armies originally part of Stavka's grand offensive design and arguably set back the projected Russian victory for a year. Whether as a function of the Soviet system, of Stalin's ruthless culling of the senior officer corps in the years of defeat, or of German tactical and operational skill, Kursk showed what the Red Army would become—not what it was.

As for Prokhorovka, both combatants' master narratives are true; both are incomplete. The Waffen SS won a tactical victory on July 12—Prokhorovka was not a Tiger graveyard, but a T-34 junkyard. Operationally, however, the palm rests with the Red Army. Prokhorovka took what the Germans had left to give. Citadel's turning point was not July 12, but July 13, when the Germans flailed desperately and vainly, like a dazed boxer, to regain even the local initiative. Operations Kutuzov and Rumyantsev would thwart them.

That leads to another myth. It has been called the myth of victory denied. It might better be described as the myth of XXIV Panzer Corps. From Citadel's beginning, Manstein saw those divisions as the lodestone of victory and bewailed their absence as the key to defeat. Apart from their crucial roles in stabilizing the sectors of Manstein's two other armies when the Soviet offensive began, nothing in the details of Citadel's final days indicate that Wiking and 23rd Panzer would have done more than commit even more of the irreplaceable mobile divisions to an already limited battle zone—from which they would have been withdrawn in any case.

As indicated throughout this text, Erich von Manstein was not a gambling man. Perhaps if poker had been his recreation, he might have remembered the game's key axioms: "Know when to hold and when to fold; know when to walk away and when to run." Like Lee at Gettysburg, he stayed for one card too many.

Winston Churchill described Kursk as heralding the downfall of the German army on the Eastern Front. This work presents Citadel as a watershed on multiple levels. Four stand out. Institutionally, the Battle of Kursk was the crossover point between two of the most formidable instruments of war the world has ever seen, built around fundamentally different paradigms. The Red Army understood war as a science, following abstract principles amenable to reason and thus dependent on planning. To the Germans, war was ultimately an art form, whose mastery required what amounted to an aesthetic sense. *Fingerspitzengefühl, Tuchfühlung,* and similar words dot Germany's military literature at critical points—euphemisms for cultivated, focused intuition.

"Paradigm" does not mean "straitjacket." In the interwar years, the Soviet Union developed concepts of mobile operations that surpassed anything in the Germans' playbook. The Red Army's theories of deep operations, conducted on multiple echelons and in combined-arms contexts, were blitzkrieg *avant la lettre.* The German campaigns of 1939–40, and to an even greater extent Operation Barbarossa, incorporated synergistic calculation far ahead of anything their opponents mustered. But when "fog and friction" reduced a campaign, a battle, or a skirmish to fundamentals, the soldiers returned to their respective taproots. Shaken to the core by the initial German successes of 1941, the USSR fell back on their system, planning complex operations to defeat and destroy the Wehrmacht as a master chess player demolishes a patzer, with no serious regard for details of implementation. The Germans, blindsided on the road to Smolensk, resorted to heroic improvisation at levels that treated panzer divisions with only a couple of dozen operational tanks and a few hundred riflemen as fully combat effective in the depths of a Russian winter.

The Battle of Kursk was fought after both armies had had two years to learn—and to suffer—from their own and each other's mistakes. Positively and negatively, neither was what it had been during Barbarossa or the struggle for Stalingrad. At Kursk, their elites met head-to-head, each with time to understand the nature of the proposed encounter and to prepare in its own fashion. The restricted size of the theater created a dueling ground. That demanded focus: neither adversary could impose its doctrine and will from the beginning. It demanded skill: slips and errors could not be compensated for by changing the battle's parameters. And it demanded will: Which side possessed the confidence and the nerve to last the course for the five final minutes? What would be the outcome? Perihelion and aphelion, or mutual standoff in the pattern of 1916: Verdun and the Somme? The Battle of Kursk sketched the answer and opened the door to a new reality. After Citadel, there was no position the Germans could defend, no line they could maintain, if the Red Army was willing to pay the price of taking it or breaking it.

Kursk's second watershed involved the German army's fundamental reconfiguration. It began World War II as an instrument of offense and exploitation. The bedrock of its command system was independent authority. Given a mission, the means of accomplishing it were the commander's responsibility. This reflected systems of training and education that meant initiative and adaptability were likely to produce favorable results at any level. It reflected a common military culture, built around the general staff. And it reflected a privileging of creativity, aggression, and major risk taking for big gains.

This mentality synergized with an institutional structure based on high-tech formations within a mass. The force multipliers developed in the 1930s, based on internal combustion engines and electronic communications, favored developing an elite—not in the racial/ideological sense of the Waffen SS, not on the basis of personnel selection, like British and American paratroopers, not even on combat performance like the Soviet Guards divisions, but rather a functional elite based on learned skills: the panzer and panzer grenadier divisions. That structure was reinforced by the long-range consequences of the much-maligned Versailles Treaty.

With conscription forbidden and the military production complex eviscerated, Germany was constrained to mobilize the bulk of its wartime army as foot-propelled infantry. Their vehicles were largely horse-drawn; their training levels varied downward from marginal; their armament depended heavily on what could be delivered by overstrained factories or salvaged from the Reich's latest conquests.

That structure's success owed much to its own quality—but no less to its obliging enemies. By 1943, the Red Army was no longer an obliging enemy. Kursk was the German army's last major, operational-level offensive. For the rest of the war, it shifted to a defensive orientation. It did so superlatively, and that is an anomaly. States as a rule may go to war with the armies they have. Armies as a rule fight wars with the tools they begin with. The U.S. Army never overcame its internal dichotomy between mobility and firepower. British shortcomings in combined-arms operations remained a constant from the evacuation of Dunkirk to the crossing of the Rhine. But after Kursk, on both major fronts, the German army remade itself.

To a degree, that process reflected Adolf Hitler's insistence that his commanders report operational particulars in detail—and state clearly when they failed to carry out assigned orders. His increasing micromanagement was a consequence of increasing amounts of information. The nearly instantaneous communication enabled by modern electronics gave not only Hitler but any senior officer direct access to subordinate echelons of command. That fact, however, did not automatically diminish German operational effectiveness. Initially, the most familiar response to the Red Army's increasing offensive capability was Erich von Manstein's concept of flexible defense: Give ground, let the enemy overreach, then hit back. When such sweeping maneuvers became impossible as Soviet numbers and flexibility increased, a new generation of Eastern Front veterans such as Erhard Raus and Walther Model developed a combined-arms zone defense that tactically frustrated the Red Army until the Reich's final breakdown in 1945—and that depended heavily on communications that throttled initiative at higher command levels.

Materially, the German army introduced a "platoon technology" that reshaped the battlefield. The MG-42, with its high cyclic rate of fire; the MP-43 and Sturmgewehr 44 assault rifles; and the Panzerfaust and Panzerschreck portable antitank rockets lifted the German infantryman to a level the rest of the world's foot soldiers would not reach for decades. In their developed versions, the Panther and Tiger tanks, with their high-velocity guns and well-sloped armor, and their first-rate radios and optics, combined fighting power and survivability to a higher degree than their counterparts. And it was at Kursk that these formidable armored vehicles, like the army as a whole, began the paradigm shift from offensive to defensive mainstays.

Kursk was a watershed for the USSR as well. It marked the first stage of the final development of the broad-front strategic grand design Stalin had sought from the war's beginning. Previous versions had foundered on poor coordination, inadequate logistics, limited tactical skills—and German fighting power. From Soviet perspectives, the Kursk salient was developed as a baited strategic trap: the greater the German commitment there, the more vulnerable they would be to attacks on the flanks. Operationally, Army Group Center managed to reestablish a front. In the south during that same time frame, Manstein managed a fighting withdrawal across the Dnieper. He celebrated this "heroic epic" in his memoirs. And the Russians had bought their initial victories in the Ukraine dearly, with more than a million and a half casualties. But in October, a series of attacks carried the Red Army across the Dnieper, setting the stage for Kursk's third watershed: the Soviet Union's valediction.

The Dnieper crossings were signposts of the Red Army's tactical progress. The flexibility suggested during Citadel came to the fore as within a week more than twenty bridgeheads, some over twenty miles deep, pocked a river line the Germans never really established in the first place. In November, Voronezh Front thrust into Kiev, liberating "the mother of Russian cities" in an operation combining, in Vatutin's words, the "speed and resolution" he had originally sought during Citadel. On December 24, the Red Army struck again, in force: four fronts, three and a quarter million men, and twenty-six hundred tanks acting in synchronization.

The Germans in the juggernaut's path made their way west as best they could. Soviet spearheads cut off sixty thousand men in one pocket, over three times as many in another. The Germans responded with two epic breakouts. Neither was more than a speed bump to an offensive that, before running out of steam, tore fifty-mile gaps in the German defenses, led to Hitler's making "stand fast" an obsession, and structured Stavka's strategic design over the next eighteen months. That plan was based on a series of mutually reinforcing strategic offensives along several axes, beginning in early 1944. Russian accounts stress a system, with one multifront thrust in the Leningrad sector and another in the Ukraine, setting the stage for a third: Operation Bagration, a massive blow against Army Group Center with the intention of annihilating the forces in that sector and compelling the Germans in the north and south to retreat or risk envelopment. The underlying concept was political as well as strategic. If success reinforced success, the way to Berlin and Western Europe might open before the British and Americans did more than gain a foothold on the continent.

Detailed analysis of newly available records, by David Glantz in particular, presents a more complex, more opportunistic strategic pattern, with new missions and objectives assigned as the initial ones developed. Whether particular initiatives were intended to exploit success blitzkrieg fashion, improve the prospects of future, systematic offensives, or simply keep the Germans guessing remains difficult to determine, especially since unsuccessful operations tended to disappear down one of the USSR's many memory holes. The end result was the same: compound, continuous overstretch of increasingly limited Wehrmacht resources. And whether interpreted as a fencer's sophisticated swordsmanship or a death by a thousand cuts, the operations that carried the Red Army to the Oder River and Budapest were as spectacular as any in the history of war making. On February 26, 1944, the siege of Leningrad was lifted. Beginning on June 22, Operation Bagration erased Army Group Center, more than thirty divisions, from the German order of battle. By December, southern Russia was German-free and the survivors were trying to hold on to Budapest, on the Reich's threshold. The two-pronged drive into Hitler's capital in the war's final months appears almost anticlimactic.

The Soviet Union's strategic approach had three taproots. One was Stalin's enduring belief that if the Germans were hit hard enough everywhere, their defenses would break somewhere—and break beyond repair. The second was an emphasis on speed and surprise that informed prewar regulations and never disappeared in the planning staffs. The third involved the field commanders' general inability to decide when and where the decisive rupture would occur and their personal ambition to be the one who made it happen. By 1944, the Soviet front commanders had in common an appetite for status and a fear of losing it. Both mentalities were created and controlled by a leader who saw himself as all-powerful. With history itself on his side, Stalin pushed the envelope of events—all the way into Berlin.

In Kursk's aftermath, the Red Army also completed its institutional transformation from a bludgeon—not to a rapier, but certainly to a katana. Russian commanders were learning how to coordinate their movements on a theater level and how to keep moving, without the unintended pauses and interruptions that characterized pre-Kursk offensives. American Lend-Lease jeeps facilitated communication; American 2.5-ton trucks set standards for reliability in the supply echelons. Air-ground cooperation steadily improved, as did artillery fire direction. Both started from far enough back to remain well below Western standards. But there were enough guns, Katyushas, and Shturmoviks that by 1944–45, that minimum efficiency was sufficient.

Technically, the armored force in particular moved to an advanced stage. In April 1943, an upgunned version of the T-34 began entering service. Its 85 mm gun was a battlefield match for both the Germans' big cats, and the JS-II gave it a formidable stablemate. Named for Joseph Stalin, the tank mounted a 122 mm gun, the heaviest of any World War II tank. A new generation of assault guns emerged, carrying 122 mm and 152 mm pieces in fixed mountings on tank hulls. First used at Kursk, they were promptly and appropriately named *zvierboy,* "animal hunters," and accounted for many a Tiger and Panther before VE Day.

The importance of mechanized mobility to the Red Army of 1944–45 overshadows in much of the literature the fact that, doctrinally, throughout the war the infantry remained the primary arm. The combined-arms tactics, the massed artillery, the close air support—all were predicated on, and grew from, the infantry's perceived needs. As late as the end of 1943, only around three hundred thousand of more than four million ground troops served in the mobile formations. In terms of technology, the infantrymen fell ever further behind the tankers, the gunners, and the airmen.

The massive losses of 1941–43 also altered the rifle units' makeup. About a million prisoners were released from the Gulag into the army. The diminishing of the preferred manpower pool of ethnic Russians led to increasing numbers of replacements drawn from Soviet Asia and from the newly liberated western regions. Their political reliability was questioned, on racial grounds for the Asians and from fear the Ukrainians and Byelorussians had been contaminated by their years under fascism. "They know absolutely nothing about fighting, military discipline, real soldiers' spirit," lamented one frustrated captain. But the Red Army's riflemen in 1944–45 were more than handmaids to the tanks, more than follow-up and mop-up troops. At the end of the war, especially in the street fighting in Vienna, Berlin, and the dozens of other built-up sites in the Reich, Red Army infantry were an adversary more determined, and more formidable, than their British and American counterparts.

In that last context, Kursk's fourth watershed involved determination. Since the Middle Ages, at least, war in the Western world had developed a culture of accommodation, of not making things worse than they had to be. Frequently honored in the breach, that culture nevertheless tended to reassert itself constantly, even during civil wars and insurrections, whether the opponents were long-service professionals or hastily uniformed civilians. From the first days of Barbarossa, however, German behavior at the front and behind the lines overtly denied accommodation even at basic levels. At Prokhorovka, a Leibstandarte tank crewman reflected that the Russian soldier fought bravely, "but when taken prisoner . . . he'd quiver like a mouse. . . ." With no sense of irony, the same crewman described a group of Russian prisoners, forty or fifty of them, walking toward the rear guarded by a single SS rifleman. "So we asked him, 'Aren't you afraid?' 'Afraid?' he asked right back. 'Watch.' " The guard said something in Russian. Two prisoners fell out. "Our guy gave them a burst in the stomach from his machine pistol and shouted, 'Now there, see just how frightened I am.' "

Russian soldiers for their part were drawn from a society and a culture where suffering pain and inflicting it were the stuff of every day. A quarter century of Soviet rule refined, legitimated, and institutionalized that mentality. On July 10, a Leibstandarte self-propelled antitank gun disappeared in a wooded area. Its four-man crew was captured. The Russians asked each man to give his age. The youngest was spared, the other three summarily shot.

After Kursk, this often documented mutual brutality metastasized and metamorphosed on both sides. From a Soviet perspective, the war was, in Stalin's words, "a just and patriotic war of liberation." However complex the conflict's origins, who had attacked whom on June 22, 1941, was not in question, any more than the United States could be accused of attacking the Japanese fleet at anchor on December 7, 1941. The theme of self-defense was reinforced by the history of German barbarity. Familiar to every man and woman in the Red Army, it was reinforced at political meetings, maintained through newspapers and radio broadcasts, and nurtured by the encouragement to keep personal records of atrocities noted and repaid. For anyone seeking tangible evidence, the Ukraine and Byelorussia provided scenes of devastation inconceivable even to survivors of the great famines. Home leaves and local furloughs were chimeras. Once at the front, men remained there. Mail delivery was haphazard; memories faded into dreams. The Soviet soldiers' horizons and expectations shrank as the war moved forward. A common meme developed, however, the closer the Red Army came to the Reich's borders. Its basis was rage at the Germans for attacking and despoiling the USSR in seeming defiance of their own immeasurably higher standard of living. Its matrix was a sense of unfettered triumph. "It was a wonderful life," recalled a lieutenant, ". . . loot, vodka, brandy, girls everywhere." Its scope was comprehensive. Civilian or soldier, German or forced laborer—it made no essential difference. The rapes, the beatings, the killings, the deportations were not even massively random. They were a final, universal, direct manifestation of total war.

The Germans too underwent a moral and behavioral transformation. Since 1941, a frontline culture had developed that combined convenience and indifference, embedded in a matrix of hardness. Hardness was neither cruelty nor fanaticism. It is best understood as will focused by intelligence for the purpose of accomplishing a task—at whatever the cost. It was a mind-set particularly enabling the brutal expediency that is an enduring aspect of war.

As the great retreat began after Kursk, the hardness earlier described as central to Wehrmacht frontline culture became the subtext of a wider mission, moral as well as military. German soldiers saw themselves as defending Western civilization, the German nation, and not least their own homes, against what Hoth called in a memo "an Asiatic mode of thinking and primitive instincts," inflamed and focused by Jewish-Bolshevik intellectuals. In the West, opponents of the Nazi regime might talk of ceasing resistance, opening the front. In the East, it was war to the knife until the final days—and often after the fighting formally ceased.

War takes two basic forms. One is a matching of superiorities and inferiorities at decisive moments. The other is a test of strengths and wills, a crisis of attrition. The Battle of Kursk was the Eastern Front's transition point—and its point of no return.

ACKNOWLEDGMENTS

This book has been a long time coming. I wish to thank my family, my colleagues at Colorado College, and my students for putting up with me during its gestation. Particular thanks to Gretchen Boger, whose professionalism and enthusiasm during her two years with the History Department reminded me why I chose that profession; and to our office coordinator, Sandy Papuga, for her goodwill and common sense.

I am grateful to Random House for its patience while the book was in progress and for its expertise once the manuscript was submitted. The copy editor deserves special praise—I would not have believed I could make so many errors of fact and generate so many clumsy sentences! The errors that remain are my responsibility several times over.

I also wish to acknowledge the staff of Tutt Library, especially Diane Armock, the interlibrary loan coordinator. Kathy Barbier and Rob Citino generously shared their knowledge of the subject and provided welcome encouragement. And Sam Lerman was during his Colorado College career a valued associate in a course on terrorism that became a joint enterprise. Sam, this book's for you. May you write a better one.

Guide to Further Reading

This is not a formal bibliography, but instead a guide incorporating some of the material I have found useful and interesting. It is meant to be reader-friendly and is correspondingly weighted toward works in English, written or translated.

The best general introduction is M. K. Barbier, *Kursk: The Greatest Tank Battle, 1943* (London: Amber Books, 2002). Noteworthy alike for accuracy, balance, and readability, it presents a seamless overview of Citadel. Will Fowler, *Kursk: The Vital 24 Hours* (London: Amber Books, 2005), uses a similar format. Despite the title, it is a well-written survey with excellent graphics and useful sidebars. Time-challenged readers may prefer Geoffrey Jukes, *Kursk: The Clash of Armour* (New York: Ballantine Books, 1969); and Mark Healy, *Kursk 1943: The Tide Turns in the East* (Oxford: Osprey Publishing, 1992). Each is part of a distinguished series: Jukes in Ballantine's Illustrated History of World War II and Healy in Osprey's Campaign Series. Both books are well written. Both were state-of-the-art scholarship when published. Both are refreshingly brief. Both remain useful, with Healy's graphics complementing the text.

Outstanding among Kursk's recent general histories is Lloyd Clark, *The Battle of the Tanks: Kursk, 1943* (London: Headline Reviews, 2011), structured heavily around interviews and narratives. Among older works with similar formats, Robin Cross, *The Battle of Kursk: Operation Citadel 1943* (London: Penguin Group, 2002), remains a useful narrative, informed by combatants' accounts. A good balance is the operationally focused Walter S. Dunn Jr., *Kursk: Hitler's Gamble, 1943* (Westport, CT: Praeger Publishers, 1997).

Still dominating the scholarly field is the brilliant overview by David M. Glantz and Jonathan M. House, *The Battle of Kursk* (Lawrence: University Press of Kansas, 1999), which broke new ground with its sophisticated use of previously unavailable Soviet archives. Its presentation and analysis continue to challenge modification. Its emphasis on numbers and statistics can be a weight, but never a burden. Mark Healy's *Zitadelle: The German Offensive Against the Kursk Salient, 4–17 July 1943* (Stroud, UK: History Press, 2008) offers a German perspective that balances the Soviet emphasis of Glantz and House.

French military historians have shown recent and worthwhile interest in Kursk. Jean Lopez, *Koursk: Les quarante jours qui ont ruiné la Wehrmacht (5 Juillet–20 aout 1943* (Paris: Economia, 2011) is an excellent analysis by a leading French scholar of the Eastern Front. And the high-end, general-audience periodical *Champs de Bataille: Seconde Guerre Mondiale* published in 2012–2013 a series of three special issues on *Koursk 1943*. Even for those blind of their French eye, the graphics, tables, and illustrations make their acquisition worthwhile.

Citadel is best understood in the general context of events in 1943 by Robert M. Citino's *The Wehrmacht Retreats: Fighting a Lost War, 1943* (Lawrence: University Press of Kansas, 2012). The author's reference apparatus is almost as useful as his text. Citino's work is buttressed by *Die Ostfront 1943/44*, edited by Karl-Heinz

Frieser, volume 8 of *Das Deutsche Reich und der Zweite Weltkrieg* (Munich: Deutsche Verlags-Anstalt, 2007). It is also one of the best contributions to the series and arguably the most informative source on the lost year on a neglected front. Boris V. Sokolov, "The Battle for Kursk, Orel, and Charkov: Strategic Intentions and Results," in *Gezeitenwechsel im Zweiten Weltkrieg?*, edited by Roland Foerster (Hamburg: Verlag E. S. Mittler & Sohn, 1996), 69–88, is worth accessing for its post-Soviet critique of the regime's falsifications.

For traditional studies from the perspective of the participants, see Ernst Klink, *Das Gesetz des Handelns: Die Operation "Zitidelle," 1943* (Stuttgart: Deutsche Verlags-Anstalt, 1966); and the translated official *The Battle for Kursk, 1943: The Soviet General Staff Study*, edited by David Glantz and Harold S. Ornstein (London: Frank Cass Publishers, 1999).

In the front rank of specialized works on Kursk itself stand Valeriy Zamulin, *Demolishing the Myth: The Tank Battle at Prokhorovka, Kursk, July 1943: An Operational Narrative*, translated and edited by Stuart Britton (Solihull, UK: Helion & Co., 2011); and George M. Nipe, *Blood, Steel and Myth: The II.SS-Panzer-Korps and the Road to Prochorowka, July 1943* (Stamford, CT: RZM Publishing, 2011). Each is a mine of detail based on previously unfamiliar material. The extensive translations of archival material in Zamulin make the work especially valuable. Steven H. Newton's *Kursk: The German View* (New York: Da Capo Press, 2002) is an equally valuable anthology of postwar reports by senior officer participants, with excellent archivally based editorial commentary. Niklas Zetterling and Anders Frankson, *Kursk 1943: A Statistical Analysis* (London: Frank Cass Publishers, 2000), provides numbers and a useful bibliography. David Porter, *Das Reich at Kursk: 12 July 1943* (London: Amber Books, 2011), and *Fifth Guards Tank Army at Kursk* (London: Amber Books, 2011), are parallel works whose texts and graphics provide a coherent overview of these formations that can be applied to their counterparts as well. Roman Töppel, "Legendenbildung in der Geschichtsschreibung—Die Schlacht von Kursk," *Militärgeschichtliche Zeitschrift* 61 (2002): 369–401, is the best analysis of the origins and refutations of Kursk's major myths.

In the second tier of specialized material, Antonius John, *Kursk '43: Szenen einer Entscheidungsschlacht* (Bonn: Konzept Verlag, 1993), has useful primary material from Model's sector during Citadel and the shift to the Orel salient. Silvester Stadler, *Die Offensive gegen Kursk 1943: II.SS-Panzerkorps als Stosskeil im Grosskampf* (Osnabrück: Munin Verlag, 1980), reprints many orders and reports. Didier Lodieu, *III. Pz. Korps at Kursk,* translated by Allan McKay (Paris: Histoire & Collections, 2007), makes good use of archival material and unit histories. Volume 2 of Helmuth Spaeter, *The History of the Panzerkorps Grossdeutschland* (Winnipeg: J. J. Fedorowicz, 1995), and Hans-Joachim Jung, *Panzer Soldiers for "God, Honor, Fatherland": The History of Panzerregiment Grossdeutschland,* translated by David Johnston (Winnipeg: J. J. Fedorowicz, 2000), combine to do well by the army's showpiece. Volume 2 of *Armored Bears: The German 3rd Panzer Division in World War II,* compiled by the division's veterans (Mechanicsburg, PA: Stackpole 2013), focuses on personal experiences and anecdotes. Christopher W. Wilbeck's *Sledgehammers: Strengths and Flaws of Tiger Tank Battalions in World War II* (Bedford, PA: Aberjona Press, 2004) includes a good analysis of the Tigers' role with Breith's corps.

Airpower, whose vital role in Citadel is often marginalized, is well presented in Christer Bergström, *Kursk: The Air Battle: July 1943* (Hersham, UK: Ian Allan Publishing, 2008). Von Hardesty and Ilya Grinberg, *Red Phoenix Rising: The Soviet Air Force in World War II* (Lawrence: University Press of Kansas, 2012), present Citadel in the context of the Red Air Force's wartime development. Richard Muller, *The German Air War in Russia* (Baltimore: Nautical & Aviation Publishing Company of America, 1992), is a solid counterpoint. And among dozens of aircraft books, Martin Pegg, *Hs 129: Panzerjäger!* (Burgess Hill, UK: Classic Publications, 1997), covers one of the less familiar types.

Among works addressing wider issues related to Kursk, Geoffrey Jukes, *Stalingrad to Kursk: Triumph of the Red Army* (Barnsley, UK: Pen & Sword Military, 2011), is excellent on the factors underlying the shift in military power on the Eastern Front. Dana V. Sadarananda, *Beyond Stalingrad: Manstein and the Operations of Army Group Don* (Westport, CT: Praeger Publishers, 1990), summarizes the experiences that directly shaped Manstein's approach to Citadel and its aftermath. George M. Nipe Jr., *Decision in the Ukraine, Summer 1943: II SS and III Panzer Korps* (Winnipeg: J. J. Fedorowicz Publishing, 1996), takes these formations through Kursk and afterward. For details of the post-Kursk fighting, Rolf Hinze, *East Front Drama, 1944: The Withdrawal Battle of Army Group Center*, translated by Joseph G. Welsh (Winnipeg: J. J. Fedorowicz Publishing, 1996), and *Crucible of Combat: Germany's Defensive Battles in the Ukraine, 1943–44*, translated and edited by F. P. Steinhardt (Solihull, UK: Helion & Co., 2009), are richly detailed, with minimal "Wehrmacht pathos."

Most of the accessible biographies and memoirs are of Germans. The best critical analysis, by a substantial distance, of Manstein's careeer and character is Mungo Melvin, *Manstein: Hitler's Greatest General* (London: Weidenfeld & Nicolson, 2010). Benoît Lemay, *Erich von Manstein: Hitler's Master Strategist*, translated by Pierce Heyward (Havertown, PA: Casement Publishers, 2010), runs an honorable second. The German original of Manstein's memoir, *Verlorene Siege* (Bonn: Athenäum Verlag, 1955), includes relevant material omitted from *Lost Victories* (Chicago: Henry Regnery, 1958). Alexander Stahlberg, *Bounden Duty: The Memoirs of a German Officer, 1932–45*, translated by Patricia Crampton (London: Brassey's, 1990), presents the ambiguities confronting a personal aide involved with the resistance to Hitler. Among the rest, Steven H. Newton, *Hitler's Commander: Field Marshal Walther Model—Hitler's Favorite General* (New York: Da Capo Press, 2006), is solid on Model. F. W. von Mellenthin was XLVIII Panzer Corps's chief of staff during Citadel. *Panzer Battles: A Study of the Employment of Armor in the Second World War* (Norman: University of Oklahoma Press, 1956) includes his perspective on the operation.

Senior Russian commanders' memoirs include Konstantin Rokossovsky, *A Soldier's Duty,* translated by Vladimir Talny (Moscow: Progress Publishers, 1970); and Pavel Rotmistrov's swashbuckling *Stal'naya gvardiya* (Moscow: Voenizdat, 1984). The more accessible *Stalin's Generals,* edited by Harold Shukman (New York: Grove Press, 1993), includes excellent chapters on Novikov, Vatutin, Vasilevsky, and Rokossovsky. Richard N. Armstrong, *Red Army Tank Commanders: The Armored Guards* (Atglen, PA: Schiffer Publishing, 1994), includes chapters on Katukov and Rotmistrov.

On the questions of motives and behaviors, Roger R. Reese, *Why Stalin's Soldiers Fought: The Red Army's Military Effectiveness in World War II* (Lawrence: University Press of Kansas, 2011), and Catherine Merridale, *Ivan's War: Life and Death in the Red Army, 1939–1945* (New York: Metropolitan Books, 2006), are a definitive combination. Omer Bartov, *Hitler's Army: Soldiers, Nazis, and War in the Third Reich* (New York: Oxford University Press, 1991), Stephen G. Fritz, *Frontsoldaten: The German Soldier in World War II* (Lexington: University Press of Kentucky, 1995), and Thomas Kühne, *Belonging and Genocide: Hitler's Community, 1918–1945* (New Haven: Yale University Press, 2010), are no less persuasive for the Wehrmacht. Sönke Neitzel and Harald Welzer's *Soldaten: On Fighting, Killing, and Dying* (New York: Alfred A. Knopf, 2012) uses tape recordings of low-ranking German POWs to convey an unfiltered version of the unreflective hardness that informed their behavior in Russia.

NOTES

Note: These references are intended primarily to serve as a guide to further reading for nonspecialists on this complex subject. As such they have been kept to a minimum, cite the most accessible sources on each subject, and take account of readers' probable language limitations by citing translations when possible. Those seeking to probe more deeply into the masses of archival data are encouraged to consult the Guide to Further Reading (page 283) as an intermediate step.

INTRODUCTION

xi **Fostering myth as much as history** Roman Töppel, "Kursk: Mythen und Wirklichkeit einer Schlacht," *Vierteljahrshefte für Zeitgeschichte* 57, no. 3 (2009): 349–384, and "Legendenbildung in der Geschichtsschreibung: Die Schlacht um Kursk," *Militärgeschichtliche Zeitschrift* 61 (2002): 369–401, are perceptive and comprehensive on this subject.

xi **In terms of page counts** Norman Davies, *No Simple Victory: World War II in Europe, 1939–1945* (London: Penguin Books, 2008), is a useful corrective for the imbalance.

xii **"Forgotten year"** Karl-Heinz Frieser et al., *Das Deutsche Reich und der Zweite Weltkrieg*, vol. 8, *Die Ostfront, 1943–44* (Munich: Deutsche Verlags-Anstalt, 2007), p. 277.

xii **Two master narratives emerged** See as typical English-language versions, and from opposite poles of the presentation spectrum, Janusz Piekalkiewicz, *Operation Citadel: Kursk and Orel: The Greatest Tank Battle of the Second World War*, trans. Michaela Nierhaus (Novato, CA: Presidio Press, 1987), and David M. Glantz and Harold L. Orenstein, eds., *The Bat-*

tle for Kursk, 1943: The Soviet General Staff Study (London: Frank Cass Publishers, 1999). One features heroic narratives and evocative photos. The other exemplifies Carlyle's "Dryasdust." Though dated, each remains useful as a portal into the former combatants' respective mentalities in the Cold War era.

xii **German monopoly of Eastern Front narratives** Ronald Smelser and Edward J. Davies II, *The Myth of the Eastern Front: The Nazi-Soviet War in American Popular Culture* (New York: Cambridge University Press, 2007), is comprehensive and perceptive.

CHAPTER 1: GENESIS

4 **Operation Barbarossa** The invasion has generated enough discussion and analysis to justify a monograph on its historiography alone. As an introduction, Geoffrey Megargee, *War of Annihilation: Combat and Genocide on the Eastern Front, 1941* (Lanham, MD: Rowman, 2006), stands out. For analysis, David Stahel, *Operation Barbarossa and Germany's Defeat in the East, 1941* (Cambridge: Cambridge University Press, 2009), is balanced and reader-friendly. Most detailed, albeit principally from a German perspective, is Horst Boog et al., *Germany and the Second World War*, vol. 4, *The Attack on the Soviet Union*, trans. Ewald Osers et al. (Oxford: Oxford University Press, 1998). David M. Glantz, *Barbarossa Derailed: The Battle for Smolensk, 10 July–10 September 1941*, 2 vols. (Solihull, UK: Helion & Co., 2011–12), is exhaustingly superlative on the tactical/operational dynamics of combat in a crucial sector and time frame. Alex J. Kay et al., eds., *Nazi Policy on the Eastern Front: Total War, Genocide, and Radicalization* (Rochester, NY: Rochester University Press, 2012), is an anthology of well-executed case studies.

5 **Hitler issued Directive 41** The basic outline of Operation Blue is reprinted in Walther Hubatsch, ed., *Hitlers Weisungen für die Kriegführung* (Frankfurt: Bernard & Graefe, 1962), pp. 183–191.

5 **A secondary objective was Stalingrad** For a strategic/operational overview of the Stalingrad campaign, the best combination of narrative and analysis is Robert M. Citino, *Death of the Wehrmacht: The German Campaigns of 1942* (Lawrence: University Press of Kansas, 2007). Joel S. A. Hayward, *Stopped at Stalingrad: The Luftwaffe and Hitler's Defeat in the*

East, 1942–1943 (Lawrence: University Press of Kansas, 1998), complements Citino's ground-oriented presentation. Bernd Wegner, "The War Against the Soviet Union," in Horst Boog et al., *Germany and the Second World War*, vol. 6, *The Global War*, trans. Ewald Osers et al. (Oxford: Oxford University Press, 2001), pp. 853–1158, is also essential.

7 **Expected the Germans to attack**   For the general background of Soviet strategic planning, see most recently Peter Mezhiritsky, *On the Precipice: Stalin, the Red Army Leadership and the Road to Stalingrad, 1931–1942*, trans. Stuart Britton (Solihull, UK: Helion & Co., 2012).

7 **A major offensive to recapture the city of Kharkov**   For Kharkov's genesis and outcome, David M. Glantz, *Kharkov 1942: Anatomy of a Military Disaster Through Soviet Eyes* (Shepperton, UK: Ian Allan Publishing, 1998), synergizes a Soviet staff study with the editor's consistently perceptive comments. Hans Doerr, "Der Ausgang der Schlacht um Charkow im Frühjahr 1942," *Wehrwissenschaftliche Rundschau* 4, no. 1 (January 1954): 9–18, much more cursory, is by the then chief of staff of a corps heavily involved in the battle.

8 **Ivan was still no match for Hitler's panzers**   The persistent and often cited German pattern of underrating its Soviet opponent is highlighted in this context by Christian Hartmann, *Halder: Generalstabschef Hitlers, 1938–1942* (Paderborn: Ferdinand Schöningh, 1991), pp. 318–319.

8 **Not mere counterattacks**   David M. Glantz offers the best account in any language: "Forgotten Battles of the German-Soviet War (1941–1945)," part 7, "The Summer Campaign, 12 May–8 November 1942: Voronezh, July 1942," *Journal of Slavic Military Studies* 14, no. 3 (2001): 150–220.

9 **Increasing division and diversion**   For a relatively brief overview of the development of the Stalingrad operation, see Wegner, "War Against the Soviet Union," in *The Global War*, pp. 958–990. David M. Glantz and Jonathan M. House, *To the Gates of Stalingrad: Soviet-German Combat Operations, April–August 1942* (Lawrence: University Press of Kansas, 2009), and *Armageddon in Stalingrad: September–November 1942* (Lawrence: University Press of Kansas, 2009), go deeper into the details. Antony Beevor, *Stalingrad: The Fateful Siege, 1942–1943* (London: Penguin Books, 1998), antedates the academic titans but is no less intellectually worthy— and a less demanding introduction for general readers.

9 **Operation Mars** David M. Glantz is definitive on this little-known operation, analyzing Rzhev in *Zhukov's Greatest Defeat: The Red Army's Epic Disaster in Operation Mars, 1942* (Lawrence: University Press of Kansas, 1999).

12 **First step in restoring the maneuver warfare** For Manstein's decision making, see his memoir *Lost Victories: The War Memoirs of Hitler's Most Brilliant General* (London: Methuen & Co., 1958), pp. 297–303. Mungo Melvin, *Manstein: Hitler's Greatest General* (London: Weidenfeld & Nicolson, 2010), pp. 287–307, is the most balanced analysis. The best critical treatment is Heinz Magenheimer, *Stalingrad* (Selent, Germany: Pour le Mérite–Verlag für Militärgeschichte, 2007).

13 **Encouraged Stavka to go a stage further** David M. Glantz, *After Stalingrad: The Red Army's Winter Offensive, 1942–43* (Solihull, UK: Helion & Co., 2009), presents the Soviet perspective. Dana V. Sadarananda, *Beyond Stalingrad: Manstein and the Operations of Army Group Don* (Westport, CT: Praeger Publishers, 1990), is economical for the other side of the front. Eberhard Schwarz, *Die Stabilisierung der Ostfront nach Stalingrad: Mansteins Gegenschlag zwischen Donez und Dnjeper im Frühjahr 1943* (Göttingen: Muster-Schmidt, 1985), is based on the records of Manstein's army group. Robert M. Citino, *The Wehrmacht Retreats: Fighting a Lost War, 1943* (Lawrence: University Press of Kansas, 2012), pp. 41–74, is excellent on "the limits of command" in the context of Manstein's counterstroke.

14 **"Miracle" . . . "genius"** Melvin, *Manstein,* pp. 344–346, summarizes Manstein's performance from the perspective of a general officer and an accomplished historian.

15 **Process of recovering from two disconnects** For the Red Army's internal dynamic, see Roger R. Reese, *Stalin's Reluctant Soldiers: A Social History of the Red Army, 1925–1941* (Lawrence: University Press of Kansas, 1996), and *Red Commanders: A Social History of the Soviet Army Officer Corps, 1918–1991* (Lawrence: University Press of Kansas, 2005), pp. 12–134. Mark von Hagen, *Soldiers in the Proletarian Dictatorship: The Red Army and the Soviet Socialist State, 1917–1930* (Ithaca, NY: Cornell University Press, 1993), covers the ideological aspects; David R. Stone, *Hammer and Rifle: The Militarization of the Soviet Union, 1926–1933* (Lawrence: Univer-

sity Press of Kansas, 2000), is excellent on the nearly disastrous distorting effects of excessive military production.

16 **Ripple effects**   David M. Glantz, *Stumbling Colossus: The Red Army on the Eve of World War* (Lawrence: University Press of Kansas, 1998), is once again the best beginning for these developments.

17 **War was not a contingency**   Richard W. Harrison, *The Russian Way of War: Operational Art, 1904–1940* (Lawrence: University Press of Kansas, 2001), is the best presentation of this process. Mary R. Habeck, *Storm of Steel: The Development of Armor Doctrine in Germany and the Soviet Union, 1919–1939* (Ithaca, NY: Cornell University Press, 2003), is an excellent comparative analysis from a technical perspective. Sally W. Stoecker, *Forging Stalin's Army: Marshal Tukhachevsky and the Politics of Military Innovation* (Boulder, CO: Westview Press, 1998), addresses the high-level infighting when the stakes were literally mortal.

19 **Rebuilding virtually from the ground up**   Steven J. Zaloga and Leland S. Ness, *Red Army Handbook 1939–1945* (Stroud, UK: Sutton, 1998), is good for the details of reorganization and rearmament.

20 **Depended on perspective**   Boris Gorbachevsky, *Through the Maelstrom: A Red Army Soldier's War on the Eastern Front, 1942–1945*, trans. and ed. Stuart Britton (Lawrence: University Press of Kansas, 2008), pp. 108–113.

20 **"Into the chopping machine"**   Ibid., p. 130.

21 **Eviscerated in a matter of weeks**   On this point, cf. David Porter, *Soviet Tank Units, 1939–45* (London: Amber Books, 2009), and Steven J. Zaloga and James Grandsen, *Soviet Tanks and Combat Vehicles of World War Two* (London: Arms and Armour Press, 1984).

22 **Unpleasant tactical surprises**   See, for example, the reports from this period abstracted in Thomas L. Jentz, ed., *Panzertruppen: The Complete Guide to the Creation & Combat Employment of Germany's Tank Force, 1933–1942*, vol. 2 (Atglen, PA: Schiffer Publishing, 1996), pp. 21–46.

22 **Four hundred thousand tankers**   Among many examples, cf. Dmitriy Loza, *Commanding the Red Army's Sherman Tanks: The World War II Memoirs of Hero of the Soviet Union Dmitriy Loza*, trans. and ed. James F. Gebhardt (Lincoln: University of Nebraska Press, 1996), and Evgeni Bessonov, *Tank Rider: Into the Reich with the Red Army* (London: Green-

hill, 2005). Both are from a later period than that covered in this book—but not many tanker veterans of the earlier years seem to have survived to record their experiences. Artem Drabkin and Oleg Sheremet, *T-34 in Action: Soviet Tank Troops in WWII* (Mechanicsburg, PA: Stackpole Books, 2008), synthesizes the stories of eleven tankers—again all but one from the war's later period.

23 **Given the right catalyst** This was increasingly provided by an emerging cadre of talented leaders. See Richard N. Armstrong, *Red Army Tank Commanders: The Armored Guards* (Atglen, PA: Schiffer Publishing, 1994).

23 **Guns had been important** Chris Bellamy, *Red God of War: Soviet Artillery and Rocket Forces* (London: Brassey's, 1986). Petr Mikhin, *Guns Against the Reich: Memoirs of an Artillery Officer on the Eastern Front* (Barnsley, UK: Pen & Sword, 2010), begins at Rzhev and takes its narrator through Stalingrad and Kursk.

24 **Russia's people behaved heroically** Nina Tumarkin, *The Living & the Dead: The Rise & Fall of the Cult of World War II in Russia* (New York: Basic Books, 1994).

26 **Hope that their sacrifices** Catherine Merridale, *Ivan's War: Life and Death in the Red Army, 1939–1945* (New York: Metropolitan Books, 2006), and Roger R. Reese, *Why Stalin's Soldiers Fought: The Red Army's Military Effectiveness in World War II* (Lawrence: University Press of Kansas, 2011), combine to present the Soviet soldiers' human dimensions.

26 **Gorbachevsky . . . recalls a postwar discussion** Gorbachevsky, *Through the Maelstrom*, p. 376.

26 **Best understood in terms of synergies** On the wider links between army and party, the best overview is Manfred Messerschmidt, "The Wehrmacht and the Volksgemeinschaft," *Journal of Contemporary History* 18, no. 4 (1983): 719–744. On the military aspects, cf. Robert M. Citino, *The Path to Blitzkrieg: Doctrine and Training in the German Army, 1920–1939* (Boulder, CO: Lynne Rienner Publishers, 1999), and James S. Corum, *The Roots of Blitzkrieg: Hans von Seeckt and German Military Reform* (Lawrence: University Press of Kansas, 1992).

28 **Soldiers were confident** Stephen G. Fritz, *Frontsoldaten: The German*

Soldier in World War II (Lexington: University Press of Kentucky, 1995), and Omer Bartov, *Hitler's Army: Soldiers, Nazis, and War in the Third Reich* (New York: Oxford University Press, 1992), retain their place as standards. On the issue of participation, see particularly Thomas Kühne, *Belonging and Genocide: Hitler's Community, 1918–1945* (New Haven: Yale University Press, 2010), pp. 95–136.

30 **"Band of brothers"**   Roger Beaumont, "On the Wehrmacht Mystique," *Military Review* 66, no. 6 (July 1986): 45–56.

31 **Mastery demanded study and reflection**   Dennis E. Showalter, "Prussian-German Operational Art, 1740–1943," in *The Evolution of Operational Art: From Napoleon to the Present,* ed. John Andreas Olsen and Martin van Creveld (Oxford: Oxford University Press, 2011), pp. 35–63. The quotation is from pp. 35–36. The meme of war as an art form is a major theme of Robert M. Citino, *The German Way of War: From the Thirty Years' War to the Third Reich* (Lawrence: University Press of Kansas, 2005). The panzer arm is discussed specifically in Dennis E. Showalter, *Hitler's Panzers: The Lightning Attacks That Revolutionized Warfare* (New York: Berkley Caliber, 2009).

32 **Product of improvisation**   Wilhelm Deist, "The Rearmament of the Wehrmacht," in Diest et al., *Germany and the Second World War,* vol. 1, *The Build-up of German Aggression,* trans. Ewald Osers et al. (Oxford: Clarendon Press, 1990), pp. 373–540.

33 **Deconstruct the concept of blitzkrieg**   Cf. Karl-Heinz Frieser, *The Blitzkrieg Legend: The 1940 Campaign in the West,* trans. J. T. Greenwood (Annapolis: Naval Institute Press, 2005), and from a broader perspective, Adam Tooze, *The Wages of Destruction: The Making and Breaking of the Nazi Economy* (London: Allen Lane, 2006).

35 **Chronic shortage of staff officers**   The problem of staff overwork is a central theme of Geoffrey P. Megargee, *Inside Hitler's High Command* (Lawrence: University Press of Kansas, 2000).

35 **A matrix of "hardness"**   The concept is best demonstrated in Sönke Neitzel and Harald Welzer, *Soldaten: On Fighting, Killing, and Dying: The Secret WWII Transcripts of German POWs,* trans. Jefferson Chase (New York: Alfred A. Knopf, 2012).

CHAPTER II: PREPARATIONS

38 **"Made a balls of it"**   Quoted in Rick Atkinson, *An Army at Dawn: The War in North Africa, 1942–1943* (New York: Henry Holt, 2002), p. 410.

38 **His most embarrassing**   Ken Ford, *The Mareth Line, 1943: The End in Africa* (Oxford: Osprey Publishing, 2012), is a good introduction to this sequence of operations.

38 **Last half million warm bodies**   Bernd Wegner, "Grundprobleme der deutschen Kriegführung nach Stalingrad," in Frieser et al., *Ostfront*, pp. 3–41.

39 **Postwar historians in general**   Alfred Zins, *Die Operation Zitadelle: Die militärgeschichtliche Diskussion und ihre Niederschlag im öffentlichen Bewusstsein als didaktisches Problem* (Frankfurt: Peter Lang, 1986).

39 **Negotiating a Russo-German peace**   Bernd Wegner, "Bündnispolitik und Friedensfrage," in Frieser et al., *Ostfront*, pp. 42–60.

41 **Hitler's iron determination**   Ian Kershaw, *Hitler, 1936–1945: Nemesis* (New York: W. W. Norton & Co., 2008), pp. 391–497.

41 **Wait until 1944**   Heinz Guderian, *Panzer Leader*, trans. Constantine Fitzgibbon (New York: Dutton, 1952), pp. 306–307.

42 **Manstein's answer was elastic defense**   Erich von Manstein, *Verlorene Siege* (Bonn: Athenäum Verlag, 1955), pp. 473–483. The English version's treatment of Kursk is one-fifth the length of the the German and far more anodyne. Cf. Melvin, *Manstein*, pp. 349–355.

43 **Operations Order No. 5**   Ernst Klink, *Das Gesetz des Handelns: Die Operation "Zitadelle," 1943* (Stuttgart: Deutsche Verlags-Anstalt, 1966), pp. 277–278.

44 **Lacked the strength to participate**   Bodo Scheurig, *Alfred Jodl: Gehorsam und Verhängnis* (Schnellbach: Verlag Bublies, 1999), pp. 225–226.

44 **"So capable and soldierly a person as Manstein"**   Guderian, *Panzer Leader*, p. 302.

44 **Minor surgery**   Alexander Stahlberg, *Bounden Duty: The Memoirs of a German Officer, 1932–45*, trans. Patricia Crampton (London: Brassey's, 1990), p. 295.

44 **Manstein's absence cleared Zeitzler's field**   Mark Healy, *Zitadelle: The German Offensive Against the Kursk Salient, 4–17 July 1943* (Stroud, UK:

History Press, 2008), pp. 45–47. The text of Operations Order No. 6, essentially Zeitzler's work, is in Klink, *Gesetz des Handelns,* pp. 292–294.

46 **Point calls for explanation** Showalter, *Hitler's Panzers,* pp. 224–238, offers an overview of the German panzers in the first half of 1943. Cf. Richard L. DiNardo, *Germany's Panzer Arm* (Westport, CT: Greenwood Press, 1997), pp. 11–20, and Thomas L. Jentz, *Germany's Panther Tank: The Quest for Combat Supremacy* (Atglen, PA: Schiffer Publishing, 1995).

48 **"The Tiger was all muscle"** Showalter, *Hitler's Panzers,* p. 232.

48 **A preferable alternative** Melvin, *Manstein,* p. 357.

49 **Model is best remembered as a tactician** Steven H. Newton, *Hitler's Commander: Field Marshal Walther Model—Hitler's Favorite General* (New York: Da Capo Press, 2006), is the best analysis in English of Model as a commander. Walter Görlitz, *Model: Strategie der Defensive* (Wiesbaden: Limes, 1975), downplays its subject's Nazi sympathies.

49 **One-on-one meeting** Healy, *Zitadelle,* pp. 79–80.

49 **Conference in Munich** Manstein, *Verlorene Siege,* pp. 488–491, and Guderian, *Panzer Leader,* pp. 306–308, are firsthand accounts, both predictably self-serving. The best analysis is Citino, *The Wehrmacht Retreats,* pp. 121–126.

50 **Well-developed approach to dealing with the senior officers** Helmut Heiber and David Glantz, eds., *Hitler and His Generals: Military Conferences, 1942–1945* (New York: Enigma, 2003), is the basic source for the Führer's approach in the war's final years.

51 **Postponed the operation** Frieser et al., *Ostfront,* p. 76.

53 **Elite Grossdeutschland Division** Michael Sharpe and Brian L. Davis, *Grossdeutschland: Guderian's Eastern Front Elite* (Hersham, UK: Ian Allan Publishing, 2001), is an economical overview. Hans-Joachim Jung, *The History of Panzerregiment "Grossdeutschland,"* trans. David Johnston (Winnipeg: J. J. Fedorowicz, 2000), is part of a subgenre of English-language publishing on the Wehrmacht and Waffen SS: narrowly focused on tactics and war stories, for practical purposes blind and deaf to the Third Reich's criminal aspects, but useful within its limits for its narrative of armored combat in Russia.

53 **SS Panzer Corps** Redesignated II SS Panzer Corps just before Citadel, it

was also widely referred to without the new number. For its recent operational background, see George M. Nipe Jr., *Last Victory in Russia: The SS-Panzerkorps and Manstein's Kharkov Counteroffensive, February–March 1943* (Atglen, PA: Schiffer Publishing, 2000).

53 **Hoth had an ample supply of it**   Hoth has kept snugly beyond the increasingly unsympathetic spotlight cast on senior Wehrmacht commanders. He has no biography and despite having served six years of a fifteen-year sentence for war crimes is a marginal presence even in Johannes Hürter's *Hitlers Heerführer: Die deutschen Oberbefehlshaber im Krieg gegen die Sowjetunion 1941/1942* (Munich: Oldenbourg, 2007)—a work focusing as much and more on its subjects' criminal behavior as their military performance.

54 **Came . . . with a string attached**   Frieser et al., *Ostfront*, p. 142.

54 **Fewer than four hundred recruits and convalescents**   Steven H. Newton, "Ninth Army and the 'Numbers Game': A Fatal Delay?," in *Kursk: The German View*, trans. and ed. Steven H. Newton (New York: Da Capo Press, 2002), pp. 371–380.

55 **Panzer divisions were ready for another battle**   Friedrich von Mellenthin, *Panzer Battles: A Study of the Employment of Armor in the Second World War* (New York: Ballantine Books, 1971), p. 215.

55 **One particular ballerina**   Gerd Schmückle, *Ohne Pauken und Trompeten: Erinnerungen an Krieg und Frieden* (Stuttgart: Deutsche Verlags-Anstalt, 1982), pp. 68–74.

56 **Soviet victories . . . had not been won in isolation**   David M. Glantz, "Prelude to Kursk: Soviet Strategic Operations, February–March 1943," *Journal of Slavic Military Studies* 8, no. 1 (1995): 1–35, and "Soviet Military Strategy During the Second Period of War (November 1942–December 1943): A Reappraisal," *Journal of Military History* 60, no 1 (1996): 115–150. Cf. A. M. Vasilevsky, *A Lifelong Cause* (Moscow: Progress Publishers, 1981), pp. 273–279.

57 **Relief of Leningrad**   David M. Glantz, *The Battle for Leningrad, 1941–1944* (Lawrence: University Press of Kansas, 2002).

57 **Contacts between the respective diplomats**   Ingeborg Fleischhauer, *Die Chance des Sonderfriedens: Deutsch-sowjetische Geheimgespräche 1941–1945* (Berlin: Siedler, 1986), contextualizes this still-open issue.

58 **Stalin sent Zhukov down from Leningrad** G. K. Zhukov, *Reminiscences and Reflections,* vol. 2 (Moscow: Progress Publishers 1985), pp. 145–148.

58 **Running a spy ring** Cf. Timothy P. Mulligan, "Spies, Ciphers and 'Zitadelle': Intelligence and the Battle of Kursk, 1943," *Journal of Contemporary History* 22, no. 2 (1987): 236–260; and in much more detail, David M. Glantz, *The Role of Intelligence in Soviet Military Strategy in World War II* (Novato, CA: Presidio Press, 1990), pp. 172–283.

59 **On April 8 he sent a message** In David M. Glantz and Jonathan M. House, *The Battle of Kursk* (Lawrence: University Press of Kansas, 1999), pp. 361–362.

60 **Zhukov and Vasilevsky entered Stalin's study** For further information on the April 12 meeting and subsequent Soviet planning, see Healy, *Zitadelle,* pp. 51–53, 61–63.

61 **Most formidable large-scale defensive system** The most complete analysis in English is—predictably—David M. Glantz, *CSI Report No. 11: Soviet Defensive Tactics at Kursk, July 1943* (Ft. Leavenworth, KS: Combat Studies Institute, 1986). Glantz and House, *Battle of Kursk,* pp. 63–78, is briefer and clearer.

66 **Partisan operations** Leonid Grenkevich, *The Soviet Partisan Movement, 1941–1944,* ed. David M. Glantz (London: Frank Cass Publishers, 1999), contextualizes the irregulars' contributions to Citadel.

67 **Operational zone of the Central Front** Glantz and House, *Battle of Kursk,* pp. 58–60, 299–306.

67 **General Konstantin K. Rokossovsky** Rokossovsky's career is summarized in Richard Wolff, "Rokossovsky," in *Stalin's Generals,* ed. Harold Shukman (New York: Grove Press, 1993), pp. 177–196, and presented in his autobiography, *A Soldier's Duty,* trans. Vladimir Talmy, ed. Robert Daglish (Moscow: Progress Publishers, 1970).

68 **Nikolai Vatutin joined the Red Army** For Vatutin, see David M. Glantz, "Vatutin," in *Stalin's Generals,* pp. 287–298. Valeriy Zamulin contributes a perceptive, positive assessment of Vatutin's performance during Citadel in "The Battle of Kursk: New Findings," *Journal of Slavic Military Studies* 25 (2012): 409–417.

69 **His front would eventually commit** For more on Voronezh Front resources, see Glantz and House, *Battle of Kursk,* pp. 60–63, 306–320.

70 **Red Air Force had taken a brutal beating** For background, see Von Hardesty and Ilya Grinberg, *Red Phoenix Rising: The Soviet Air Force in World War II* (Lawrence: University of Kansas Press, 2012), especially pp. 223–234; Dmitriy Khazanov and Aleksander Medved, *La-5/7 vs. FW 190: Eastern Front, 1942–45* (Oxford: Osprey Publishing, 2011), is a useful introduction to technical and institutional details.

71 **"Night witches"** See generally Reina Pennington, *Wings, Women, & War: Soviet Airwomen in World War II Combat* (Lawrence: University of Kansas Press, 2001).

71 **Initially, German air offensives** Christer Bergström, *Kursk: The Air Battle, July 1943* (Hersham, UK: Classic Publications, 2008), pp. 18–25; and more generally, Hermann Plocher, *The German Air Force Versus Russia, 1943* (New York: Arno Press, 1968).

71 **He escaped by "mere chance"** Rokossovsky in Daglish, *A Soldier's Duty*, p. 194.

72 **Fighter squadrons were the Luftwaffe's elite** See most recently Colin D. Heaton and Anne-Marie Heaton, *The German Aces Speak: World War II Through the Eyes of Four of the Luftwaffe's Most Important Commanders* (Minneapolis: Zenith Press, 2011).

72 **Luftwaffe higher command for Citadel** For details of organization and equipment, see Bergström, *Kursk: The Air Battle*, pp. 123–128.

73 **Air force possessed a counterpart to Zhukov** John Erickson, "Novikov," in Harold Shukman, ed. *Stalin's Generals*, pp. 155–174.

73 **Shturmovik** Yefim Gordon, *Ilyushin Il2-Il10* (Hinckley, UK: Midland Publishing, 2010), is definitive on this famous but relatively unfamiliar aircraft.

74 **The Oberkommando der Wehrmacht** For more on the OKW's input, see Citino, *The Wehrmacht Retreats*, pp. 170–175, and Walter Warlimont, *Inside Hitler's Headquarters, 1939–45*, trans. R. H. Barry (Novato, CA: Presidio Press, 1991), p. 333. For background, see Geoffrey P. Megargee, "Triumph of the Null: Structure and Conflict in the Command of German Land Forces, 1939–1945," *War in History* 4, no. 1 (1997): 60–80.

74 **Zeitzler too was having second thoughts** Healy, *Zitadelle*, p. 88.

74 **Model weighed in** Peter von der Groeben, "Ninth Army and Second

Panzer Army," in *Kursk: The German View,* pp. 102–105; and Newton, *Hitler's Commander,* pp. 219–223.

75 **On July 1, the Führer summoned the senior generals** Manstein, *Verlorene Siege,* pp. 495–497.

76 **"The German Supreme Command could think of nothing better"** Mellenthin, *Panzer Battles,* p. 217.

76 **By the time the preparations for Kursk were complete** Frieser et al., *Ostfront,* pp. 95–97.

CHAPTER III: STRIKE

78 **Central Front's counterbarrage opened** Rokossovsky, *A Soldier's Duty,* p. 195.

79 **Agreed to delay the attack** Glantz and House, *Battle of Kursk,* pp. 85, 400.

79 **1st Air Division received a surprise** Bergström, *Kursk: The Air Battle,* pp. 34–36.

79 *Landser* **soon found the going heavy** Healy, *Zitadelle,* pp. 220–222.

80 **[Ferdinands] began life as a competitor to the Tigers** For this unfortunate AFV, later renamed Elefant, see Walter J. Spielberger, "Panzerjaeger Tiger (p) Elefant," no. 20 in *Armour in Profile,* ed. Stevenson Pugh (Letterhead, UK: Profile Publications, 1968).

80 **Remote-controlled wire-guided mine-clearing vehicle** Healy, *Zitadelle,* pp. 222–226.

80 **Ninth Army's initial** *Schwerpunkt* Ibid., pp. 226–229; Glantz and House, *Battle of Kursk,* pp. 86–91; and, more closely focused, Christopher W. Wilbeck, *Sledgehammers: Strengths and Flaws of Tiger Tank Battalions in World War II* (Bedford, PA: Aberjona Press, 2004), pp. 69–71.

82 **Red Air Force was becoming a presence** Hardesty and Grinberg, *Red Phoenix Rising,* pp. 241–243.

83 **Model was anything but a rear-echelon commando** Newton, *Hitler's Commander,* pp. 228–234, reconstructs and analyzes Model's command behaviors on July 5, 6, and 7 on the basis of a barely legible penciled *"Notz für Kriegstagebuch"* ("Notes for the War Diary") that survived the nearly total loss of Ninth Army's relevant records later in the war. The document

302 · NOTES

can be found in captured German records, National Archives, T-312, roll 322.

84 **Rudenko quickly proposed mass attacks** Bergström, *Kursk: The Air Battle,* pp. 40–43.

85 **The only way out was through** Newton, *Hitler's Commander,* pp. 233–244, and Glantz and House, *Battle of Kursk,* pp. 91–93, present the head-quarters' perspectives. The excerpts from the war diary of Panzer Battalion 21 in 20th Panzer Division (Jentz, *Panzertruppen,* vol. 2, pp. 75, 83–84) convey some of the sense of the seesaw fighting that characterized July 6 in Model's sector.

85 **Luftwaffe threw in every flyable plane** Bergström, *Kursk: The Air Battle,* pp. 43–49.

87 **The 6th Infantry Division** Figures from Newton, *Kursk: The German View,* p. 409.

87 **Rokossovsky handled his reserves effectively** Rokossovsky, *A Soldier's Duty,* pp. 197–201.

88 **Model phoned Army Group Center** Newton, *Hitler's Commander,* pp. 237–239.

88 **Committed to a mental hospital** It is worth noting that a year later, Schmidt was briefly considered as a candidate for chief of the general staff! Hürter, *Hitlers Heerführer,* pp. 602–603.

89 **Ninth Army was running out of infantry** Ibid., p. 243.

90 **Ponyri as the key to Central Front's position** Frieser et al., *Ostfront,* pp. 109–110; Glantz and House, *Battle of Kursk,* pp. 115–117.

91 **Model's intended *Schwerpunkt* for July 7** Glantz and House, *Battle of Kursk,* pp. 117–120; Newton, *Hitler's Commander,* pp. 239–245.

92 **Intended to work with the tanks** Matthew Hughes and Chris Mann, *Fighting Techniques of a Panzergrenadier: 1941–1945* (Osceola, WI: MBI Publishing Company, 2000), is a useful introduction.

93 **Ninth Army had taken more than thirteen thousand casualties** Niklas Zetterling and Anders Frankson, *Kursk 1943: A Statistical Analysis* (London: Frank Cass Publishers, 2000), pp. 113, 120–121.

94 **Fourth Panzer Army already had the heaviest hammer** Ibid., p. 18; Frieser et al., *Ostfront,* pp. 90–93.

95 **On May 10, Manstein met with Hoth** Melvin, *Manstein,* pp. 360–361.

95 *Ein alter Hase*   Hoth's reservations are discussed by his chief of staff; see General of Infantry Friedrich Fangohr, "Fourth Panzer Army," in *Kursk: The German View*, pp. 77–79.

96 **Manstein understood the problem**   Manstein, *Verlorene Siege*, p. 494; Melvin, *Manstein*, p. 362.

96 **Manstein's May 10–11 visit**   Fifth Panzer Army's war diary, May 11, 1944, in National Archives, T-313, reel 65. The most detailed analysis of the genesis of the "Hoth variant" is Steven H. Newton, "Hoth, von Manstein, and Prokhorovka: A Revision in Need of Revising," in *Kursk: The German View*, pp. 357–363.

97 **Manstein was horsey**   Stahlberg, *Bounden Duty*, pp. 299–301.

98 **The train he adopted as his mobile headquarters**   Manstein, *Verlorene Siege*, p. 498.

98 **Army Group South's attack**   Helmuth Spaeter, *The History of the Panzerkorps Grossdeutschland*, vol. 2, trans. David Johnston (Winnipeg: J. J. Fedorowicz, 1995), pp. 113–115.

98 **XLVIII Panzer Corps's sector**   "KTB, 4. Panzerarmee, 4.7.1943," National Archives, T-313, roll 396; Spaeter, *Grossdeutschland*, vol. 2, pp. 116–120; Healy, *Zitadelle*, pp. 201–207. For the Russian side, see Glantz and House, *Battle of Kursk*, pp. 94–99.

98 **The Stukas and medium bombers**   Bergström, *Kursk: The Air Battle*, pp. 26–34; Hardesty and Grinberg, *Red Phoenix Rising*, pp. 239–240, 250–251.

100 **Hoth's decision to attack**   "KTB, 4. Panzerarmee, 27.6.1943," National Archives, T-313, reel 365; and Steven H. Newton, "Army Group South's Initial Assault: Analysis and Critique," in *Kursk: The German View*, pp. 382–385.

100 **Major General Friedrich Fangohr**   Fangohr, "Fourth Panzer Army," in *Kursk: The German View*, pp. 77–79.

100 **Panthers had reached Army Group South on July 1**   Jentz, *Panzertruppen*, vol. 2, pp. 96–100, excerpts reports describing technical and tactical issues in detail.

102 **Hoth's final attack orders**   Silvester Stadler, *Die Offensive gegen Kursk 1943: II.SS-Panzerkorps als Stosskeil im Grosskampf* (Osnabrück: Munin-Verlag, 1980), pp. 23–27.

102 **Constructed around its panzer divisions**   Showalter, *Hitler's Panzers*, pp. 242–252 passim, is a bare-bones overview. Among the massive body of

literature on the Waffen SS, the best overview remains Bernd Wegner, *The Waffen SS: Organization, Ideology, and Function,* trans. Ronald Webster (London: Blackwell Publishing, 1990). It is supplemented and developed by René Rohrkamp, *"Weltanschaulich gefestigte Kämpfer": Die Soldaten der Waffen-SS 1933–1945* (Paderborn: Ferdinand Schöningh, 2010). For details of organization and equipment during Citadel, David Porter, *Das Reich at Kursk: 12 July 1943* (London: Amber Books, 2011), is excellent and generally applicable to Leibstandarte and Totenkopf as well.

104 **Mass and fighting spirit** George M. Nipe, *Blood, Steel, and Myth: The II. SS-Panzer-Korps and the Road to Prochorowka, July 1943* (Stamford, CT: RZM Publishing, 2012), pp. 65–84, is detailed, clearly presented, and generally eschews SS mythmaking. Valeriy Zamulin, *Demolishing the Myth: The Tank Battle at Prokhorovka, Kursk, July 1943: An Operational Narrative,* trans. and ed. Stuart Britton (Solihull, UK: Helion & Co., 2011), pp. 92–102, presents the Russian perspective.

105 **Third German trump card was the Luftwaffe** Bergström, *Kursk: The Air Battle,* p. 30.

106 **Army Detachment Kempf** Cf. Colonel General Ehrhard Raus, *"Armeeabteilung* Kempf," in *Kursk: The German View,* pp. 47–53, for a command perspective; Didier Lodieu, *III. Pz. Korps at Kursk,* trans. Alan Mackay (Paris: Histoire and Collections, 2007), for a tactical overview based heavily on unit war diaries; and Franz-Wilhelm Lochmann et al., *The Combat History of German Tiger Tank Battalion 503 in World War II,* trans. Fred Steinhardt (Mechanicsburg, PA: Stackpole Books, 2008), pp. 107–108, for the role of the Tigers.

CHAPTER IV: GRAPPLE

111 **Katukov, working in his undershirt** "Katukov," in Armstrong, *Red Army Tank Commanders,* pp. 58–59.

111 **Vatutin's high-risk decision** Zamulin, *Demolishing the Myth,* pp. 104–110; Glantz and House, *Battle of Kursk,* pp. 101–103.

111 **"Flying light"** Bergström, *Kursk: The Air Battle,* pp. 56–57.

112 **A strongpoint in itself** Spaeter, *Grossdeutschland,* pp. 120–123; Mellenthin, *Panzer Battles,* pp. 55–56.

113 **To the Pena River** Traditionsverband der Ehemaligen 3. Panzer-

Division, *Geschichte der 3: Panzer Division Berlin-Brandenburg, 1935–1945* (Berlin: Buchhandlung G. Richter, 1967), p. 375; Zamulin, *Demolishing the Myth*, p. 116.

113 **Infantryman who did not expect miracles** Healy, *Zitadelle*, p. 236.

114 **A network of fortified heights** Cf. the day's combat reports in Stadler, *Offensive gegen Kursk*, pp. 49–53, and the narrative in Nipe, *Blood, Steel, and Myth*, pp. 114–141, and Zamulin, *Demolishing the Myth*, pp. 114–133.

115 **"Tough and determined resistance"** "18:00 Uhr., Tagesmeldung 'LSSAH,'" in Stadler, *Offensive gegen Kursk*, p. 43.

116 **Hoth's orders for the next day** "Panzerarmeebefehl Nr. 2," in ibid., pp. 52–53.

116 **"A complete success"** KTB, 4, Panzerarmee, Chefnotizen für 6.7.1943, National Archives T-313, roll 369.

116 **Zeitzler refused** Melvin, *Manstein*, p. 373.

116 **Easier stated than achieved** Lodieu, *III. Pz. Korps*, pp. 30–46.

117 **Arguing with his superiors** Glantz and House, *Battle of Kursk*, pp. 113–115.

118 **"Pick up the pace!"** "Panzerarmeebefehl Nr. 2," in Stadler, *Offensive gegen Kursk*, p. 53.

118 **Stukas were overhead** Bergström, *Kursk: The Air Battle*, p. 59.

118 **Grossdeutschland was stopped in its tracks** Spaeter, *Grossdeutschland*, pp. 121–122; Jentz, *Panzertruppen*, vol. 2, p. 96; Glantz and House, *Battle of Kursk*, pp. 126–129.

119 **Success won by finesse and maneuver** Spaeter, *Grossdeutschland*, p. 123.

120 **Tigers at the apex** Nile, *Blood, Steel, and Myth*, pp. 169–175; Zamulin, *Demolishing the Myth*, pp. 134–137.

120 **"Excellent Luftwaffe support"** "18.00 Uhr.: Div. 'Das Reich' Tagesmeldung," in Stadler, *Offensive gegen Kursk*, p. 60.

121 **Corridor the Russians were determined to shut** Ibid., p. 57.

121 **Naked from shirttail to boots** Otto Weidinger, *Division Das Reich* (Osnabrück: Munin-Verlag, 1969), pp. 177–178.

122 **Hausser submitted his report to Hoth** "22.40 Uhr.: Tagesmeldung an die Armee," in Stadler, *Offensive gegen Kursk*, p. 61.

122 **Fourth Panzer Army must be stopped** Glantz and House, *Battle of Kursk*, pp. 113–114; Zamulin, *Demolishing the Myth*, pp. 138–139.

122 **One of the hardest days in the Battle of Kursk** Zamulin, *Demolishing the Myth,* pp. 95–96.

122 **"Larger units" and "heavier tanks"** Armstrong, *Red Army Tank Commanders,* pp. 58–59.

123 **Crews could often repair track damage themselves** Zetterling and Frankson, *Kursk 1943,* pp. 120–123; Healy, *Zitadelle,* p. 258.

124 **The Russians had other ideas** Cf. Lodieu, *III. Pz. Korps,* pp. 46–57, and Nipe, *Blood, Steel, and Myth,* pp. 175–182.

126 **"Keep a few for interrogation"** Erhard Raus, *Panzer Operations: The Eastern Front Memoir of General Raus, 1941–1945,* comp. and trans. Steven H. Newton (New York: Da Capo Press, 2003), p. 203.

126 **A disconcerting image** Manstein, *Verlorene Siege,* p. 499; Melvin, *Manstein,* pp. 373–374.

127 **The image of a tar baby** "Panzerarmeebefehl Nr. 3," in Stadler, *Offensive gegen Kursk,* pp. 57–58.

127 **Transferred the bulk of their respective mobile forces** Healy, *Zitadelle,* p. 271; Nipe, *Blood, Steel, and Myth,* pp. 216–217.

128 **Syrzevo itself held out** Spaeter, *Grossdeutschland,* pp. 123–124; Healy, *Zitadelle,* pp. 271–272.

128 **Mistakes are in the nature of war** Mellenthin, *Panzer Battles,* p. 233.

128 **Division ordered the battle group to hold its ground** Spaeter, *Grossdeutschland,* p. 124; Healy, *Zitadelle,* pp. 272–274; Bergström, *Kursk: The Air Battle,* pp. 62–64.

129 **No fewer than twelve attacks** Glantz and House, *Battle of Kursk,* p. 135.

130 **Warriors for the working day** Nipe, *Blood, Steel, and Myth,* pp. 216–219.

130 **For July 8, Hausser proposed** "Aufträge für die 8.7," in Stadler, *Offensive gegen Kursk,* p. 62.

131 **Pushed forward in stops and starts** Nipe, *Blood, Steel, and Myth,* pp. 194–202.

131 **An immediate counterattack** Glantz and House, *Battle of Kursk,* p. 133; Weidinger, *Division Das Reich,* p. 182.

132 **One of Das Reich's panzer grenadier regiments** Weidinger, *Division Das Reich,* p. 181.

132 **Front orders issued at 11:00 P.M.** Glantz and House, *Battle of Kursk,* p. 134; Zamulin, *Demolishing the Myth,* pp. 139–142.

133 **Most spectacular initial results of Vatutin's counterattack** Martin Pegg, *Hs 129 Panzerjäger!* (Burgess Hill, UK: Classic Publications, 1997), pp. 145–149; Weidinger, *Division Das Reich*, pp. 182–184; and from the targets' perspective, Zamulin, *Demolishing the Myth*, pp. 143–147.

134 **"Good cooperation with the Luftwaffe"** Stadler, *Offensive gegen Kursk*, p. 63.

134 **New, potentially decisive surge** Lodieu, *III. Pz. Korps*, pp. 58–73, provides tactical details for the panzers; Erhard Raus, "*Armeeabteilung Kempf*," in *Kursk: The German View*, p. 54, refers to leading the counterattack—not exactly a normal job for a corps commander, though Raus presents it as all in a day's work on the Russian front.

135 **Army group commander consulted Zeitzler** Melvin, *Manstein*, p. 373.

136 **The bottom of Central Front's barrel** Rokossovsky, *A Soldier's Duty*, pp. 200–201.

137 **Luftwaffe radio intelligence scored the first points** Bergström, *Kursk: The Air Battle*, pp. 53–54.

137 **Red Army riflemen in possession of part of Ponyri** Glantz and House, *Battle of Kursk*, pp. 120–121.

137 **A modest operation** Paul Carell, *Scorched Earth: Hitler's War on Russia*, vol. 2, trans. Ewald Osers (London: G. G. Harrap, 1970).

137 **Shuttled from place to place** Excerpt in Jentz, *Panzertruppen*, vol. 2, p. 84.

137 **The 4th Panzer Division's prospects** Carell, *Scorched Earth*, p. 47; Healy, *Zitadelle*, pp. 281–285; Piekalkiewicz, *Operation Citadel*, pp. 159–161; Newton, *Hitler's Commander*, pp. 249–250.

138 **Model's first reaction to another futile day** Newton, *Hitler's Commander*, pp. 250–251.

139 **Everywhere except around Ponyri** Healy, *Zitadelle*, p. 286.

139 **Senior officers' conference** Newton, *Hitler's Commander*, pp. 252–253. The phrase *rollenden Materialabnützungsschlacht* also appears in the Ninth Army's war diary for September 7, 1943 (Frieser et al., *Ostfront*, p. 110).

139 **No sign of a smoke screen** Bergström, *Kursk: The Air Battle*, p. 71.

140 **Model replicated Lemelsen's action** Healy, *Zitadelle*, p. 287; Newton, *Hitler's Commander*, p. 253; Rokossovsky, *A Soldier's Duty*, p. 201.

140 **A series of counterattacks** Klink, *Gesetz des Handelns,* p. 261.

141 **"Chain dogs"** Literally *Kettenhünde:* Wehrmacht slang for "military police."

141 **Fighters were defensively minded** Bergström, *Kursk: The Air Battle,* p. 73.

141 **Model responded with a revised plan** Frieser et al., *Ostfront,* p. 111; Zins, *Operation Zitadelle,* pp. 58–59.

142 **Strength figures for the Central Front** Zetterling and Frankson, *Kursk 1943,* p. 118.

142 **Forced him to commit reserves** Rokossovsky, *A Soldier's Duty,* pp. 200–201.

142 **Offensive in the Orel sector was ripe for launching** Glantz and House, *Battle of Kursk,* p. 233.

CHAPTER V: DECISIONS

144 **That in turn required shuffling** Glantz and House, *Battle of Kursk,* p. 139.

145 **Fifth Guards Tank was a high card** David Porter, *Fifth Guards Tank Army at Kursk: 12 July 1943* (London: Amber Books, 2011), is a detailed overview of Fifth Guards Tank Army's genesis and structure, a companion volume to his earlier-cited work on Das Reich.

145 **Hoth too was testing the wind** Healy, *Zitadelle,* p. 288; KTB, 4, Panzerarmee, Chefnotizen für, 9.7.1943, National Archives T-313, roll 369.

146 **No aircraft could be spared** The improving performance of the Soviet air force also drew off German planes. Cf. Hardesty and Grinberg, *Red Phoenix Rising,* pp. 254–255; Bergström, *Kursk: The Air Battle,* pp. 67–69.

146 **Hoth's original concept** Fangohr, "Fourth Panzer Army," in *Kursk: The German View,* pp. 77–80.

146 **Order No. 4 . . . was ambiguous** "Panzerarmeebefehl Nr. 4, 20.20 Uhr., 8.7.1943," in Stadler, *Offensive gegen Kursk,* pp. 69–70.

147 **Breith had to clear his own sector** Lodieu, *III. Pz. Korps,* pp. 58–73; Nipe, *Blood, Steel, and Myth,* pp. 211–212.

148 **Knobelsdorff initially responded** Spaeter, *Grossdeutschland,* pp. 125–127; Glantz and House, *Battle of Kursk,* pp. 142–144; Healy, *Zitadelle,* pp. 290–291; Nipe, *Blood, Steel, and Myth,* pp. 216–219.

150 **Hausser's orders** "Korps-Befehl für den Angriff am 9.7.1943," in Stadler, *Offensive gegen Kursk,* p. 71.

150 **Leibstandarte advanced** Nipe, *Blood, Steel, and Myth,* pp. 192–211, is exhaustive; Healy, *Zitadelle,* pp. 294–296, is a more economical overview.

151 **Confirming major armor movements** "Feindlage 9.7.1943, Stand 19.00 Uhr.," in Stadler, *Offensive gegen Kursk,* pp. 79–80.

151 **July 9 was a long day** Glantz and House, *Battle of Kursk,* pp. 138–140.

152 **2nd Tank Corps** Zamulin, *Demolishing the Myth,* pp. 185–186.

152 **Fourth Panzer Army had received a maximum effort** Bergström, *Kursk: The Air Battle,* pp. 67–69; Hardesty and Grinberg, *Red Phoenix Rising,* pp. 247–248, 251–253.

155 **Time had come to throw the switch** The most detailed analysis of this issue is Newton, "Hoth, von Manstein, and Prokhorovka," in *Kursk: The German View,* pp. 358–369.

156 **Sometime between noon and 1:30** Ibid., pp. 368, 452.

156 **Army Order No. 5** "Panzerarmeebefehl Nr. 5, 20:30, 9.7.1943," in Stadler, *Offensive gegen Kursk,* p. 79.

157 **Loss/recovery/repair figures** Glantz and House, *Battle of Kursk,* pp. 351–352; Frieser et al., *Ostfront,* pp. 117–118.

158 **Citadel's outcome depended on using XXIV Panzer Corps** Manstein, *Verlorene Siege,* p. 501.

158 **Came closest to enabling a meaningful breakout** Cf. particularly Newton, *Kursk: The German View,* p. 369.

159 **Avoid a simple battle of attrition** Robert Forczyk, *Sevastopol 1942: Von Manstein's Triumph* (Oxford: Osprey Publishing, 2008), is a solid, brief, accessible overview.

159 **Hoth's trump card** Spaeter, *Grossdeutschland,* pp. 127–128; Glantz and House, *Battle of Kursk,* pp. 153–157; Nipe, *Blood, Steel, and Myth,* pp. 270–275.

161 **Visible through binoculars** Carell, *Scorched Earth,* p. 72.

161 **The 11th Panzer Division spent July 11** Nipe, *Blood, Steel, and Myth,* pp. 301–303.

161 **Guderian . . . had been recalled** See Guderian, *Panzer Leader,* p. 303, and his July 17, 1943, "Report on the Operations of Panzer-Regiment (Panther) von Lauchert," in Jentz, *Panzertruppen,* vol. 2, pp. 98–99.

162 **Material reason for optimism**   Guderian, "Operations of Panzer-Regiment (Panther) von Lauchert," p. 99; Zetterling and Frankson, *Kursk 1943*, p. 123.

163 **He did some serious thinking**   Given the absence of a general written plan, Zamulin, *Demolishing the Myth*, pp. 258–263, is the clearest reconstruction of Voronezh Front's decision-making processes at this juncture.

164 **Citadel in reverse**   Citino, *The Wehrmacht Retreats*, p. 212, and the comprehensive bibliographic analysis on pp. 345–346. For strategic context and operational concept, see Glantz and House, *Battle of Kursk*, pp. 227–234.

165 **If the Germans broke into Voronezh Front's rear areas**   Zamulin, *Demolishing the Myth*, p. 262.

165 **Necessary to inform Stavka**   Ibid., pp. 263–268; Glantz and House, *Battle of Kursk*, pp. 159–161.

167 **Rotmistrov's Guardsmen were the key**   English-language versions of Rotmistrov's account of the meeting are in Armstrong, *Red Army Tank Commanders*, pp. 247–348, and Zamulin, *Demolishing the Myth*, pp. 268–269.

167 **Met with Rotmistrov's corps commanders**   Zamulin, *Demolishing the Myth*, pp. 269–270.

168 **Nearly blitzkrieg-level standard**   Ibid., pp. 270–278.

169 **Hausser's final orders**   "Aufträge an die Divisionen für 10.7.1943," in Stadler, *Offensive gegen Kursk*, pp. 81–82.

170 **Leibstandarte's attack**   Nipe, *Blood, Steel, and Myth*, pp. 254–291; Zamulin, *Demolishing the Myth*, pp. 183–187, 192.

171 **Checked by a Guards heavy tank regiment**   Zamulin, *Demolishing the Myth*, pp. 192–193.

171 **Orders were to force a crossing**   "Auftraege an die Divisionen für 10.7.1943," in Stadler, *Offensive gegen Kursk*, p. 83.

171 **The weather and the Russians**   Nipe, *Blood, Steel, and Myth*, pp. 263–268; Zamulin, *Demolishing the Myth*, pp. 187–189.

172 **"Bitter fighting"**   "18.00 Uhr. von Div. 'Totenkopf,' " in Stadler, *Offensive gegen Kursk*, p. 88.

172 **Holding its positions as ordered**   Nipe, *Blood, Steel, and Myth*, pp. 260–262.

172 **Hausser reported to Hoth** "19.25 Uhr. Tagesmeldung an Armee," in Stadler, *Offensive gegen Kursk*, pp. 88–89.

173 **Seems to have encouraged Hoth** "20:30 Uhr. Tagesmeldung der Armee," in ibid., pp. 89–90; Nipe, *Blood, Steel, and Myth*, p. 281.

173 **A five-hundred-yard mudflat** Nipe, *Blood, Steel, and Myth*, pp. 292–293.

173 **Leibstandarte was on its own** Ibid., pp. 281–285.

174 **Russian situation brightened around dawn** Glantz and House, *Battle of Kursk*, pp. 167–168.

175 **His real message** Zamulin, *Demolishing the Myth*, pp. 208–209.

175 **Leibstandarte had to provide its own flank security** Nipe, *Blood, Steel, and Myth*, pp. 285–290; Zamulin, *Demolishing the Myth*, pp. 214–226.

177 **Prokhorovka remained just out of German reach** Zamulin, *Demolishing the Myth*, pp. 235–241.

177 **Leibstandarte blamed what it called limited success** "16.40 bis 17.00 Uhr. Tagesmeldungen der Divisionen Leibstandarte" and "Auftrag des II. SS-Pz.-Korps für 12.7," in Stadler, *Offensive gegen Kursk*, pp. 95, 97–98.

177 **A long, hard day in the mud** Nipe, *Blood, Steel, and Myth*, pp. 292–297.

178 **Das Reich spent most of July 11** "16.40 bis 17.00 Uhr. Tagesmeldungen der Divisionen. Das Reich" and "17.30 Uhr. Tagesmeldung an der Armee," in Stadler, *Offensive gegen Kursk*, pp. 96, 97–98.

179 **The Russians were explaining defeat** Zamulin, *Demolishing the Myth*, pp. 231–234.

179 **Rotmistrov's counterattack** Rotmistrov's account in his memoirs is translated in Glantz and House, *Battle of Kursk*, pp. 175–176.

180 **Revised the details of their tactical plan** Zamulin, *Demolishing the Myth*, pp. 278–279.

CHAPTER VI: HARD POUNDING

182 *Klotzen, nicht kleckern* "Auftrag II.SS-Pz.-Korps für 12.7," in Stadler, *Offensive gegen Kursk*, pp. 97–98; Nipe, *Blood, Steel, and Myth*, pp. 314–316; Rudolf Lehmann, *The Leibstandarte*, vol. III, trans. Nick Olcott (Winnipeg: J. J. Fedorowicz, 1990), p. 233.

183 **Three panzer divisions' worth of shovels** Lodieu, *III. Pz. Korps*, pp. 74–81; Healy, *Zitadelle*, pp. 308–309; Zamulin, *Demolishing the Myth*, pp. 250–252.

184 **Manstein . . . met with Hoth and Kempf** General of Infantry Theodor Busse, "Operation Citadel Overview," in *Kursk: The German View,* pp. 22–23; Raus, *Panzer Operations,* pp. 207–208; Manstein, *Verlorene Siege,* p. 500.

184 **Rapid intervention of III Panzer Corps** Lodieu, *III. Pz. Korps,* pp. 92–103; Zamulin, *Demolishing the Myth,* pp. 252–255.

185 **Citadel's forgotten divisions** Lodieu, *III. Pz. Korps,* pp. 87–88, 90–91, 96–100.

186 *Immer bereit, still zu verbluten im feldgrauen Kleid* "Ihr Musstet Marschieren," Frank Rennicke's tribute to Germany's World War II infantry, is one of the signature songs of Germany's contemporary Far Right. That does not diminish the occasionally powerful effect of its images.

186 **"Asians"** The "Description of Combat Operations of the 19th Panzer Division Between 5 July and 18 July 1943" is cited in Zamulin, *Demolishing the Myth,* p. 252.

186 **Rolled into Olkhovatka** Lodieu, *III. Pz. Korps,* p. 96.

187 **The commanding general . . . concurred** Manstein, *Verlorene Siege,* p. 500; Melvin, *Manstein,* p. 376.

187 **According to Hoth's chief of staff** Fangohr, "Fourth Panzer Army," in *Kursk: The German View,* pp. 89–90.

188 **Sixty-ninth Army had managed** Glantz and House, *Battle of Kursk,* p. 163.

188 **A high-risk, high-gain nighttime operation** Described eloquently in Carell, *Scorched Earth,* pp. 84–86 passim, and more soberly in Franz Kurowski, *Panzer Aces: Battle Stories of German Tank Commanders of WWII,* trans. David Johnston (Mechanicsburg, PA: Stackpole Books, 2004), pp. 52–54. The Russian side of the story is told in Zamulin, *Demolishing the Myth,* pp. 402–407.

190 **They mistook the Germans for Russians** Zamulin, *Demolishing the Myth,* p. 419; Bergström, *Kursk: The Air Battle,* p. 79. The truck carrying the air liaison officer had broken down during the advance, breaking the division's air–ground link as well.

192 **"Where was everybody else?"** "KTB. Tagesmeldung III.Panzer-korps am 12.7.1943," National Archives, T-314, roll 197; Klink, *Gesetz des Handelns,* pp. 243–244; Nipe, *Blood, Steel, and Myth,* pp. 314–315; Lodieu, *III. Pz.*

Korps, pp. 103–109 passim; Zamulin, *Demolishing the Myth,* pp. 407–426 passim; Glantz and House, *Battle of Kursk,* pp. 202–204.

192 **Unexpectedly successful advance**   Lodieu, *III. Pz. Korps,* pp. 115–116; Zamulin, *Demolishing the Myth,* p. 406.

193 **Stalin . . . issued orders to Steppe Front**   Zamulin, *Demolishing the Myth,* pp. 409–410.

193 **About two hundred tanks**   Ibid., p. 410.

193 **Dispatch a strong force**   Ibid., p. 413.

193 **Trufanov's fire brigade arrived in increments**   Ibid., pp. 419–423.

194 **"Introduce the strictest discipline"**   Ibid., pp. 425, 486–487. An English translation of the "Order for the National Commissar for the Defense of the Soviet Union, July 28, 1942" is accessible on the Internet at http://www.stalingrad-info.com and independently under "Order 227."

195 **Vasilevsky informed Stalin**   Zamulin, *Demolishing the Myth,* p. 426.

196 **Providing the muscle for the straight right-hand punch**   Ibid., pp. 204–205.

196 **Grossdeutschland's sideways shuffle**   For the confusing events of July 12 in this sector, cf. "KTB: Darstellung der Erignsse XLVIII Panzer-Korps am 12.7.1943," National Archives, T-314, roll 1170; "XLVIII Panzerkorps Tagesmeldungen an Pz.AOK, 12.7.1943," National Archives, T-314, roll 1171; the published material in Spaeter, *Grossdeutschland,* pp. 129–130; Mellenthin, *Panzer Battles,* 224; Glantz and House, *Battle of Kursk,* pp. 202–208; and Nipe, *Blood, Steel, and Myth,* pp. 351–353.

197 **The corps commander failed**   Zamulin, *Demolishing the Myth,* pp. 430–431.

197 **"Temporarily compelled . . . to withdraw"**   Spaeter, *Grossdeutschland,* p. 130; Zamulin, *Demolishing the Myth,* pp. 432–434.

198 **He could no longer advance**   Zamulin, *Demolishing the Myth,* pp. 430, 434.

198 **More cobbler than blacksmith**   Cf. Armstrong, *Red Army Tank Commanders,* pp. 94–95.

199 **Shifting to a defensive posture**   Spaeter, *Grossdeutschland,* p. 130.

199 **Manstein appeared at corps headquarters**   Nipe, *Blood, Steel, and Myth,* p. 353.

199 **Knobelsdorff's eventual orders**   Ibid., p. 353; Mellenthin, *Panzer Battles*, pp. 126–128.

200 **Swan song of the panzers**   Ivan S. Konev, *Aufzeichnungen eines Front-oberbefehlshabers 1943/44*, trans. Irmgard Zeisler, 2nd ed. (Berlin: Militärverlag der DDR, 1983), p. 43.

201 **Leibstandarte and Das Reich were kept awake**   Nipe, *Blood, Steel, and Myth*, pp. 315–317.

202 **Rotmistrov's tankers were no less nervous**   Cf. the accounts in Zamulin, *Demolishing the Myth*, p. 298, and Lloyd Clark, *The Battle of the Tanks: Kursk, 1943* (New York: Atlantic Monthly Press, 2011), pp. 314–315. Porter, *Fifth Guards Tank Army*, p. 56, refers to the hatch problem.

202 **Not all the Russian tankers . . . were men**   Anna Krylova, *Soviet Women in Combat: A History of Violence on the Eastern Front* (New York: Cambridge University Press, 2010), brilliantly contextualizes the general subject.

203 **Rotmistrov arrived at the command post**   Zamulin, *Demolishing the Myth*, p. 299.

203 **Caught in their blankets**   Ribbentrop's narrative begins in Kurowski, *Panzer Aces*, pp. 174–178.

203 **Only seven tanks that morning**   "KTB 4th Panzerarmee, Chefnotizen für 12.7.1943," National Archives T-313, reel 369.

204 **Soviet barrage was falling short**   Zamulin, *Demolishing the Myth*, pp. 284–385, 301–306.

204 **Fifth Guards Tank Army's first battle**   Ibid., pp. 306–307.

205 **"Steel! Steel! Steel!"**   Ibid., pp. 308–309. Though Zamulin deftly corrects the details of Rotmistrov's colorful, frequently cited account of the jump-off, its ambience remains.

205 **A massive air attack**   Bergström, *Kursk: The Air Battle*, pp. 79–81.

206 **None was better than Hans-Ulrich Rudel**   Hans-Ulrich Rudel, *Stuka Pilot*, trans. Lynton Hudson (New York: Ballantine Books, 1958), pp. 85–86. Bergström, *Kursk: The Air Battle*, p. 79, establishes July 12, rather than the more generally cited July 5, as the most likely date for this.

206 **"The first flight flies behind me"**   Rudel, *Stuka Pilot*, p. 85.

207 **"It was like a giant had grabbed"**   Interview quoted in Clark, *Battle of the Tanks*, p. 345.

207 **Russians were advancing almost blindly**   An easily accessible overview of the technical and operational capacities of the T-34/76 at this period is Robert K. Forczyk, *Panther vs T-34: Ukraine 1943* (Oxford: Osprey Publishing, 2007).

207 **Puts 234 tanks in the first attack wave**   Zamulin, *Demolishing the Myth,* pp. 309–310.

208 **"The field . . . sprang to life"**   Ibid., p. 321.

208 **"Alone at Prokhorovka"**   His actual title is "Born Again at Prokhorowka." Kurowski, *Panzer Aces,* pp. 178–180.

208 **No knowledge of its presence**   Zamulin, *Demolishing the Myth,* pp. 327–328.

209 **"Inferno of fire, smoke, burning T-34s"**   Kurowski, *Panzer Aces,* p. 181.

209 **Command and control eroded**   Zamulin, *Demolishing the Myth,* pp. 319–320.

209 **Some of Citadel's fiercest fighting**   Ibid., pp. 315–328 passim.

210 **Personally took out a T-34**   Patrick Agte, *Jochen Peiper: Commander, Panzerregiment Leibstandarte,* trans. Robert Dohrenwend (Winnipeg: J. J. Fedorowicz, 1999), p. 176.

210 **Situational awareness and a cool head**   Patrick Agte, *Michael Wittmann and the Waffen SS Tiger Commanders of the Leibstandarte in WWII,* vol. 1. (Mechanicsburg, PA: Stackpole Books, 2006), specifically pp. 85–132 passim, contextualizes Wittmann's Citadel experience with a minimum of the Waffen-SS-flavored heroic pathos common in this genre. T-shirts celebrating Wittmann are nevertheless available at a number of commercial and commemorative Internet sites.

211 **Halt at an angle**   Nipe, *Blood, Steel, and Myth,* p. 330.

211 **Citadel's defining incident**   Zamulin, *Demolishing the Myth,* pp. 352–353; Kurowski, *Panzer Aces,* p. 205.

211 **The still-desperate melee**   Nipe, *Blood, Steel, and Myth,* p. 332; Agte, *Jochen Peiper,* p. 176.

212 **Ran full tilt into**   Zamulin, *Demolishing the Myth,* pp. 332–334; Lehmann, *Leibstandarte,* pp. 234–235.

212 **A veteran of the 10th Tank Corps . . . wrote**   Quoted in Zamulin, *Demolishing the Myth,* p. 335.

212 **Ramming a German AFV**   Ibid., p. 333.

214 **The relationship of myth and reality was closer**   Ibid., pp. 364–370; Nipe, *Blood, Steel, and Myth,* pp. 340–343.

214 **Improvised company of captured T-34s**   Weidinger, *Das Reich,* pp. 199–200.

215 **Rotmistrov arrived**   Zamulin, *Demolishing the Myth,* pp. 377–378, 456–457.

215 **Heavily contingent on Totenkopf's performance**   Nipe, *Blood, Steel, and Myth,* pp. 343–349, 381–398.

216 **Not all the comrades were valiant**   Ibid., pp. 356, 389–90. Paul Wanke, *Russian/Soviet Military Psychiatry, 1904–1945* (London: Routledge, 2012), surveys the USSR's approach to psychiatric casualties.

216 **As of 10:45 P.M.**   Totenkopf's report of 22.45 in Stadler, *Offensive gegen Kursk,* p. 105; Nipe, *Blood, Steel, and Myth,* pp. 349–350.

217 **Spent time in a mental hospital**   Charles W. Sydnor, Jr., *Soldiers of Destruction: The SS Death's Head Division, 1933–1945* (Princeton, NJ: Princeton University Press, 1977), p. 8.

217 **The original, Soviet version**   Zamulin, *Demolishing the Myth,* pp. 516–543, covers Russian mythology; Frieser et al., *Ostfront,* pp. 129–135, is the German counterpoint. Nipe, *Blood, Steel, and Myth,* pp. 326–327, focuses on the number of tanks directly involved.

218 **Noted only one for July 12**   Ralf Tiemann, *Chronicle of the 7. Panzer-Kompanie I. SS-Panzer Division "Leibstandarte,"* trans. Allen Brandt (Atglen, PA: Schiffer Publishing, 2004), p. 60.

218 **Demanding to know what had happened**   Glantz and House, *Battle of Kursk,* p. 428, fn. 31; Frieser et al., *Ostfront,* pp. 132–133; Zamulin, *Demolishing the Myth,* pp. 441, 507.

218 **Rotmistrov shaking from the stress**   Armstrong, *Red Army Tank Commanders,* pp. 320–322. In the course of World War II, over 250 Russian generals were executed or sent to penal units. Christopher N. Donnelly, "The Soviet Attitude Toward Stress in Battle," in *Contemporary Studies in Combat Psychiatry,* ed. Gregory Belenky (Westport, CT: Greenwood Press, 1987), p. 233.

218 **Stalin remained sufficiently disturbed**   Zamulin, *Demolishing the Myth,* p. 457; Zhukov, *Reminiscences and Reflections,* p. 190.

219 **Manstein "thanked and praised"**   "Generalkommando II. SS. Pz.-Korps, 22.00 Uhr.," in Stadler, *Offensive gegen Kursk*, p. 104.

219 **Hoth was edgy**   "KTB 4th Panzerarmee, Chefnotizen für 21.7.1943," National Archives, T-314, roll 1170.

220 **"Nothing mattered to me any more"**   Lochmann et al., *Tiger Tank Battalion 503*, pp. 116–117. Nipe, *Blood, Steel, and Myth*, p. 363, summarizes the state of the SS; conditions were no better in the army formations.

220 **Ideological racism and cultural arrogance**   Cf. Neitzel and Welzer, *Soldaten*, p. 317–343.

221 **Delivered by phone**   Stadler, *Offensive gegen Kursk*, p. 103.

221 **Solid prospects existed for a breakthrough**   Glantz and House, *Battle of Kursk*, p. 209, speak of "cautious optimism." Nipe, *Blood, Steel, and Myth*, p. 353, stresses the shock effects of July 12 on Hoth and his staff.

221 **Hoth's final orders arrived**   "Durch FS um 20.45 Uhr.: An II-SS Pz.-Korps," in Stadler, *Offensive gegen Kursk*, p. 103.

221 **Corps intelligence summary**   "Feindlage 12.7.1943, Stand: 21.00 Uhr.," in ibid., pp. 105–106.

222 **Hausser responded to Hoth**   "Auftraege für 13.7.43" (the "14" in the text is an obvious misprint), in ibid., p. 105; "KTB II. SS-Panzerkorps an SS Divisionen 'LSAH,' 'DR,' und 'T' . . . Auftraege für 13.7.43," National Archives, T-354, roll 605.

Chapter VII: Crossovers

224 **The Russians came to it**   Cf. Harrison, *Russian Way of War*, and the more comprehensive overview by Jacob Kipp, "The Tsarist and Soviet Operational Art, 1853–1991," in *Evolution of Operational Art*, pp. 64–95.

224 **Its rebirth was a two-year process**   "Rebirth" is the central theme of Glantz, *Stumbling Colossus*.

225 **Preparations for Kutuzov**   Glantz and House, *Battle of Kursk*, pp. 227–232; and Glantz, "Soviet Military Strategy," *Journal of Military History* 60, no 1 (1996).

226 **An inactive sector**   That description is relative. See Franz Kurowski, *Deadlock Before Moscow: Army Group Center, 1942/1942*, trans. Joseph G. Welsh (Atglen, PA: Schiffer Publishing, 1992).

226 **Locus of a serious plot**   Peter Hoffmann, "Trecksow and Army Group Center," in *The History of the German Resistance, 1933–1945,* trans. Richard Barry (Cambridge, MA: MIT Press, 1977), pp. 264–289.

227 **Confronted Operation Kutuzov**   For the final balance of forces, see Frieser et al., *Ostfront,* pp. 98–99.

227 **Achieved almost complete surprise**   David M. Glantz, *Soviet Military Deception in the Second World War* (London: Routledge, 1989), pp. 160–193.

227 **Launch time was determined**   For a general operational overview, see John Erickson, *The Road to Berlin: Continuing the History of Stalin's War with Germany* (Boulder, CO: Westview Press, 1983), p. 108. Major General Peter von der Groeben, "Ninth Army and Second Panzer Army," in *Kursk: The German View,* pp. 108–112, gives a German staff officer's perspective.

229 **Airpower played a major role**   Bergström, *Kursk: The Air Battle,* pp. 82–84; Hardesty and Grinberg, *Red Phoenix Rising,* pp. 261–265.

229 **Had his ups and downs**   Geoffrey Jukes, "Bagramyan," in Harold Shukman, ed., *Stalin's Generals,* pp. 26–27.

230 **Bryansk Front found the going tougher**   Lothar Rendulic, "Die Schlacht von Orel, Juli 1943: Wahl und Bildung des Schwerpunktes," *Österreichische Militärische Zeitschrift* 1 (1963): 130–138.

230 **Owed a good part of their success**   Bergström, *Kursk: The Air Battle,* pp. 85–86.

231 **A rapidity . . . Newton, calls suspicious**   Newton, *Hitler's Commander,* pp. 253–255.

232 **The 12th Panzer had spent a week**   The division's records are summarized in Antonius John, *Kursk '43: Szenen einer Entscheidungsschlacht* (Bonn: H&H Konzept Verlag, 1993), pp. 106–118.

233 **"The threshold to battle hell"**   Ibid., pp. 117, 120. The 5th Panzer Grenadier Regiment was part of 12th Panzer Division.

234 **In a strategic . . . cleft stick**   Simon Ball, *The Bitter Sea: The Struggle for Mastery in the Mediterranean, 1935–1949* (London: HarperPress, 2010), and Douglas Porch, *The Path to Victory: The Mediterranean Theater in World War II* (New York: Farrar, Straus & Giroux, 2004), are the best overviews from, respectively, a policy/strategy and a strategic/operational

perspective. Citino, *The Wehrmacht Retreats,* brilliantly integrates the synergies of the Mediterranean theater and the Russian front.

234 **Italy was a broken reed**   MacGregor Knox, *Hitler's Italian Allies: Royal Armed Forces, Fascist Regime, and the War of 1940–1943* (New York: Cambridge University Press, 2000), is an analytical overview. Gerhard Schreiber, "Das Ende des nordafrikanischen Feldzugs und der Krieg in Italien 1943 bis 1945," in Frieser et al., *Ostfront,* pp. 1100–1114, summarizes the German perspective of the Axis endgame.

234 **But where?**   Citino, *The Wehrmacht Retreats,* pp. 172–175, presents the options.

235 **His reputation for optimism**   Albert Kesselring, *Kesselring: A Soldier's Record,* trans. Lynton Hudson (New York: William Morrow, 1954), pp. 196–198; Schreiber, "Ende des nordafrikanischen Feldzugs," in Frieser et al., *Ostfront,* p. 1113.

235 **Hitler should have come forward**   Manstein, *Verlorene Siege,* p. 501.

236 **"Under the sun-ray lamp"**   Stahlberg, *Bounden Duty,* p. 307.

236 **Hitler's presentation**   Manstein, *Verlorene Siege,* pp. 501–503; Frieser et al., *Ostfront,* pp. 141–142.

238 **Too late in the day**   Stahlberg, *Bounden Duty,* pp. 309–310.

238 **An increasing number of similar ones**   Dennis E. Showalter, "Conscience, Honor, and Expediency: The German Army's Resistance to Hitler," in *Confront!: Resistance in Nazi Germany,* ed. John J. Michalczyk (New York: Peter Lang, 2004), pp. 62–79.

239 **To define his own place in history**   Melvin's excellent biography may be complemented by Benoît Lemay, *Erich von Manstein: Hitler's Master Strategist* (Havertown, PA: Casemate, 2010), and Marcel Stein, *Field Marshal von Manstein: The Janus Head—A Portrait,* ed. Gwyneth Fairbank, trans. Marcel Stein (Solihull, UK: Helion & Co., 2007).

239 **Vatutin's headquarters had been doing the same thing**   Glantz and House, *Battle of Kursk,* p. 208; Zamulin, *Demolishing the Myth,* pp. 426, 460–461.

240 **Vatutin requested reinforcements**   Zamulin, *Demolishing the Myth,* pp. 456–457.

241 **Stated purpose of the meeting**   Ibid., pp. 457, 470–471.

241 **Lack of specialized recovery vehicles** Ibid., pp. 447–449. Gary A. Dickson, "Tank Repair and the Red Army in World War II," *Journal of Slavic Military Studies* 25 (2012): 381–392, is an overview of Red Army maintenance methods.

241 **Quiet in the SS sector** Nipe, *Blood, Steel, and Myth*, pp. 366–371.

242 **"I couldn't deal with it"** Agte, *Jochen Peiper*, pp. 176–179.

243 **On Totenkopf's front** Zamulin, *Demolishing the Myth*, pp. 460–466; Nipe, *Blood, Steel, and Myth*, pp. 378–382.

244 **Taken at all costs** Nipe, *Blood, Steel, and Myth*, p. 382.

245 **Soviet attacks began** Zamulin, *Demolishing the Myth*, pp. 469–473; Nipe, *Blood, Steel, and Myth*, pp. 372–374.

245 **Fourth Panzer Army's daily report** "KTB 4.Panzerarmee, Chefnotizen für 13.7.1943," National Archives, T-313, roll 369.

245 **Suggested an opportunity** At least to Manstein. Manstein, *Verlorene Siege*, p. 501.

246 **Dazed and mechanical** Mellenthin, *Panzer Battles*, p. 226; Glantz and House, *Battle of Kursk*, p. 210; cf. "Darstellung der Ereignisse XLVIII Panzer-Korps am 13.7.1943," National Archives, T-314, roll 1170; and Nipe, *Blood, Steel, and Myth*, pp. 384–388.

246 **Nowhere near in any of its divisional sectors** Lodieu, *III. Pz. Korps*, pp. 121–126; Zamulin, *Demolishing the Myth*, pp. 474–480.

246 **A revised plan** Manstein, *Verlorene Siege*, pp. 500–501; Melvin, *Manstein*, p. 376; Frieser et al., *Ostfront*, pp. 141–144.

247 **Strained to its limits** Nipe, *Blood, Steel, and Myth*, p. 382.

247 **It was Grossdeutschland's turn** Ibid., pp. 412–413; Spaeter, *Grossdeutschland*, pp. 131–132; Mellenthin, *Panzer Battles*, pp. 228–229; Bergström, *Kursk: The Air Battle*, pp. 99–100.

248 **First Tank Army . . . had done its job** Armstrong, *Red Army Tank Commanders*, p. 63.

249 **"The stubborn defense of its current lines"** Zamulin, *Demolishing the Myth*, pp. 513–514.

249 **Rhetoric of attack was challenged** Ibid., pp. 486–487.

250 **Breith was on his own** Ibid., pp. 495–496; Lodieu, *III. Pz. Korps*, pp. 126–140; Nipe, *Blood, Steel, and Myth*, pp. 409–411.

251 **"Behaving splendidly"** Zamulin, *Demolishing the Myth*, p. 489.

251 **Vatutin responded**   Ibid., pp. 503–504.

252 **Withdrawal to a new defensive line**   Ibid., pp. 504–512.

252 **Das Reich's panzer grenadiers**   Nipe, *Blood, Steel, and Myth*, pp. 398–405; Lodier, *III. Pz. Korps*, p. 139.

253 **Further refined and reconceptualized**   Cf. the summaries in Frieser et al., *Ostfront*, p. 145, and Nipe, *Blood, Steel, and Myth*, pp. 413, 417–418, with "Vorschlag für Operation Roland am 16.7.1943, KTB Panzerarmeeoberkommando 4 an Heeresgruppe Süd," National Archives, T-313, roll 382.

255 **Stavka's planned offensive**   David M. Glantz, *From the Don to the Dnepr: Soviet Offensive Operations, December 1942–August 1943* (London: Frank Cass Publishers, 1991), pp. 229–252.

255 **Unlikely to encourage a narrow focus**   Nipe, *Blood, Steel, and Myth*, p. 445, revising his earlier judgment in *Decision in the Ukraine: German Panzer Operations on the Eastern Front, Summer 1943* (Winnipeg: J. J. Fedorowicz, 1996), pp. 55–56, 67.

255 **Limited prospects for Manstein's projected revision of Citadel**   Nipe, *Blood, Steel, and Myth*, pp. 421–422.

256 **Citadel's file of might-have-beens**   Weidinger, *Division Das Reich*, pp. 213, 216.

256 **Stalin and Stavka were anxious**   Zhukov, *Reminiscences and Reflections*, p. 194.

256 **Southern Front attacked the Sixth Army**   Major Dr. Martin Francke, "Sixth Army Defends the Mius River Line," in *Kursk: The German View*, pp. 306–324.

256 **Finally recognized the obvious**   Frieser et al., *Ostfront*, pp. 191–193; Glantz and House, *Battle of Kursk*, pp. 244–246.

258 **Out of touch with reality**   Newton, *Hitler's Commander*, pp. 256–262; Frieser et al., *Ostfront*, pp. 185–190; Bergström, *Kursk: The Air Battle*, pp. 90–95; Hardesty and Grinberg, *Red Phoenix Rising*, pp. 262–267.

259 **To change the Führer's mind**   Glantz and House, *Battle of Kursk*, p. 238.

259 **Position in the Mediterranean was steadily eroding**   Citino, *The Wehrmacht Retreats*, pp. 238–254, reconstructs and contextualizes admirably the quandary facing the German high command at this period. For a staff officer's on-the-ground perspective of the situation in Italy, see Siegfried

Westphal, *Heer in Fesseln: Aus den Papieren des Stabschefs von Rommel, Kesselring und Rundstedt* (Bonn: Athenäum Verlag, 1952), pp. 214–226.

259 **Grew increasingly tenuous** For details and background, see Josef Schröder, *Italiens Kriegsaustritt 1943: Die deutschen Gegenmassnahmen im italienischen Raum: Fall "Alarich" und "Achse"* (Göttingen: Musterschmidt-Verlag, 1969).

260 **He summoned Kluge** Frieser et al., *Ostfront,* pp. 219–220.

260 **No pressure was applied for close pursuit** Zamulin, *Demolishing the Myth,* pp. 458–459, 515.

261 **Germany's ultimate assets** Manstein, *Verlorene Siege,* pp. 516–517.

261 **Fighting Manstein's war** For the German perspective, cf. Frieser et al., *Ostfront,* pp. 193–200, and Melvin, *Manstein,* pp. 382–387. The Russian side is predictably well and exhaustively presented in Glantz, *Don to the Dnepr,* pp. 251–365.

262 **"A blizzard of red arrows"** Citino, *The Wehrmacht Retreats,* p. 232.

262 **Zeitzler paid an unannounced visit** Manstein, *Verlorene Siege,* pp. 518–519.

262 **Hitler flew to Vinnitsa** Ibid., pp. 522–529; Melvin, *Manstein,* pp. 387–388, 391–394.

264 **Demanded a private meeting with the Führer** Manstein, *Verlorene Siege,* pp. 529–530.

264 **No dictator can accept such a challenge** Melvin, *Manstein,* pp. 394–395.

264 **Close to throwing the Salerno landing into the sea** Angus Konstam, *Salerno 1943: The Allied Invasion of Italy* (Barnsley, UK: Pen & Sword Military, 2007), is an economical overview.

264 **Gersdorff . . . had gone so far** His version of the following events is in Rudolf-Christof Gersdorff, *Soldat im Untergang* (Frankfurt: Ullstein, 1977), pp. 134–136; cf. Hoffmann, *German Resistance,* p. 290.

266 **"One-sided actionism"** Isabel V. Hull, *Absolute Destruction: Military Culture and the Practices of War in Imperial Germany* (Ithaca, NY: Cornell University Press, 2005), p. 170.

266 **Is an oath one-sided?** Robert B. Kane, *Disobedience and Conspiracy in the German Army, 1918–1945* (Jefferson, NC: McFarland & Co., 2002), analyzes and contextualizes this morally complex question.

266 **They scorched the earth** For Manstein's definition and description, see

Manstein, *Verlorene Siege*, pp. 539–540. Broader analyses include Bernd Wegner, "Die Aporie des Krieges," in Frieser et al., *Ostfront*, pp. 256–269; and from a unit perspective, Christoph Rass, *"Menschenmaterial": Deutsche Soldaten an der Ostfront: Innenansichten einer Infanteriedivision, 1939–1945* (Paderborn: Ferdinand Schöningh, 2003), pp. 365–385.

266 **"Field of rubble"** Cited in Stephen G. Fritz, *Ostkrieg: Hitler's War of Extermination in the East* (Lexington: University Press of Kentucky, 2011), p. 372.

267 **"Burning our bread"** Quoted in David M. Glantz and Jonathan House, *When Titans Clashed: How the Red Army Stopped Hitler* (Lawrence: University Press of Kansas, 1995), p. 172.

267 **By the time Army Group South reached the Dnieper** Frieser et al., *Ostfront*, pp. 360–367 and 301–308, discusses the situation of Army Groups South and Center.

Conclusion: Watersheds

268 **First come statistics** Zamulin, *Demolishing the Myth*, pp. 530–546; Frieser et al., *Ostfront*, pp. 150–159; Zetterling and Frankson, *Kursk 1943*, pp. 111–131.

273 **"Platoon technology"** Dennis E. Showalter, "More than Nuts and Bolts: Technology and the German Army, 1870–1945," *Historian* 65, no. 1 (2002): 139–142.

273 **Signposts of the Red Army's tactical progress** Frieser et al., *Ostfront*, pp. 301–490, is the best analysis; Rolf Hinze, *Crucible of Combat: Germany's Defensive Battles in the Ukraine, 1943–1944*, trans. and ed. Frederick P. Steinhardt (Solihull, UK: Helion & Co., 2009), is the most detailed account in English.

274 **Russian accounts stress a system** Glantz and House, *When Titans Clashed*, pp. 196–201; Karl-Heinz Frieser, "Der Zusammenbruch im Osten," in Frieser et al., *Ostfront*, pp. 493ff. passim. Useful as well are Gerd Niepold, *Battle for White Russia: The Destruction of Army Group Centre June 1944*, trans. Richard Simpkin (London: Brassey's, 1987), and Walter S. Dunn Jr., *Soviet Blitzkrieg: The Battle for White Russia, 1944* (Boulder, CO: Lynne Rienner Publishers, 2000).

275 **Three taproots** Cf. David M. Glantz, *The Military Strategy of the Soviet Union: A History* (London: Frank Cass Publishers, 1992).

275 **Armored force in particular moved to an advanced stage**   Porter, *Soviet Tank Units*, is a useful introduction to a subject bidding fair to eclipse its German counterpart in specialized literature and on websites.

276 **Altered the rifle units' makeup**   David Glantz, "Soviet Use of 'Substandard' Manpower in the Red Army, 1941–1945," in *Scraping the Barrel: The Military Use of Substandard Manpower, 1860–1960*, ed. Sanders Marble (New York: Fordham University Press, 2012), pp. 151–178.

276 **"They know absolutely nothing"**   Quoted in Max Hastings, *Armageddon: The Battle for Germany, 1944–1945* (New York: Alfred A. Knopf, 2004), p. 124.

277 **A culture of accommodation**   See particularly Martin van Creveld, *The Culture of War* (New York: Presidio Press/Ballantine Books, 2008).

277 **"Quiver like a mouse"**   Cited in Zamulin, *Demolishing the Myth*, p. 450.

277 **Asked each man to give his age**   Lehmann, *Leibstandarte*, p. 230.

277 **"A just and patriotic war"**   Reese, *Why Stalin's Soldiers Fought*, pp. 176–200; Merridale, *Ivan's War*, p. 282 passim.

278 **Defending Western civilization**   David K. Yelton, *Hitler's Volkssturm: The Nazi Militia and the Fall of Germany, 1944–1945* (Lawrence: University Press of Kansas, 2002), and Robert S. Rush, "A Different Perspective: Cohesion, Morale, and Operational Effectiveness in the German Army, Fall 1944," *Armed Forces & Society* 25, no. 3 (1999): 477–508, combine to depict a reality much more nuanced and far less exalted. The matrix of Nazi Germany's endgame of "war to the knife" is exhaustively presented in Ralf Blank et al., *Germany and the Second World War*, vol. 9/1, *German Wartime Society, 1939–1945: Politicization, Disintegration, and the Struggle for Survival*, trans. Derry Cook-Radmore (Oxford: Oxford University Press, 2008).

INDEX

ABOUT THE AUTHOR

DENNIS E. SHOWALTER has taught history at Colorado College since 1969 and is joint editor of the journal *War in History*. He was president of the Society for Military History from 1997 to 2001. In addition, Showalter has taught at the United States Air Force Academy, the United States Military Academy, and the Marine Corps University. He has written extensively on the wars of Frederick the Great, the German Wars of Unification, World War I, and World War II. *Tannenberg: Clash of Empires* won the American Historical Association's Paul Birdsall Prize for best new book of 1992.

ABOUT THE TYPE

This book was set in Minion, a 1990 Adobe Originals typeface by Robert Slimback (b. 1956). Minion is inspired by classical, old-style typefaces of the late Renaissance, a period of elegant, beautiful, and highly readable type designs. Created primarily for text setting, Minion combines the aesthetic and functional qualities that make text type highly readable with the versatility of digital technology.